Treatment of Addiction

The treatment of drug and alcohol addiction is highly complex. Changing trends in policy and models of treatment reflect a fragmented view of the problem, and practitioners offering alternative approaches risk being isolated from the mainstream. To counter this, *Treatment of Addiction* examines the issues as they relate to the clinical practice of arts therapies which, it is argued, have an especially relevant contribution to make.

Using research, discussion of related literature and clinical examples to illustrate theoretical positions, the book explores why arts therapies offer such an appropriate and effective treatment approach. The authors show how psychotherapeutic thinking contributes to the understanding of the difficulties experienced by this client group and discuss the importance of group therapy in this area of work. Contributors look at the different arts therapies and how they are developing in a number of different treatment settings.

This book provides a lively and challenging view of professional approaches to difficult treatment issues, and will be of value to practitioners in all branches of psychotherapy.

Diane Waller is Reader in Art Psychotherapy at Goldsmiths College, University of London, and the President of the British Association of Art Therapists. **Jacky Mahony** is Head of Art Psychotherapy for Oxleas NHS Trust.

Contributors: **Tim Cantopher, Angelika Groterath, Corrie McClean, Jacky Mahony, Marcia Pleven, Neil Springham, Diane Waller, Gary Winship**

Treatment of Addiction

Current issues for arts therapies

Edited by
Diane Waller and
Jacky Mahony

ROUTLEDGE

London and New York

MT

First published 1999
by Routledge
11 New Fetter Lane, London EC4P 4EE

Simultaneously published in the USA and Canada
by Routledge
29 West 35th Street, New York, NY 10001

Typeset in Times by Routledge
Printed and bound in Great Britain by TJ International Ltd,
Padstow, Cornwall

British Library Cataloguing in Publication Data
A catalogue record for this book is available from the
British Library

Library of Congress Cataloguing in Publication Data
Treatment of Addiction: Current issues for arts therapies/edited
by Diane Waller and Jacky Mahony.
Includes bibliographical references and index.
1. Substance abuse – Treatment. 2. Art therapy. 3. Addicts –
Counselling of. 4. Group psychotherapy. I. Waller, Diane.
II. Mahony, Jacky.
RC564.T737 1998
616.86'0651—dc21   98 17017

ISBN 0–415–16996–8 (hbk)
ISBN 0–415–16997–6 (pbk)

12/22/04

Contents

Illustrations

Tables

Contributors

Tim Cantopher is a consultant psychiatrist working in the independent sector in Surrey. He has links with a number of psychotherapists who use different theoretical models. His special interests are in the treatment of drug and alcohol problems and of depression, and in service organisation in all areas, in which he is widely published. He has recently published *Dying For a Drink*, which looks at alcoholism, and in particular its psychodynamic roots.

Angelika Groterath took degrees in psychology and sociology in Germany and worked as a clinical psychologist. She went on to study psychotherapy, graduating as a psychodramatist from the Moreno Institute in Stuttgart in 1984 and gaining her PhD in Sociology in 1986. She also studied classical psychodrama with Zerka Moreno in Germany and Switzerland. She has lectured extensively throughout Europe on sociology, sociodrama and psychodrama. Since 1990 she has worked at the Centro Italiano di Solidarieta in Rome and has published works in German, English and Italian.

Corrie McClean studied sociology and politics at the University of Essex and visual arts at the University of Sussex. She trained as an art psychotherapist at Goldsmiths College and specialised in work with terminally ill patients, and in hospice work with clients having HIV/AIDS related cancers. She held the Corinne Burton Award for hospice work whilst a trainee, and continues to provide art therapy, aromatherapy and massage for AIDS sufferers in Brighton. She has also been a playworker, and run art and art therapy groups for adolescents and young offenders and women drug users and their children.

Jacky Mahony is an art therapist and works as Deputy Manager of a community mental health centre for Oxleas NHS Trust in Kent. Previously she worked for nine years at the Henderson Hospital Therapeutic Community. At the same time she worked part-time as a tutor in the Art Psychotherapy Unit of Goldsmiths College where she completed her MA in 1992. The research described in this book was carried out during this period. Over the past year she has been establishing an Art Psychotherapy Department for Bromley Mental Health Services. She has published several papers and chapters on institutional dynamics and alcoholism in relation to art therapy.

Marcia Pleven trained as a dancer in the US and worked professionally throughout the States and Europe for many years. She trained as a dance/movement therapist at Art Therapy Italiana in Bologna and gained the postgraduate Diploma in Art Psychotherapy (Dance/Movement Therapy) of Goldsmiths College. Marcia has pioneered DMT in Italy, and has worked both privately and for the Centro Italiano di Solidarieta since 1990. She also teaches modern dance and composition at the Academia Nazionale di Danza Rome, and gives courses in DMT in Rome and at ATI in Bologna.

Neil Springham studied visual arts before training as an art psychotherapist at Goldsmiths College, and gaining his MA in 1992. He has since worked as an art therapist in both general psychiatry and drug and alcohol services. He currently divides his time between being head of art therapy at Bournewood NHS Trust, tutoring at Goldsmiths College art psychotherapy unit, and offering clinical supervision privately.

Diane Waller is an art therapist and group psychotherapist, as well as Reader at Goldsmiths College and President of the British Association of Art Therapists. She has helped to develop many art psychotherapy programmes in the UK and Europe, particularly in former Yugoslavia, Bulgaria, Italy and Switzerland and currently in Germany (Berlin). Her professional interests are in the sociology of art therapy as a profession, in training, groups, intercultural psychotherapy, the treatment of addictions and eating disorders. She has contributed to and published several books on these subjects. Her parallel interest is in the ethnography of the Balkans, particularly in dance and textiles.

Gary Winship trained in Group Psychotherapy at Goldsmiths College and took his Masters Degree at the Tavistock Clinic. He worked for fourteen years at the Maudsley Hospital, and in 1980 he began to specialise in the treatment of drug users. He is currently employed by West Berkshire NHS Trust, as a psychotherapist with adult clients. He has co-led workshops using art media, and has written and published many papers on group work, therapeutic communities and drug addiction. He is a visiting tutor to the MA Group Psychotherapy at Goldsmiths College.

Acknowledgements

From Jacky Mahony to Nick Mahony, Keith Miller and Anna Rowe for their help and support in the preparation of this book.

From Diane Waller to the late Dan Lumley, Juan Corelli and the staff and trainees of the art therapy programme at CEIS, and to Brighton Oasis Project from whom I have learned so much about the complexities of addiction.

From both authors to Routledge, especially Hannah Dyson, Kate Hawes and Edwina Welham for their help throughout.

Note: We have usually referred to 'client' in the book, to represent those who use the services described, although individual contributors may have used 'patient' or 'resident' or 'addict' according to the context.

Introduction

Diane Waller and Jacky Mahony

We assume that the first question people will ask when they consider the title of this book is, what do the authors mean by addiction? This particular question is posed and addressed by several of the contributing authors, especially by Angelika Groterath in her forthright essay about concepts of addiction and dependence (Chapter 1), and by Tim Cantopher (Chapter 2) who explores this question as well as the place of the psychotherapies in treating people who have drug problems. The fact that we have linked addiction with treatment and arts therapies implies that we are writing specifically about people whose addictions cause them serious life problems, including physical and mental illness, and in *Treatment of Addiction* we focus on addiction to substances such as alcohol, heroine, cocaine and other so-called 'hard drugs'.

We have been asking many questions ourselves since we became interested in this area of work 'accidentally': in the case of Diane Waller, this was through an invitation to work at the Centro Italiano di Solidarieta in the mid-1980s, and for Jacky Mahony, a chance assignment to review the literature on art therapy and alcoholism as part of her MA in Art Psychotherapy in 1992, discussed in Chapter 6. In this book we have not discussed the many addictions which are sanctioned in our society, such as addiction to tobacco, shopping (noticed especially in the weeks before and immediately following Christmas), gambling, food, coffee, exercise and even work. Any of these, in excess, can produce serious difficulties (in the examples of gambling and excessive shopping the end result can sometimes lead to debt and bankruptcy, prison and possible suicide).

We found it a problem when thinking about 'drugs' as there are so many, and decided to concentrate on aspects of illegal use, criminality adding another dimension to the addict's problem, and on alcohol. Being addicted to alcohol may in fact produce more anti-social behaviour and carry a greater risk of developing a life-threatening illness than an addiction to cocaine or cannabis. In *Dealing with Drugs*, published in 1987 but still relevant in the 1990s and highly recommended, Annas Dixon puts this issue in perspective:

> If we compare the damage caused by alcohol and cigarettes in society with the recent statistics on deaths related to controlled drugs, the current public concern over illicit drug use seems somewhat hypocritical...While cigarette smoking may become an increasingly deviant activity, alcohol consumption continues to increase despite the obvious damage to individuals, families and society.
>
> (Dixon 1987:11)

She continues:

> The use of drugs such as heroin and cocaine that provoke fear and righteous indignation needs to be seen against a background of a drug oriented society which both depends on drugs to aid social interaction and pleasure, and has also come to want 'a pill for every ill'. It is tempting to take an aspirin to prevent an anticipated tension headache, or a sleeping pill to avoid a sleepless night, rather than look at alternative ways of solving problems.
>
> (ibid.)

Many more deaths are caused to others as a result of people being drunk – for example, drunk driving, manslaughter following fights and beatings – than by people on heroin. Crack-cocaine can stimulate such violent and anti-social behaviour as mugging, robbery and 'joy riding', and it is a drug which has a high media profile, particularly in the US, in its association with gangs of young people who are perceived as being out of control and dangerous. There seems little evidence, however, to support the fear that is generated by sensational articles.

We considered the widespread use of drugs like valium and barbiturates which have been found to have withdrawal symptoms of such severity that, in the case of barbiturates can be fatal, and in the case of valium, withdrawal can cause anxiety and panic similar to that for which the drug was originally prescribed. So many 'drug problems' were caused through administration, in good faith, by medical practitioners. Dixon explores the pertinent question: 'What is a drug problem?' She points out that, as workers in this field, we need to consider whose problem it is: is it the client's, the parents' or the worker's? If the problem rests with the worker, then this could be due to personal beliefs, experiences, values and attitudes which are possibly influenced by media-hype. There must be some agreement between the worker and the client that there is a problem needing attention, otherwise it would be useless to try to work together (Dixon 1987: 15). When the use of a drug becomes a problem to the client it is usually because first, he/she is psychologically and physically dependent on it; second, he/she can no longer afford to buy the drug; and third, his/her life has been taken over by the drug resulting in the break-down of relationships (for example, the loss of a partner, children taken into care and so on). Loss of the drug, however, causes overwhelming feelings similar to those following a bereavement, as well as physical withdrawal symptoms. It is during the period after a decision has been made to give up the drug that the person is at his/her most vulnerable. Gary Winship explores some of these issues in Chapter 3, while discussing group therapy.

It seems that 'addicts', including alcoholics, are not a popular client group and punitive attitudes can be observed among workers: 'They brought it on themselves', 'they have no self-control', 'they are junkies, layabouts, a drain on society', are just some of the comments one hears. The addicts' often ambivalent attitude regarding giving up their habit makes them a difficult group to work with, and is possibly one of the reasons why psychotherapists have fought shy of taking on addicted clients. It is often social workers, youth workers, teachers or workers in specialised 'drug centres' who are required to 'do something'. As Dixon points out:

> Some [clients] may still be fairly committed to drug taking and put over very confused messages to the worker because they believe that all social workers want to hear clients express a desire to 'kick' the habit. This may be bewildering and frustrating for someone who perceives their role to be one of helping people to stop their drug use... As with all clients, the first interview is extremely important, for drug users often expect to be rejected as undesirable by professionals if they

confess to the sort of lifestyle they have been leading...They
often feel rejected by the caring professions.

(Dixon 1987: 44)

This experience of feeling rejected, even though it may be a perception of the client and not intended by the worker, can cause a client
to give up at the first attempt to seek help, once they have a glimmer
of motivation to do so.

There are few services for the older drug user with a family, and
in particular for women and children. Residential centres are often
designed with young adults in mind. Women drug users with children are particularly vulnerable because they often have difficulties
over and above the addiction: for example, being in an abusive relationship, having to resort to prostitution to pay for the drugs or
being in a relationship with a pimp, fearing that the child will be
taken away and, in the worst cases, engaging in child abuse either
through neglect or violence, or else witnessing a partner abuse the
child. The extent of such devastating problems became clear to
Diane Waller through working with the staff of the Oasis project in
Brighton, England.

The innovative Oasis project offers a part-time service to women
with current and past drug problems and their children. It currently
has a staff of six full-time posts and several sessional workers
offering complementary therapies (including art therapy) and yoga.
To date the project has achieved funding from several sources,
including the UK National Lottery, but the continuing struggle
with poor resources and time pressure have resulted in low staff
morale. In order to counteract the sense of rejection experienced by
the clients who would use the centre, the project team have gone out
of their way to make the service 'user friendly' and to set up
networks with other agencies, the project's belief being:

that people have the power and choice to make positive changes
in their lives. It aims to create a holistic healthy environment in
which people can engage and participate in various aspects of
the programme for the mutual benefit of both themselves as
individuals and the community as a whole. The project is
committed to providing a confidential person-centred, high
quality and cost effective service...Brighton Oasis Project is
keen to promote the participation of our clients in the planning

and implementation of the services we offer and also in their evaluation.

(Brighton Oasis Project 1997: 3)

We have noted that this 'belief' is one shared by the older and larger Centro Italiano di Solidarieta in Rome, whose humanistic philosophy has had a considerable influence on Diane Waller, Marcia Pleven and Angelika Groterath (see Chapter 4). The 'treatment' philosophies of such programmes are a long way from those of Concept Houses, which are often staffed by ex-addicts who have been through similarly tough regimes themselves. Although these Concept centres incorporate the notion of self-help, their highly structured and confrontative programmes are not suitable for psychiatrically disturbed or severely depressed people, nor, we would suggest, for older addicts and especially those with children.

Since writing a chapter together in 1992 about the use (or non-use) of art therapy in centres for alcohol and drug addicts, which included a review of both American and British literature on art therapy in the treatment of alcohol and drug abuse, we have been preoccupied by why so little work has been done with these client groups. During our research, we discovered that first, there wasn't much literature available, and second, the majority which was available was somewhat puzzling, in that the stated theoretical orientation of the art therapist was not borne out in the description of practice. In the chapter we noted that:

> Albert-Puleo's (1980) discussion of transference illuminates what seems to us to be a major theoretical issue in working with problems of drug and alcohol dependency: i.e., resistance, narcissism, manipulative behaviour. Other art therapists described seem to approach these difficulties by employing controlling, structured and confrontative methods, without conceptualizing a framework to rationalize their approach. Whilst intuition and pragmatism may provide what the client needs in a treatment situation, unless there is a conceptual framework to provide a rationale for interventions and therapeutic technique, the therapeutic relationship is open to misuse and abuse.

(Waller and Gilroy 1992: 181)

We both felt that this had much to do with art therapists trying to adapt their approach to Concept House or 'Daytop' models of treatment. The majority of the papers we found were from the US, where these models and their derivatives were influential. Donnellan and Toon (1986) offered a challenge to this approach by suggesting that some of the techniques used were potentially counter-productive and that staff may be inadequately trained in their use. The hierarchical nature of some of the approaches in therapeutic communities and the potential for abuse of power is a cause for concern.

A sentence in an article titled, 'The Art Experience in Addict Rehabilitation', in the *American Journal of Art Therapy* which, although written in 1976, we suspect is still representative of attitudes found today in many treatment centres, stimulated us to explore further, and to the eventual writing of this book. The sentence in question read: 'Exploratory psychotherapy, stripped of confrontative aspects, has also been notably unsuccessful in therapeutic work with addicts' (Foulke and Keller 1976: 75).

Diane Waller's experience of conducting interactive art therapy groups does not bear out this statement, but this could be because these groups were able to contain the pain caused by reactivating early life disturbances and enable discovery of vulnerable, sensitive areas of self which had previously been disowned. This was indeed difficult for the group members, who found it easier to confront and dissect each other's art work in the first few sessions than to face their own vulnerability. As an 'outsider' in a highly confrontative culture, and indeed the first time that she had worked with staff and residents in a therapeutic community (TC) for drug addicts, Waller found this startling in that she was expected (by the clients) to demand from them an explanation and justification of their work. Her relaxed group-oriented approach was perceived as 'not doing anything' and was the cause of much anxiety, and indeed rage, in the initial period of the group. She was able to manage this situation by asking the group members about their past experience of groups, including art therapy groups, and enlisting their help in understanding what expectations they had and why they had them, and in modifying the highly confrontative and intrusive questioning that was the norm. The group members were able to see that they had many resources which could be used to support each other, without becoming persecutory, and that the images were a valuable extension of themselves which could be explored in an atmosphere of 'interest' and lack of judgement (Waller 1993). It was important to ensure that such groups were conducted in a treatment culture which is able to support the very child-like, raw feelings which can be activated.

A strong case for group work is made by Gary Winship in Chapter 3, in which he describes experiences with clients in a hospital ward structured on a TC model, and in Chapter 5, where the viewing of certain films stimulates strong emotions and interactions in this context. Corrie McClean and Marcia Pleven, on the other hand, focus on individual clients' process using visual art therapy and dance/movement therapy respectively. McClean uses an object-relations model to inform her work, which takes place in individual sessions and Pleven uses a psychoanalytically-oriented dance/movement therapy approach to her client within the context of a women's group. Both McClean and Pleven carried out this work in centres which were unfamiliar with psychoanalytic methods and each found that they had to struggle to maintain their focus. In Chapter 7, Neil Springham, who has worked for several years with both drug and alcohol addicted clients, focuses on an art therapy group within a programme which includes a broad mix of groups from skills-based to psychodynamically oriented. Springham has explored how narcissism operates in the area of addiction and is manifested in the clients' images.

It was as a direct outcome of our explorations into the complex world of addictions that we decided to put together this series of papers which would, we anticipated, through their multidisciplinary nature, begin to counteract the isolation which is often experienced by workers in this field, and particularly by arts therapists. Many workers report feeling overwhelmed by the traumatic life stories of their clients and at the same time angered by the client's 'resistance' to what the worker is offering. In an attempt to 'help' the client they subvert their discipline in a way which renders it useless – as we have noted from the existing art therapy literature. The notion of 'partnership' in treatment seems to be replaced by controlling, intrusive approaches to counselling, a technique which we believe is like throwing the baby out with the bath water. On the other hand, we hear that drug addicts and alcoholics are 'not suited to' psychotherapy, at least not to psychodynamic psychotherapy because of their lack of motivation, ambivalence etc. By bringing together the contributions in this book which, although targeted towards arts therapists will we hope be of interest to others, our aim is to stimulate discussion and further investigations to which arts therapists can contribute effectively.

Having outlined the scheme of the book and the rationale behind its conception, we would like now to draw the reader's attention to some of the literature by arts therapists which has addressed work with drug addicts.

Difficulties experienced by people with addiction related problems as seen by art therapists

In talking about the characteristics found in people with problems related to addiction, it is relevant to refer to the difficulty of separating the idea of personality traits that might make the individual susceptible to becoming dependent on a substance – from problems arising directly as a result of being addicted. Studies addressing the hypothesis of an 'addictive personality' are discussed by Lavelle, Hammersley and Forsyth (1993) who state that the literature has produced contradictory evidence with many methodological flaws. Although it seems that psychological characteristics of problem drinkers and problem drug users do differ from controls, a unique addictive personality has not been defined. Their own interesting study of adolescent licit and illicit drug users in Glasgow in Scotland addresses some of these issues. One of their conclusions suggests, for instance, that the Minnesota Multiphasic Personality Inventory, which is frequently used in research with drug misusers, only measures 'delinquency' instead of a more permanent personality type.

For the purposes of this book, we will briefly describe the difficulties of people with drug and alcohol dependence-related problems as seen by art therapists and how these are addressed in treatment by art therapy.

Moore's (1983) review of the substance abuse literature considers that the characteristics of those addicted makes art therapy a particularly appropriate treatment method. Traits include: loneliness, low self-esteem, helplessness, an inability to communicate in a genuine way and the loss or lack of a sense of control. Further examination of the literature reveals several themes regarding the relevance of art therapy in the treatment of this client group with regard to their particular difficulties. We will examine each aspect separately.

Difficulties in expression and communication of emotion

1   Facilitating expression
    Self-expression can be facilitated by the use of art materials in art therapy sessions (Adelman and Castricone 1986: 53), helping people become more aware of their feelings and to gain insight. Kaufman (1981: 353) considers that art expression is particularly effective when verbal expression is difficult, when words are used to hide feelings or when there is a lack of awareness of thoughts and feelings. Head (1975: 44) describes meaning in a picture being revealed almost without the patient's knowledge. Moore (1983: 251) finds art can make issues more accessible for discussion by making them concrete or symbolic, and Wadeson (1980: 233) finds expression through art to provide a sensitive instrument for 'tapping' complex emotions. It is seen to enhance the quality of communication and reduce confusion (Moore 1983: 251).

2   Protecting defences
    In the implication that there is a need to protect defences, many art therapists see the art therapy as providing a less threatening way of exploring difficulties than more directly verbal means. Mahony and Waller (1992: 186) describe how if necessary, defences can be protected by the artwork, providing a concrete aesthetic level at which to relate, while at the same time both therapist and client can be aware of the underlying message. Similarly, Albert-Puleo (1980: 47) sees the artwork as providing a non-threatening focus where objects can be talked about rather than contacting the ego, with repressed material becoming more acceptable to consciousness. In a similar vein, Springham (1992: 15) refers to the artwork as providing 'metaphors' to members of a group.

3   Providing containment
    Art therapy is seen to be particularly helpful in addressing the characteristic difficulty found in substance misuse states of experiencing and expressing strong emotions. Johnson (1990: 300) says that recovering addicts often disclose extreme shame, anguish and rage. The artwork is seen to provide containment to the expression or communication of potentially difficult material: Donnenberg (1978: 39) regards the non-verbal aspect

of art therapy as offering a non-threatening and socially acceptable form of expression; and Albert-Puleo (1980: 51) believes
aggression can be externalised 'appropriately'. Foulke and
Keller (1976: 80) write that spontaneous feeling can be experienced in a 'safely' controlled way; and Potocek and Wilder
(1989: 100) describe how expression and behaviour can be
explored and experimented with in a less threatening framework than a group which is primarily a verbal forum.

Loss of control

Distancing, experimentation and redirecting

The characteristic fear of those with substance misuse difficulties,
of being overwhelmed by painful and confusing emotions, is seen to
be addressed in several ways. Moore (1983: 251) sees the artwork
acting as an aid to the recognition and differentiation of feeling
states, the clarification of which brings an increased sense of
mastery. Head (1975: 48) defines this more simply as the artwork
providing 'some distancing' thereby giving a more objective view of
conflicts which will then be less threatening. Ways of experimenting
seem to be provided by the artmaking: Adelman and Castricone
(1986: 58) consider their approach supports independence and risk-
taking; and Ulman (1953: 61) describes how intuitive, non-verbal
expression in drawing provides a new sense of being able to trust
feelings. Mahony and Waller (1992: 186) describe a process of
initially feeling overwhelmed by the image, coming to terms with it,
and then wanting to experiment. Foulke and Keller (1976: 75)
consider that the act of painting may serve to control the release of
strong feelings; and Spring (1985: 100) says that art therapy can
provide a 'model' for achieving a sense of control. Another aspect
of gaining control is illustrated by Albert-Puleo (1980: 51) who
describes impulsive actions and behaviour being redirected into
pictorial expression.

Low self-esteem

Developing and building on resources

The development of self-esteem is described by several art therapists: Kaufman (1981: 359) sees art therapy as being able to reveal

strengths; Head (1975: 48) considers that it can add the stimulation needed to function in a more productive or satisfying way; and Mahony and Waller (1992: 186) describe how the development of skills increases self-esteem. Albert-Puleo (1980: 50) describes how her model of art therapy was able to address particularly low self-esteem, thus enabling the client to express previously internalised anger and feelings of inadequacy. Johnson (1990: 301) considers shame to be a core issue in alcoholism which can be addressed through art. Foulke and Keller (1976: 80) describe how art therapy in a supportive environment can be used tentatively to test feared emotions resulting in enhanced self-esteem by the increased capacity to experience these emotions.

Isolation

Symbolic expression and communication

Adelman and Castricone (1986: 53) regard those who are addicted to substances as suffering from profound social isolation, but they believe that expression of this isolation in symbolic form can begin a process of communication and social interaction. Luzzatto (1989) extends the concept of isolation when she describes 'withdrawal' and 'clinging' as two basic emotional positions of people with drinking problems. Short-term art therapy work is focussed on the experimentation with symbolic images of the two positions. The actual making of art is seen as lessening isolation (Allen 1985: 11) through providing a basis for sociable exchange (Ulman 1953: 59) and interaction (Head 1975: 54). Similarly, Foulke and Keller (1976: 80) suggest that creating artwork in a group provides opportunities for sharing and validating experiences; and Springham (1992: 16) finds initial reactions to art therapy can be used by members of a short-term group as a unifying experience. Potocek and Wilder (1989: 100) describe how through art and without the need for verbalisation, dependence on a substance can be redirected to reliance on appropriate relationships for emotional needs.

It can be seen from the literature that art therapists consider there are specific and unique benefits to be offered by art therapy to the treatment of people with drug and alcohol related problems and detailed discussion of specific aspects will be provided by several authors in this book.

Bibliography

Adelman, E. and Castricone, L. (1986) 'An expressive arts model for substance abuse group training and treatment', *The Arts in Psychotherapy*, 13: 53–9.

Albert-Puleo, N. (1980) 'Modern psychoanalytic art therapy and its application to drug abuse', *The Arts in Psychotherapy*, 7 (1): 43–52.

Allen, P.B. (1985) 'Integrating art therapy into an alcoholism treatment program', *American Journal of Art Therapy*, 24: 10–12.

Brighton Oasis Project (1997) 'Service Specification', October, 22 Richmond Place, Brighton BN2 2NA.

Dixon, A. (1987) *Dealing with Drugs*, London: BBC Books.

Donnellan, B. and Toon, P. (1986) 'The use of "therapeutic techniques" in the Concept House model of therapeutic community for drug abusers: For whose benefit – staff or resident?', *International Journal of Therapeutic Communities*, 7 (3): 183–9.

Donnenberg, D. (1978) 'Art Therapy in a Drug Community', *Confinia Psychiat.*, 21: 37–44.

Foulke, W.E. and Keller, T.W. (1976) 'The Art experience in addict rehabilitation', *American Journal of Art Therapy*, 15(3): 75–80.

Head, V.B. (1975) 'Experiences with art therapy in short-term groups of day clinic addicted patients', *The Ontario Psychologist*, 7(4): 42–9.

Johnson, L. (1990) 'Creative therapies in the treatment of addictions: The art of transforming shame', *The Arts in Psychotherapy*, 17: 299–308.

Kaufman, G.H. (1981) 'Art therapy with the addicted', *Journal of Psychoactive Drugs*, 13(4): 353–60.

Lavelle, T., Hammersley, R. and Forsyth, A. (1993) 'Is the "addictive personality" merely delinquency?', *Addiction Research*, 1(1): 27–37.

Luzzatto, P. (1989) 'Drinking problems and short-term art therapy: Working with images of withdrawal and clinging', in A. Gilroy and T. Dalley (eds) *Pictures at an Exhibition*, London: Tavistock/Routledge, 207–19.

Mahony, J. and Waller, D.E. (1992, reprinted 1994) 'Art therapy in the treatment of alcohol and drug abuse', in D.E. Waller and A. Gilroy (eds) *Art Therapy: A Handbook*, Buckingham: Open University Press, pp. 173–88

Moore, R.W. (1983) 'Art therapy with substance abusers: A review of the literature', *The Arts in Pychotherapy*, 10: 251–60.

Potocek, J. and Wilder, V.N. (1989) 'Art/Movement psychotherapy in the treatment of the chemically dependent patient', *The Arts in Psychotherapy*, 16: 99–103.

Spring, D. (1985) 'Sexually abused, chemically dependent women', *American Journal of Art Therapy*, 24: 13–21.

Springham, N. (1992) 'Short term group processes in art therapy for people with substance misuse problems', *Inscape*, Spring: 8–16.

Ulman, E. (1953) 'Art therapy at an outpatient clinic', *Psychiatry*, 16: 55–64.

Wadeson, H. (1980) *Art Psychotherapy* (Chapter 18), Wiley: Interscience Publications.

Waller, D.E. (1993) *Group Interactive Art Therapy: Its Use in Training and Treatment,* London and New York: Routledge.

Waller, D.E. and Gilroy, A. (1992) *Art Therapy: A Handbook*, Buckingham and Philadelphia: Open University Press.

Chapter 1

Conceptions of addiction and implications for treatment approaches

Angelika Groterath

Addiction

For many years addiction has been considered a disease of modern western society. In 1964 when the World Health Organisation recommended recognising drug addiction as an illness, it referred explicitly to the physical diseases which result from drug addiction. In the years since this recommendation, drug addiction has come to be regarded as a form of mental illness in some European countries. What is surprising is that this has happened not as a result of scientific research, but as a result of theorisation and mystification. In Germany in the late 1990s, for example, there is still no professorship and consequently no discrete university research unit concerned with addiction. Nevertheless addiction therapy in Germany – as in many other countries – is carried out professionally. Residential treatment centres are publicly financed only when the director is a medical doctor and the centre is staffed by professionals such as doctors, psychologists and social workers. These professionals frequently base their therapeutic work on the hypotheses or even myths of therapeutic theories, but use therapeutic instruments which don't necessarily comply with these theories (Groterath 1993: 250–2). One can find similar examples of this non-rational approach to addiction treatment elsewhere in Europe, such as the presence of gurus or so-called 'charismatic' leaders in some treatment centres in France and Italy, which surprisingly meets with the approval of health administrators.

The truth, however, is that we assume a great deal about addiction but in fact do not know why some people become addicted to drugs, whereas others, who have experienced similar life circumstances and have had the same access to drugs, do not. Georges

Estievenart, from the drug department of the European Commission, probably best summed up our knowledge about addiction at a conference in 1993 in Florence, Italy, with the suggestion that we have come to realise that there is a close relationship between the use of drugs by individuals and the production and trafficking of drugs (Estievenart 1993: 9). To put it another way, '...we have known for a long time that offer and demand are in a mutual relation' (Groterath 1996: 8). But this connection has, apparently, nothing to do with the numerous questions of addiction therapy which have been discussed for at least twenty-five years in scientific and therapeutic literature.

The user population

Illegal drug use first emerged in western European countries as a significant social phenomenon among the youth population in the late 1960s and early 1970s – mainly on the wave of the protest movements. During this period, the addict acquired a special social 'function' in society: he/she was held up as an example of abnormal and deviant behaviour in a 'normal' society, a kind of 'scarecrow' figure. Heroin is still perceived as the main problem drug in that it is regarded as the force behind drug-related crime and is implicated in health indicators such as treatment admissions, physical complications and drug-related death. Nevertheless, the 'scarecrow' has become a historical figure as:'Throughout the 1980s, the age range and demographic and social characteristics of drug consumers tended to broaden and diversify' (European Communities 1996: 5).

Statistical information taken from the European Communities Report quoted here, can be translated in social terms as follows: there is a tendency in western European societies to absorb addiction into normality. An addict of the 1990s, even a heroin user, can be a 'normal' citizen. Drug use is no longer seen as a problem solely confined to social outsiders or to the younger generation. Indeed, the average age of people entering treatment centres today (for example, in Denmark, the Netherlands and Sweden) is 30 years and over (ibid.: 18). Furthermore, in many countries it would appear that older drug users are not seeking help from traditional treatment services, mainly because they are designed for younger people, and therefore not perceived as suitable or appropriate by or for older people.

In the late 1980s, the Centro Italiano di Solidarieta[1] in Rome created a non-residential Evening Programme for adults who, to all intents and purposes, were 'normal' members of society. To quote Paolo Pacchiarotti, the manager of the programme:

> We got more and more telephone calls from adults looking for help, mainly women and men aged between 35 and 40, but some over 50 years old. We had to deal with people who had good jobs and clearly defined professional status. Most of them were married or lived in stable relationships, others were separated, divorced or widowed. Nearly all of them had children. ... Their financial situation was good, they could buy the drugs and were not constrained to join the subculture of drug-criminality. All of them had relationships with persons who had nothing to do with drugs.
>
> (Pacchiarotti 1995: 2)

> Indeed, it might so happen that at the same time as an older man or woman in the Evening Programme was being treated, his or her son or daughter could be found in treatment in the non-residential Koiné – a programme for adolescents with school problems at risk of becoming, or who have already become drug users.
>
> (Pacchiarotti 1995: 2)

Treatment services

The Evening Programme example given in the preceding section, which involves the creation of various therapeutic programmes for different user types, cannot be considered representative of treatment centres throughout Europe. It is fair to say that treatment services in Europe have changed in the past few years, but they have done so in another way: 'in many countries methadone programmes are expanding and new "low threshold" services make entry into treatment easier' (European Communities 1996: 16).

The debate around methadone programmes quickly became a political issue, and unfortunately the arguments for and against often lacked a sense of perspective, as could be observed from the many conferences on the subject over the years. Turning the debate about methadone into a simplistic pro and anti one means that the drug is not seen for what it really is: just one possibility among many options – neither a magic potion, nor a force for evil.

How did the question of how to treat drug addiction become such a strongly political issue, and why is it treated in such a simplistic manner? The answers are not yet available, and maybe the question has yet to be formulated in many parts of the scientific and/or therapeutic world. On the one hand, it seems unavoidable that the 'methadone discussion' or the discussion about 'harm reduction' in general must become a political issue all over the world, following on from the fact that the US, still the 'super power', continues to commit a lot of money to the concept of 'harm reduction'. On the other hand, many European professionals in the field lose their sense of perspective when discussing the subject, and campaign strenuously against methadone – maybe in part because they fear job losses as more treatment centres lose patients or fail to attract them.

For many years addiction treatment has been the treatment – or perhaps more precisely, the social control – of people on the margins of society. Many treatment centres were conceived as 'islands' removed from mainstream society, and many so-called therapeutic instruments were developed especially (and almost exclusively) for treating addicts. Today's addicts are no longer protesting against society, and instead, frequently fit into the 1990s culture of consumerism – with drugs perceived as being just another consumer item promising happiness and freedom. This could be one reason why some of the therapeutic or educational instruments that have been developed for therapeutic communities or similar institutions are no longer effective. A socially well-adapted person with a good capacity for intellectual insight and a moderate system of psychological defenses (characteristics of many addicts today) does not require strong social control, nor will the client tolerate heavily directive interventions.

I would suggest that the tendencies towards liberalisation in Europe are one symptom of the process of 'normalization' of addiction, but it is not the only symptom, and that 'addicts themselves present a lot of symptoms, and many of them today could be treated with psychotherapeutic methods' (Groterath 1995a: 3). 'Traditional' psychotherapy has, however, never played a considerable role in addiction treatment.

Psychotherapy

It is worth considering some particularities of psychotherapeutic methods. Psychotherapy is a product of the twentieth century and has its theoretical roots in central European culture. European culture is grounded in the fourfold heritage of Greek philosophy, Roman law, German concepts about society, and the Christian religion. Even today this mixture gives rise to certain characteristics: for example, a tendency towards individuality, rationality and ethics of work and performance.

To what degree psychology and psychotherapy is influenced by such a mixture, or is culturally biased by it, cannot be easily quantified. This is due to the fact that mainstream psychology and psychotherapy tend to regard themselves as sciences or at the very least disciplines of universal value. Furthermore, there is still some confusion about the definition of psychotherapy, and what is recognised in one country as a psychotherapeutic method ('professional' psychotherapy), can be considered a supplementary approach in another, or even charlatanism in a third.

What nearly all psychotherapeutic methods have in common is that they diagnose personal deficiencies and tend to locate the 'problem' in the individual. Some psychotherapists are aware of the social nature of their clients' problems, but feel – and with their mostly individual-centered methods, often are – impotent to do anything about it. At present, the so-called systems approaches, with family therapy as its protagonist, are appreciated by those professionals who criticise the individualism of traditional psychotherapy. But even though this approach avoids attaching a 'guilty' label to one individual in particular and tries to avoid the imbalance of the traditional doctor–patient relationship, it fails to break substantially with the principles of psychotherapy. Deficiency is still always diagnosed, what has changed is the unit, with the whole family seen as the 'patient'.

Relationships between individual members of family units at least in part reflect relationships existing at higher levels in the organisation of a society. Yet society is never seen as a 'patient' of psychotherapy.

Psychotherapeutic methods in addiction treatment

Many of today's addicts, even though apparently 'normal' citizens, are as socially ill as addicts of the past, and although they can be helped by psychotherapeutic methods, these need to be combined with social or educational programmes which can deal with the social aspects of drug addiction.

The question of how to change the treatment and which psychotherapeutic methods to integrate cannot be answered in a general way since individual countries have specific legal, social and cultural conditions which need to be addressed. Therapeutic services have to be developed in the context of these conditions. This applies in particular to therapeutic communities or similar nearly 'total' social institutions, for although many of them define themselves as 'alternatives to society', they are nearly always a form of (human) laboratory or cultural mediation agency for the society they are situated in, and by which in most cases they are paid.

In virtually all cases, psychotherapeutic methods are conceptualised around an out-patient setting, and they imply a close and often exclusive doctor–patient relationship. They are therefore too 'weak' to survive in institutions which don't share their basic assumptions about people and their potential. If placed within a social structure that operates under other principles, psychotherapeutic methods will often change and cease to become effective. One can see this in the example of psychodrama (a topic which I have expanded on in Chapter 4):

> As for classical psychodrama, according to Moreno it can be effective only in an institutional structure that shares its main assumptions about man being potentially creative, able to relate himself to others and to act together with them, and able to find his own resources, his own way. If put into a social structure that starts from other principles psychodrama suffers changes and often is not effective any more. To agree theoretically with the above mentioned assumptions of psychodrama is not enough. A social institution must be measured by the methodology that translates its philosophy into practice. As for TCs. we know that most of them define themselves as human, jointly responsible and so on. But what about directive or even violent interventions in those TCs? And what about tendencies

of staff members to feel and behave as super-parents? The effectiveness of classical psychodrama is more than limited when a group member who leaves the psychodramatic session and has experienced that it is he who finds his own way in life, joins another group where whoever conducts the group is and knows all and where group members are and know nothing.

(Groterath 1995b: 3)

Psychodrama has experienced a great deal of change in the context of addiction treatment; changes that are as diverse as the strongly directive versions found in some American Therapeutic Communities to the more psychoanalytic psychodrama style of some European treatment centres. But other psychotherapeutic methods have also suffered. The transference relationship of classical psychoanalysis, for example, cannot be established in a treatment centre nor in a similar social institution, because doctors involved in the institutional setting cannot be considered 'white walls of projection', but at most 'grey (eminence) walls', as men and women who react and express themselves in a therapeutic situation not only in a counter-transference way, but also in a very human and personally involved manner.

The integration of psychotherapeutic methods in institutions such as therapeutic communities requires first of all a precise analysis of their compatibility with that institution's philosophy and methodology. And something is also required from the psychotherapist: he/she must give up the pretension of being exclusive. Psychotherapists working in addiction treatment centres must be constantly aware of their intervention being only one factor in a complex system of therapeutic factors, and they must also recognise the fact that therapeutic factors interfere with one another.

Once a basis has been established, that is, once it has been ascertained that different therapeutic instruments are compatible with one another, many psychotherapeutic methods can be integrated in addiction treatment. Even though therapeutic communities seems to favour group methods, brief individual therapy carried out in the Rogerian style, for example, can be integrated – maybe not as a complete 'Rogerian therapy', but as an opportunity for patients to temporarily disengage themselves from the embedding and caring group arrangements of the therapeutic institution and to concentrate on their own feelings. This method could be particularly appropriate at the end of a course of treatment when a client is preparing to integrate back into society – a society that often leaves them alone and doesn't provide so many opportunities to be embedded.

Even though art therapies are rarely valued by the 'establishment' of psychotherapy (which has a tendency to absorb them or to use them as 'supplementary methods'), or by the establishment of addiction treatment (which until recently, seemed to consider all addiction treatment 'home-made' or own property), these methods have for many years been important elements in addiction treatment programmes – often in clandestine ways. It is time to reassess their value and see them as psychotherapeutic methods which can be used in group settings; which can be combined easily with other methods (perhaps because they do not make so many claims for exclusivity as the 'masters' of psychotherapy); and, finally, because they seem, on the basis of our experience, to be highly appropriate for addiction treatment. Although we still lack statistical data about the effectiveness of these methods, some reflections about their nature can at least support the hypothesis of their being appropriate for addiction treatment.

Many addicts, though perhaps less so than in the past, suffer from a sense of failure and rejection by society. It is well known that they are afraid of being judged by others and as a result they themselves often judge and criticise. Verbal psychotherapeutic methods tend to re-enact a school or even tribunal situation: the emphasis is on what is said in these sessions. Neurotic patients, and mainly those with a high level of education, normally feel quite comfortable on this 'stage of words' and can use it for therapeutic work. In contrast, addicts often feel uncomfortable on this 'stage' and tend to refuse it. This phenomenon has been called therapeutic resistance by some, and 'non-treatability' of addicts by others. The important thing is that we have noticed that even so-called 'untreatable' addicts react positively and often in a highly differentiated way to psychotherapy as soon as the 'stage' shifts, i.e. when the therapeutic situation doesn't re-enact the traumatic situation of judgement or exams and the risk of failing, and instead offers a more permissive 'stage'. That is what the arts therapies do – with colours and forms, movement, music and play. Furthermore, in that they involve not only the mind but also the body of the patients, these methods are more 'lively' than verbal psychotherapeutic methods, more closely connected to the vital expressions of the individual. Addicts have an urgent need to come in contact with such expressions: drug addiction can be a suicide by degrees. Addicts have treated their bodies very badly, and even though they may be 'clean' during treatment, many of them are still threatened by the risk of HIV infection or other diseases. Maybe their 'liveliness' is another reason for the arts therapies' success in addiction treatment.

Note

1 See Chapter 4 for a description of the structure and function of CEIS.

Bibliography

Estievenart, G. (1993) 'The European Community and the Global Drug Phenomenon', in G. Estievenart (ed.) *Policies and Strategies to Combat Drugs in Europe. The Treaty on European Union: Framework for a New European Strategy to Combat Drugs?*, European Commission.
European Communities (1996) 'Annual Report on the State of the Drugs Problem in the European Union', E.E.C.D.D.A., European Commission.
Groterath, A. (1993) 'Und wenn sie nun doch nicht krank sind? Psychodrama als Probe für das Leben im Centro Di Solidarietà in Rom', *Psychodrama* 6, 2: 246–9.
——(1995a) 'The Use of Psychotherapy in Addiction Treatment', unpublished conference paper, Dealing with Addiction: What Measures At What Price?, The Institutes of ICAA, 11–16 June 1995, Trieste, Italy.
——(1995b) 'It Shouldn't Be Always a Drama. The Use of Psychodrama in Therapeutic Communities', unpublished conference paper, Europe Against Drug Abuse, EFTC, 28 May–2 June 1995, Thessaloniki, Greece.
——(1996) 'Die Unschuld verloren', Suchtreport, 6: 6–13.
Pacchiarotti, P. (1995) 'Adults, the Labour World, Drug Addiction: The Need for an Out-Patient Treatment Perspective', unpublished conference paper, Europe Against Drug Abuse, EFTC, 28 May–2 June 1995, Thessaloniki, Greece.

Chapter 2

The philosophy of treatment of people with alcohol or drug problems and the place of the psychotherapies in their care

Tim Cantopher

Introduction

The further back in history one goes, the more primitive and less constructive is the approach taken by society to the treatment of addiction, whether it's to alcohol or other drugs (Royal College of Psychiatrists 1986). In Peru in the fifteenth century, the approved treatment for drunkenness was to have the offender taken to the market square and beaten to death. Until the third decade of this century, management of alcoholism and illicit drug dependence was only slightly more positive. Although most drug dependence was iatrogenic in the early part of the twentieth century, the attitude of the authorities was to focus on the damage done by the addict to society and to punish him/her for it. The same was true for people with drink related problems; those who were afflicted aroused concern only when falling foul of the laws governing drunkenness in a public place.

The problem was that nobody knew how to help people with addictions. For people with a drink problem the turning point came in the 1930s with the introduction of Alcoholics Anonymous (AA) in the UK from the States. In 1926 the Rolleston Committee, which was set up to find ways of dealing with the escalating problem of opiate dependence, published a report. This report signalled a similar shift in the fortunes of those dependent on morphine, heroin and other additive drugs (Report of the Rolleston Committee 1926). Alcoholics were now seen to be suffering from a disease which, although incurable, could be controlled by following the prescribed AA 'twelve steps of recovery' programme (Alcoholics Anonymous 1988). In addition, opiate addicts were seen as 'not merely suffering from some vicious form of indulgence', but suffering from a medical condition which required treatment. Thus doctors were given the authority to prescribe addictive drugs including opiates for their patients for the control and treatment of their addiction.

This system, in contrast to the one operating in the US whereby all opiates were restricted for use only in pain relief, was known as 'the British System' and was envied by helping professionals around the world until, decades later, America and other countries followed suit. Since this time the mainstay of the British approach to the treatment of opiate addiction has been the prescribing of substitutes, such as methadone, under controlled conditions. However, with the significant rise in the number of opiate addicts in the 1960s, the problem threatened to become uncontrollable with doctors receiving the blame for fuelling the problem through excessive and injudicious prescribing. This led to the setting up of specialist drug clinics where prescribing could be centred. Since their creation, these clinics have become overwhelmed by the continuing expansion of the problem, and so treatment has again devolved in part to other doctors, including GPs. However, the specialist clinics remain and have over the years developed a range of treatments. Research has shown that treatment which involves counselling together with prescribing approaches is more effective than prescribing alone (Jaffe 1995: 861). In treatment centres as a result, a range of different therapies have been developed, not only to help addicts control their dependence but also to move toward abstinence and to maintain it. Unfortunately, no body of research is available on what form of 'counselling' is most effective or whether specific or more exploratory therapies may be particularly useful. Research in the medical literature tends to concentrate on comparisons between particular treatment types, for example, 'counselling' versus 'drug treatment', and to date it has not focused on which elements of exploratory therapy may help people to overcome their addiction. We are, therefore, largely reliant on clinical experience in deciding on the types of therapies to incorporate into a treatment programme.

With other drugs of abuse, such as amphetamines, LSD, cocaine and Ecstasy, our length of experience in treating dependent individuals is even less. Drug substitution is not an option. While there is a great paucity of evidence available on treatment efficacy, most treatment centres recognise that treatment based on some form of psychotherapy, whether it be supportive counselling, behavioural, cognitive or psychodynamic psychotherapy, is central to provision of services for this group.

For people with alcohol related problems in Britain there was no effective help available other than through the AA until the 1950s when the first Alcohol Treatment Unit (ATU) was opened at Warlingham Park Hospital, Surrey, England. A number of similar units followed. Most were based on a six- to eight-week programme involving both individual and group psychotherapies on a residential basis, following detoxification from alcohol. A number of different models and therapies were used depending on the training and orientation of the senior staff in these units. In the private sector, most in-patient/residential programmes were founded on the 'Minnesota Model', a treatment which is based on a total abstinence from alcohol as a lifelong aim and incorporates the twelve steps of recovery.

Unfortunately, such units are expensive and have a limited volume. Alcoholism is common and so clearly more was needed to deal effectively with the problem. When research emerged which apparently showed that the ATUs were no more effective than much briefer and less expensive alternatives, their fate was largely sealed. In recent years, with their closure and replacement by solely community based approaches, much of the development of intensive programmes using psychodynamic and other therapies has ceased.

Recent trends, research and current services

Since the advent of HIV/AIDS, services for drug abusers have attracted more interest and funds. At the same time the focus has changed. No longer is total and permanent cessation of drug use the sole aim of treatment. The new emphasis is on 'harm reduction'. An implicit assumption has been made that not all drug users can or even want to stop their drug use. These individuals are now targeted by services in an attempt to reduce the harm to them and to society caused by their dependence. Although approximately two per cent of illicit drug users die each year, most of these addicts succumb to effects other than those of the drug itself, such as poisoning from additives (known as 'cutting'), infection from contaminated injection equipment or changes in purity of street supplies leading to overdosing. A change of behaviour of addicts, away from injection and toward other forms of administration (for example, oral, inhalation or smoking) can therefore greatly reduce morbidity and mortality. This was always the case, but it took the emergence of HIV/AIDS for services to be directed primarily toward changing the way in which drugs are taken.

In their first publication on the subject, the British Government was clear about its priorities in dealing with drug treatment (Advisory Council on Misuse of Drugs 1988: 2). Where a conflict arose between good clinical practice and the prevention of the spread of HIV/AIDS, the latter was to take priority. As a result a great deal of attention in recent years has been paid to educating drug users about HIV/AIDS: making services easily accessible and user-friendly, encouraging methadone prescribing services and setting up needle and syringe exchange schemes. While these schemes have often proved highly effective in changing behaviour away from the sharing of injection equipment, many feel that the other important aim – to encourage addicts away from their dependence on illicit drugs – has been lost. This was recognised by a working group on drug services commissioned by the British Government in 1991 who acknowledged that a variety of services are necessary for drug users with a range of aims, depending on the needs of the individual (Department of Health 1991).

The concentration on harm reduction since the late 1980s has tended to reduce the level of attention given to treatment of drug addictions, especially through the psychotherapies. This is a shame, since it has been well established for some years that such 'non-medical' approaches can be highly effective (Rathod 1977).

In 1977, Edwards et al. published the result of a study of 100 male alcoholics which looked at the effectiveness of intensive treatments, including a range of therapies and in-patient treatment as against a session of simple advice giving (Edwards et al. 1977). One year in to the study they found no significant difference in outcome between the two groups. This study, and similar ones which have followed, have radically changed the emphasis away from intensive treatment approaches involving prolonged therapies, including psychotherapies, toward much cheaper 'minimal interventions'. Community Alcohol Teams were set up to replace the closing ATUs. Their main aim was to ensure that people with drink related problems were identified quickly, as doing so not only minimises the time for physical, psychological and social morbidity to occur, but also renders treatment more effective. In the first year of heavy drinking, merely giving appropriate advice to individuals picked up through screening leads to a significant reduction in levels of drinking in nearly fifty per cent of patients (Wallace *et al.* 1988). However, until recently it took approximately ten years from the onset of the problem for the average alcohol dependent patient to enter treatment, by which time treatment ceased to be very effective.

Clearly, therefore, an emphasis on early intervention, often of a fairly simple type and at a primary care level, was and is the right way forward. However, in the last decade, there has been an increasing awareness on both sides of the Atlantic that the baby has been thrown out with the bath water, as it were. That is to say, while intensive therapies and ATUs should not form the central plank of a treatment service, there are some people who need this kind of treatment. As such services are not often available under the National Health Service in many parts of the UK, community alcohol teams are now finding that a small number of people with a severe and long-standing dependence on alcohol are simply not manageable on a 'brief intervention' basis in the community.

In the US the concept that patients/clients may need to be matched to appropriate treatments was first aired in the 1980s. While everyone in the alcohol treatment field was attempting to shift the emphasis of services away from the residential toward early community based interventions, the numbers of patients in in-patient treatment units were stubbornly refusing to fall.

The response of the US Government was to set up 'Project MATCH' (Matching Alcoholism Treatments to Client Heterogeneity), with funding of US$45 million; a study on such a large scale that it could not be conceived of in the UK, or anywhere else in the world. The results were reported in January 1997 (Project MATCH Research Group 1977). While disappointingly few concrete conclusions were reached, what did emerge was that the twelve step treatment is particularly successful for patients with no symptoms of psychopathology. Unfortunately a comprehensive treatment programme incorporating psychotherapies of more than one kind (including art therapy) was not included in the list of approaches matched with different patient/client types. However, this study has sparked a different way of thinking and a new line of research, working to offer each patient the treatment best suited to his or her needs.

Increasingly workers in the field are recognising that some patients/clients do need intensive programmes, including psychotherapies. We need to ask ourselves not whether this is so, but who these individuals are and how these therapies are best delivered.

In the meantime, the author of the report argues for the preservation of residential treatment programmes for the minority of patients/clients who fail to respond to brief and/or community based approaches. The decision about what form of psychotherapy to use should be based on a sound appraisal of the background to the individual's drink or drug problem. Hence, in my view, an appreciation of the basic models of how someone may develop addiction to a substance is an essential prerequisite for matching the therapy to the individual. Moreover, the author and many of his colleagues (one of whom is represented later in this volume – Neil Springham, Chapter 7) are agreed that one major purpose of therapy is to enable the patient/client to gain an understanding of the background to his addiction, in order to be able to work on the specific changes necessary for his recovery.[1] A brief outline of some of the models which have applied to patients in our unit follows.

Some models of addiction and their implications for the individual

Models related to the effect of the drug:

The opponent process

All drugs which carry a capacity for addiction demonstrate this process. The more addictive a drug the faster and more powerful is the opponent process. The opponent process for heroin is rapid and extreme while for alcohol it is relatively slow. For a person not previously dependent on alcohol it usually takes the consumption of over 50 units a week, with few drink-free days, over a period of at least several months for the opponent process to operate.

The process is that by which a drug taken regularly will reverse its initial effects in the long term. Each time the drug is administered it has an effect or a range of effects. As the drug leaves the system these effects wear off and there is a small overshoot, which in less addictive drugs is so small as often to be undetectable by the person. For example, the effects of alcohol on most people are to cause a lowering of tension and anxiety, a pleasant rise in mood, encouragement of sleep, dulling of pain, muscle relaxation, enhancement of confidence and a rise in the epileptic threshold (that is a lowering of the tendency to have a seizure in an epileptic patient). A person drinking regularly to excess over a long enough period will gradually suffer a reversal of these acute effects, experiencing a rise in anxiety, depression, poor sleep, aches and pains, tense crampy muscles, a collapse in confidence and (eventually) a risk of developing epileptic seizures.

Hence the long-term effects of any addictive drug used to excess can be predicted on the basis of a reversal of the immediate effects. This process, however, is not just obscure to the sufferer; it will usually appear that the opposite effect is occurring. For example, most alcoholic patients are convinced that alcohol is the only drug effectively to lower their anxiety, raise their mood and enable them to sleep. Indeed, in the short term this is the case, but in the longer term the reverse is true.

On suffering withdrawal a more extreme rebound reversal of the effects of the drug occurs, increasing the sufferer's impression that the drug is helping. So long as he takes the drug he will feel all right, whereas without it he will suffer a range of severe symptoms. This is the trap of addiction. Once the opponent process has started to operate it is inevitable that the symptoms will get worse, either slowly if the person continues regular usage, or rapidly if he stops.

Fortunately the process of detoxification can mitigate these withdrawal symptoms. By giving a drug with tranquillising, sleep inducing, muscle relaxant and anti-epileptic properties, at first in a high dosage then dwindling to nothing over a week-long period, the worst symptoms of alcohol withdrawal can be avoided. For heroin – a longer acting opiate compound without the capacity to induce euphoria – methadone is used.

While immediate withdrawal symptoms usually fade quite quickly (five days to a week for alcohol), more subtle effects can last for a longer period. Some alcoholic patients suffer a general feeling of malaise and being 'out of sorts' for six weeks or even three months after withdrawal. This is even more common in the case of highly addictive drugs such as heroin. However, if the sufferer succeeds in maintaining abstinence, these symptoms will eventually disappear. For example, an alcoholic patient's level of anxiety will return to the state it was at before regular heavy drinking started. Relaxation and anxiety management therapy can further aid this process so that the sufferer may eventually achieve levels of anxiety lower than he has experienced at any previous time.

One other phenomenon which occurs within the opponent process and which has been taken to confirm the disease model of addiction is that, after a period of abstinence following the induction of the opponent process through regular drug usage, relapse causes a rapid rise in the severity of the symptoms; not in the same way as the first time, but within days the symptoms rise to a level more severe than the last episode. It seems, for example, that an alcoholic patient who relapses suffers a rise in anxiety within a few days up to the level which would have occurred had he never stopped drinking. Thus it would appear that a disease process is continuing even during the period of abstinence.

Individual differences

In any population, most individual characteristics will vary between people in the form of a normal distribution. This means that there will be large numbers of individuals in the average range for the particular trait studied and only a few in the extreme ranges, either high or low. As an example, the normal distribution curve for height in a population is given below:

The same principle applies for any trait distributed in this way within a population, such as weight, IQ, etc.

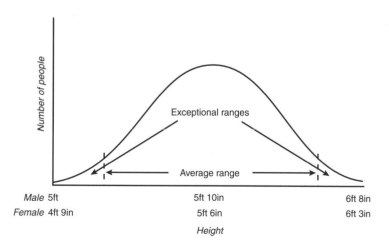

Figure 2.1 Normal distribution curve for height

The general rule is that any person falling outside the average range with respect to any trait will tend to suffer problems related to it as a result (this applies even to unexpected traits such as an exceptionally high IQ or to low levels of anxiety) (Cantopher: 1996). Relevant examples in the addiction field include being over anxious, sleeping poorly, a tendency towards extreme depressive moods, needing high levels of stimulation, being exceptionally susceptible to the anxiety-lowering effect of the drug used (especially relevant with relation to alcohol), and many others.

The implication for the individual addict is that, in the words of AA, 'a fearless personal inventory' needs to be made (AA 1988). One of the roles of an addiction treatment programme is to enable patients to see themselves in an accurate light and in particular to identify those personality traits which they possess to an exceptionally high or low degree and which have relevance to their drug use or drinking.

In facilitating the change in behaviour necessary to achieve and maintain abstinence a common misconception must be overcome: that is the assumption that personality cannot change. Personality can change – most people are different from the way they were twenty years ago. In any case, personality can only be defined as a product of a person's behaviours as it is only behaviour, rather than what a person subjectively feels like, that can be measured. Any person struggling with how to change aspects of his personality should be advised to *act differently*. This is based on the established tenet of psychology that you become the way that you act. The central factor, therefore, in changing internally is to change externally, or as the AA organisation has succinctly said: 'fake it to make it' (AA 1988). While this principle may be an anathema to some psychodynamic psychotherapists, others are very clear that behaviour change is an essential component of effective psychotherapy.

Increased salience

Any addictive drug can become more important to its user over time. For some drugs, such as alcohol, this requires excessive use over an extended period, for others – such as crack cocaine – only one dose is needed for the drug to become the most important thing in the victim's life. This is the phenomenon which destroys families. Documented accounts exist of opium smokers in ancient China selling their families in order to procure a supply of the drug. Today we see with depressing frequency accounts of abuse and neglect of children through a redirection of parental focus toward their drug of abuse.

Alcoholic patients/clients exhibit this effect in often subtle ways, through their capacity to deny and hide their problem. Many alcoholics will plan their day meticulously in order to hide their dependence on alcohol. A trip to the theatre, a children's party or a visit to friends will be organised so as to ensure that the person's blood alcohol level never falls below a comfortable limit. If challenged, the alcoholic will angrily rebut the charge. Thus families and friends are cowed into acceptance of the alcoholic's drinking pattern or even come to be a part of it. This is why Al-Anon, the sister organisation to AA for family members of alcoholics, considers alcoholism a family disease in which every member is affected and in need of help. Once an alcoholic/addict has, through treatment or otherwise, become abstinent, an enormous gap in their life is revealed. This hole, previously occupied by the drug of abuse, has to be filled if relapse is to be avoided. This can be done through generating internal change in psychotherapy, or more straightforwardly through filling it with AA/NA. The remedy of ninety meetings in ninety days has been a route to continued abstinence for many AA members. Alternatively aspects of a person's life which have withered or been pushed out through the increased salience of the drug can be rediscovered, such as interests, relationships, friends, work, etc. What isn't successful is for a person in a treatment programme to 'hope for the best'. Active steps have to be taken for recovery to be maintained.

Awareness reduction

Drugs of abuse all have two properties in common; they alter one's level of consciousness and they can cause euphoria. The most obvious route into addiction is by drug or alcohol use as a means of escape from discomfort, either physical or mental. Thus someone who has suffered a painful rejection or personal failure may drink to dull their feelings of sadness. Although the awareness of this unpleasant feeling will be reduced, the awareness of the needs of their position also disappear. Under the influence of alcohol, a person's judgement is impaired and their levels of performance become poor. He is unaware that he is compounding his problems until he sobers up – when the reality of failure hits with renewed force. By drinking more, he attempts to escape the pain of this realisation, and so a vicious circle begins with a return to sober consciousness becoming ever less possible.

The only way out of this trap is for the sufferer to sober up/stop using drugs and then, with sympathetic help, to face up to the pain of realisation of the mess that he has created. One of the key aims of any therapeutic programme should therefore be to facilitate a move away from a position of seeking immediate removal of discomfort. In my experience, patients who do well deal with the issue of feeling anxious or depressed by self-reassurance, along the lines of, 'if I put up with feeling like this today, I will feel better tomorrow'. Those who demand instant relief through tranquillisers, sleeping tablets or simply reassurance, tend to relapse as soon as they meet their first adverse life event following discharge.

Models which relate to individual life experience

Learnt helplessness

This is a concept arising from social learning theory and, at a more basic level, from operant conditioning principles. Any animal can be taught rules of behaviour through selective administration of rewards or avoidance of punishment. For example, a mouse can be trained to press a T-bar mechanism in its cage if by pressing the bar it switches off the current to a device which delivers electric shocks to the animal for a limited period. Equally, this action can be stimulated through a reward system, such as the administration of a pleasant drug (for example, heroin) each time the bar is pressed. If the mouse is trained to press the bar at a certain frequency and then the rules are changed – for example, by administering shocks independently of the frequency of bar pressing – a state of learnt helplessness can be induced. Under such conditions the animal will withdraw into a state of inactivity and lose previously learnt adoptive behaviours. For example, if a cat is introduced into the laboratory, the mouse will make no effort to avoid being eaten. It has learnt to be helpless because it has been taught a set of rules and then has had them broken. It has learnt that there is nothing it can do to alter or control its environment; sometimes pleasant things will happen and sometimes unpleasant things, but it cannot influence these events.

In adult humans it is difficult to induce learnt helplessness if given a happy and nurtured background. However, it can be brought about by repeated losses, major disasters or torture (indeed induction of learnt helplessness is a central aspect of torture), but it would involve an extreme experience in a healthy person for it to occur. However, in children it is easy to induce, requiring not even cruelty, but simply inconsistency and chaotic parenting.

A child who is inconsistently rewarded, not for good behaviour or achievement but at the whim of the parent, and punished in an equally capricious and random manner, will quickly develop a pattern of learnt helplessness. The overriding feeling will be one of having no control over the world or what happens. This child will progressively withdraw into apathy. He will be difficult to teach or to motivate, and will cope only when things are going well, meeting problems with a shrug of the shoulders and passivity. As the child grows into adulthood he will develop a range of avoidance behaviours in response to any difficulties which may arise, including drinking or drug use. This is substance abuse as an escape in a person who has retreated into the apparently safe position of giving up.

The longer and more completely a person withdraws into helplessness, the fewer positive life experiences he will enjoy, the less expertise and confidence he will gain in ordinary life skills, and the more likely it is that he will fail when he does emerge from passivity to try to do something about his situation. Thus the person's view of the world is confirmed and the learnt helplessness is underlined.

In my experience, the key to overcoming this state is through taking emotional risks and accepting failure as a necessary part of making progress. Someone who emerges from years of passivity will not be as able as their peers at activities from which they have withdrawn. Engaging in these activities none the less, and accepting that early efforts will generally end in failure, is the gateway to a return or a first discovery of personal effectiveness. The development of coping and problem solving strategies in spite of feeling like 'there isn't any point, it will all go wrong in the end' is equally crucial. One of the key roles in therapy is, therefore, to facilitate new ways of behaving and responding to challenges. The group setting of an addiction treatment programme is an ideal setting for this exploration to occur.

Psychoanalytic theory

This is an area with which art therapists are usually more familiar than are psychiatrists, and many of the issues raised in this section are dealt with more fully elsewhere in this book. However, four particular models from psychoanalytic theory are of relevance to many substance-dependent patients and so are worth mentioning here.

ORAL DEPRIVATION (FIXATION)

Freud saw the oral stage as being the earliest phase of psychosexual development, occurring in babies and small toddlers. The infant's world is entirely to do with the satisfaction of needs, in particular comfort, warmth, satiation and well-being. The crying baby's hunger, discomfort or frustration is satisfied by the breast (or the bottle) and the warm security of the parent's body. If this is provided dependably this phase is passed and the baby eventually moves to the next stage of psychosexual development, the anal stage (Freud 1914). If, however, there is no reliable parent able to dependably satisfy the baby's oral needs, he will remain fixated at this stage of development until and unless he can learn and experience the necessary issues later on in his development. If at no point is he given the means to learn that the world is essentially a safe place, where his needs for security, emotional warmth and well-being will eventually be satisfied, his view will continue to be one in which he believes that things have to be grabbed at every possible opportunity for instant gratification. Frustration and dsyphoria will be intolerable and a desperation to feel good all the time will set in. This is, of course, impossible through ordinary means, so as he grows up he will tend to turn to alcohol or other drugs for the instant gratification he craves.

For the individual who recognises this type of deprivation in his background the implications are that he needs to work on his feelings of neediness and emptiness and to develop the capacity to defer gratification. This may be achieved through therapy, through a relationship, or through AA or NA (Narcotics Anonymous). In any case, the feelings fuelling his dependence will need to be worked through for abstinence to be maintained.

IMBALANCE OF DRIVES

Psychoanalytic theory suggests that some individuals suffering from addiction are following an unconscious drive toward death, represented by their recklessly dangerous abuse of their drug. The life drive (or libido) is seen in healthy individuals as being in balance with the death drive. While the libido is the creative, competitive, life-generating force, the death drive represents both the risk-taking part of a person and also his unconscious yearning for the quietness and peace of the inorganic state to which the body returns after death.

Many patients in addiction treatment programmes recognise a strongly self-destructive, reckless and self-defeating side to themselves. The model suggests that this drive, if over-represented, should be identified. It can then be sublimated through more worthwhile or less self-destructive risk-taking or work can be done on the other side of the balance, that is the creative, competitive and/or sexual side of the person's life.

NARCISSISM

This model will be touched on only very briefly here as it is the subject of another chapter in this book (see Chapter 7). In my interpretation of the term, it implies a failure of the infant to gain the attention and nurturing that he requires from his parents. The baby screams in his cot until his frustration, anger, neediness and desperation can no longer be endured. He then passes into that emotional space beyond the extremes of emotion, which Neil Springham and others have called 'the idle interval'. Presuming the pattern of neglect continues, he will oscillate between extreme demands and attention-seeking behaviour on the one hand and the state of total detachment and self-absorption which the idle interval represents on the other. As the child gets older, this oscillation will continue. His gauche efforts to gain affection, attention and approval will cause him to be shunned by peers. His frustration grows and again he disappears into his own emotional world. As he enters adulthood, problems and frustrations are dealt with by a retreat from consciousness. Alcohol and other drugs perform this role and enable rapid withdrawal from awareness and interaction with the world.

Some patients on the programme will openly admit that they do not know how to be interested in people. This is not surprising, as a person starved of attention and affection will not have learnt how to give these commodities to others. Hence their emotional life is largely internal and mediated through substances. Emergence from this state may be achieved through psychotherapy. It can also be facilitated through 'acting as if': a person who acts as if he is concerned and involved with others will over a period of time genuinely learn how to be so. AA/NA meetings and addiction treatment programmes are ideal settings for trying out these new behaviour patterns.

IDENTIFICATION WITH THE HATED PERSON

The stage of identification begins in childhood at around five years of age and is most marked between about six and nine years. At this stage a child begins to define who he is. He does this with reference to those around him, including peers, siblings, relations and parents. Children at this age form gangs and other groupings and gain a sense of identity and self-worth from them. Those within one's own grouping are seen as good while others are looked down on: 'I'm part of his gang and we're really cool', 'I wouldn't be seen dead with him, we'd never let him into our group'. Some people never leave this stage and the extremes of this can be seen at football matches abroad or at National Front marches.

Children who are emotionally, physically or sexually abused, bullied, picked on or regularly ill-treated in any other way are unable to identify in a normal manner with role models. At this early age children are almost totally egocentric and take ill-treatment as evidence, not of the perpetrator's badness, but of their own culpability: 'I must be bad to be treated like this'.

Such a child will, at this stage, tend to identify only with others whom he views as of little worth as himself. This will often be the person who is abusing him. If, as is often the case, his abuser is a parent who is dependent on alcohol or drugs, he will tend to take on an increasing number of this person's behaviours over time. In due course he will unconsciously start to copy the abuser's drinking or drug-taking habits and later his own children may also be at risk. Hence most people who abuse children have been abused themselves.

Within treatment, a person for whom this model applies will need help to identify his behaviours and to make the link with the person or people who blighted his early experiences. Once this has become conscious he has a choice of modifying his unconsciously driven behaviours. A counsellor, therapist or sponsor will be very helpful in guiding him through this change.

Transactional analysis theory

THE ALCOHOLIC GAME (BERNE 1966)

Transactional analysts see an individual's problems as fully understandable only with reference to his relationship with significant others. Eric Berne, foremost among this group and author of the book, *Games People Play*, outlined various ways in which relationships become dysfunctional.

Berne sees the best close relationships (marriages and close partnerships) as being based on spontaneity (saying what you mean when you feel it) and intimacy (real emotional and physical closeness). More distant relationships (between acquaintances, in work settings, etc.) and close relationships which have deteriorated are based on formality (emotional and physical distance) and ritual (prescribed and pre-determined actions). This includes shaking hands, formal greetings such as 'how do you do?', and so forth. In a close relationship which has deteriorated, the lowest level of interaction, 'game playing' predominates.

In this context, a 'game' is a covert set of words or actions designed to put the victim into a position which he would not voluntarily accept were the interaction straightforward. Berne also describes a further paradigm on which relationships exist on three levels. Each person in a relationship occupies the position of a parent, adult or child, and behaves to his partner as if he were one of these three. Most good relationships are at an adult–adult level with both parties acting like and treating each other as grown-ups. 'Crossed' relationships, such as one person wanting to be treated as an adult while the other occupies a parental position, treating his partner as a child, will lead to conflict. However, where one partner wants to occupy a child-like position and the other wants a child-like figure to parent, a type of stability occurs, often buttressed by game playing. These are the positions occupied in the 'alcoholic game'.

My account of the alcoholic game is slightly different from that described by Berne, probably owing to transatlantic culture differences. For convenience, the 'child' will be male and the 'parent' female.

The 'child' is someone who has abandoned normal adult responsibility. He drinks irresponsibly and excessively as part of his child-like hedonism. The 'parent' is usually someone of weak self-esteem who 'cares' for the alcoholic 'child' as a role which makes her feel important, needed and powerful. She covertly supports the child's drinking while affecting to disapprove. When the inevitable crisis occurs she transmutes herself into 'saviour' and will do whatever it takes to ensure that the child is saved from his folly, such as getting him admitted to a detoxification unit. She delivers a metaphorical slapped wrist, blaming him for putting her to so much trouble and causing chaos and distress. He accepts this punishment, confirming the parent–child roles. He is 'good' in treatment and emerges sober, receiving a metaphorical pat on the head on his return home. As his period of sobriety extends, however, the roles in the relationship are put under strain, as the child no longer needs or wants this role, or if he does, others will begin to challenge him on why he is allowing himself to be dominated. Sabotage ensues from the parent in the form of drinks left out, drinking friends invited round or such comments as, 'don't be such a wet rag, just one drink, it is Christmas'. The child relapses into alcoholism, the roles are re-established and the cycle starts again.

I have seen this cycle completed up to eight times. For those caught up in the alcoholic game the first step is to enable them to recognise what is happening and their roles within the game. The second is to identify any available 'antitheses'. An antithesis is a manoeuvre which prevents the smooth operation of the game. Examples would be for the child to refuse to accept the child role, to reject the punishment or reward in the game cycle, to expose the sabotage, or to enlist the support of AA. There are many others in individual cases.

'OK-NESS' (HARRIS 1995)

The important concept of 'OK-ness' also arises out of the discipline of transactional analysis. Though simple, it is profound. Unless a person has a solid sense of his own worth, he will be vulnerable to the opinions of others. A person who only feels as good as the last thing that somebody said about him is condemned to an existence in which he must always act so as to please the people around him. On the contrary, a person who is 'OK' is aware of his strengths and weaknesses and can live with them. He is free to act in whichever way he chooses that is most appropriate to the situation he is in at the time.

Alcohol and drugs are often used to induce a temporary sense of OK-ness. Treatment programmes which address this issue are more effective than those which do not. A good example is the AA twelve step programme. Those who progress to working on all twelve steps invariably, in my experience, develop a sense of OK-ness; so much so in fact that many professionals feel somewhat disempowered by their solid self-belief and faith in the AA philosophy. Psychotherapeutic methods within treatment programmes, particularly group work, can also have a big influence.

Family systems theory

This branch of psychology sees individuals and their problems as part of a family system and the workings and difficulties of this system as understandable only with reference to the wider systems of the extended family, friends, acquaintances and others.

The central concept is one of 'scapegoating' in a family generating and maintaining an alcoholic member. A dysfunctional family will develop a number of abnormal patterns and behaviours over time which are outside the scope of this text. These patterns will become ingrained and assumptions will be generated which cannot be challenged by family members. However, the wider system of non-family members will tend to threaten the dysfunctional system by pointing it out. The family cannot face its problems when put under a spotlight in this way, because to do so would lead to open conflict, recrimination and allocation of guilt.

If one family member drinks heavily or uses illicit drugs he will represent an answer to the dilemma. When challenged the family can deny its responsibility for its problems: 'We were fine until he became a drug addict', 'It's not our fault we don't get on, it's all down to him', are typical refrains. The addict's behaviour will be both criticised and covertly encouraged as his role is crucial in maintaining the tenuous integrity of the family system. If he becomes abstinent, for example after a course of treatment, he will tend to be sabotaged in a covert way (see 'The alcoholic game', p. 38).

An individual in treatment will need help in looking at his family system and identifying his role of scapegoat, if it exists. On leaving the programme he will have to concentrate solely on his recovery, rather than trying to sort out the family's problems, which will have come into painful focus during his absence. He will need a lot of help with this through aftercare and/or AA/NA involvement.

Self-handicapping

This model shows up most commonly in the offspring of professional, middle-class families. Powerful, successful parents do everything possible for the welfare of their child, but forget to notice or be impressed by him. As a result he has a weak sense of self-worth but continually searches for ways of gaining parental approval. Eventually he succeeds, by extreme levels of effort in whatever area his parents particularly value, often that of academic success. The first time he does well, for example in an exam, his parents are proud, excited and show him off. From this moment he is addicted. At last he has fuel for his self-esteem and a sense of self-definition. He pursues further success with enormous diligence, putting himself under increasing strain and being subject to escalating parental expectation. As an adult he succeeds in university, at least in academic terms, and is rapidly promoted in his career. However, inevitably he is finally promoted to a level at which he cannot cope. His colleagues are more able and achieve more by doing less work. He cannot work harder or he will break down, but he cannot fail either as this would cause the collapse of his self-esteem which is based on constant success.

One way out is to drink to excess (or abuse drugs). When he loses his job he is able to maintain his false self image while blaming alcohol for his failure, saying, 'I would have made managing director if the booze hadn't stopped me'.

In a treatment programme such a person should be encouraged to identify this pattern and to explore other ways of gaining a satisfactory self-definition and good self-esteem. This will demand a move away from the pursuit of constant success and the development of realistic goals and values.

Personality research

In the comparison of people who have suffered from addictions with those who have not, certain personality and behavioural traits are over-represented in the addicted group. This does not imply the existence of an 'addictive personality' since in reality alcoholics and addicts are a diverse group with most personality types represented. However, an individual who has strong personality traits of the types listed may consider that this side of his character has a bearing on his dependence.

The over-represented traits are: low self-esteem, rebelliousness, impulsiveness, stimulus augmentation and external locus of control.

Stimulus augmentation refers to a person's tendency to over-rate a standard stimulus. For example, a jab in the hand with a pin will on average be rated as more painful by the addicted group than by the control group. The phenomenon also refers to the tendency of the addict to increase the power of his experiences, for example, capping a good day with a drink so as to make it marvellous, or compounding a problem caused by poor performance at work by getting drunk and being sent home for intoxication.

The locus of control refers to a person's view of his influence on his environment and its influence on him. The person with an internal locus of control feels in control of his environment, for example, 'I will have to talk to my wife, to help her to help me in my recovery and will enlist the help of AA to protect me when problems arise'. On the contrary, the person with an external locus of control is at the mercy of his environment, for example, 'I will be all right so long as my wife is nice to me. If she goes on at me, I will have to drink to cope'. The locus of control is the best predictor of success or failure of an individual in maintaining abstinence, so it is crucial for any treatment programme to focus on this issue and to move the locus of control internally.

Again the key to treatment is to help the individual identify his traits and behaviour and facilitate change through the therapeutic components of the programme.

Incorporating models of addiction into a treatment programme

The models that I have just outlined in the previous section are, for the sake of necessity, brief, sketchy and in some cases simplified.

The reader may consider some of the descriptions overly simplistic or may even disagree with certain details. This, however, would be to miss the point. The models outlined are the ones which I use in my day-to-day practice within an addiction treatment programme. Other people may have a broader appreciation of any of these or other models of addiction, and may consider some of the models which I have described to be inapplicable. This does not matter.

What is crucial, in my opinion, is that any treatment programme should either focus on one model as the complete answer, with a highly structured and well developed set of principles and practical measures to be followed by all (for example, the twelve step, 'Minnesota Model' programmes), or it should encourage a thorough analysis of an individual's route into addiction using a range of different theoretical frameworks. I have actually combined the two in the treatment programme that I am involved with. This may appear contradictory, but it is not. While AA are unequivocal about what addiction is (a disease) and the way to deal with it (the twelve steps of recovery), the model they use does not proscribe a search for the reasons why an individual develops his addiction.

The way this end is reached – of understanding the reasons for a person's addiction – is equally optional. In my view the exact components of a treatment programme are less important than the skills of the staff who run it. However, it is important that staffing should be multidisciplinary as many alcoholics/addicts are very skilful at developing strategies to avoid experiencing the impact of one particular therapeutic style or treatment strategy.

In this regard art therapy is particularly useful. In my experience resistant patients and those in denial dislike it intensely. Later on, if they survive the initial discomfort, they come to value this form of therapy. The reason for their discomfort is to do with the fact that over a long period of time they have become used to covering over their feelings with substances, with intellectualisation or with denial. Art therapy seems to cut through these defences, to get through to feeling, and in due course sometimes to understanding.

Once understanding is reached this must be used to create change. Insight without corresponding behaviour change is ineffectual. The programmes and individuals within the programmes which/who do well are those which/who generate change in an active way, while those who just 'hope for the best' do badly.

Conclusion

In this chapter I have outlined some of the history behind the trend in recent years toward exclusively community based and more 'minimal' models of treatment of people suffering from addictions and have suggested that this may be a mistake. I have outlined some of the ways in which an individual may develop an addiction, demonstrating how the roots may reach back to early childhood. Finally, I have suggested that a consideration of these models of addiction may enable the generation of change which is required for a person to become and stay sober/drug free.

I would argue that, while many people can adjust their drinking or stop using drugs through 'just saying no', there are some who need much more support. People who come from dysfunctional backgrounds or whose present life patterns are disturbed need a greater degree of help and this can sometimes be given only in the setting of an intensive treatment programme.

Note

1 Gender, where not specific, will be expressed as male for the sake of brevity. This does not imply any sex difference in the treatment of addictive problems.

Bibliography

Advisory Council on Misuse of Drugs (1988) *Aids and Drug Misuse*, London: HMSO.

Alcoholics Anonymous (1988) *The Big Book* (third edition), New York: A.A. World Services Inc.

Berne, E. (1966) *Games People Play*, London: André Deutsch.

Cantopher, T. (1996) *Dying for a Drink*, Lewes: The Book Guild.

Department of Health (1991) *Drug Misuse and Dependence – Guidelines on Clinical Management*, London: HMSO.

Edwards, G., Egert, S., Guthrie, S., Hawker, A., Hensman, C., Micheson, M., Orford, J., Oppenheimer, E. and Taylor, C. (1977) 'Alcoholism; a Controlled Trial of "Treatment" and "Advice"', *Journal of Studies on Alcohol*, 39: 1004–31.

Freud, S. (1914) *Psychopathology of Everyday Life*, London: Fisher Unwin.

Harris, T. (1995) *I'm O.K., You're O.K.*, London: Arrow Books.

Jaffe, J. (1995) 'Opioid-Related Disorders', in H. Kaplan and B. Sadock (eds) *The Comprehensive Textbook of Psychiatry* (sixth edition), Baltimore: Williams and Wilkins.

Project MATCH (1997) 'Matching Alcoholism Treatment to Client Hetero-geneity: Project MATCH Post-Treatment Drinking Outcomes', *Journal of Studies on Alcohol*, 58: 1: 7–29.

Rathod, N. (1977) 'Follow up study of injection in a provincial town', *Drug and Alcohol Dependence*, 2: 1–21.

Report of the Rolleston Committee (1926) London: HMSO.

Royal College of Psychiatrists (1986) *Alcohol, Our Favourite Drug*, London: Tavistock.

Wallace, P., Cutler, S. and Haynes, A. (1988) 'Randomised Controlled Trial of G.P.'s In-Patients with Excessive Alcohol Consumption', *British Medical Journal*, 297: 663–8.

Chapter 3

Group therapy in the treatment of drug addiction

Gary Winship

When I think of my experiences of group work with drug users, I am struck by the fact that it is not the group *per se* which is contained in my memory. I remember individuals whom I associate with other individuals who were in treatment at the same time. I often have reservations about the conception of a group: it has been described as a faceless entity, a mass or a crowd that inspires fear. I think the conception of a group is numb unless we keep in mind that it is a living and breathing affiliation of people. However, reservations aside, I shall continue to use the term 'group' in this chapter with the proviso that I mean it to refer to something that has a human interactional quality.

I am struck also that my memory of group work with drug dependent patients is for the most part rather benign. I am not suggesting that the groups with addicts have always been a joy to work with, indeed at the time they were often painfully silent, sometimes explosive, and at other moments, tedious and repetitive. But in the end, the rewards were worthwhile. Those occasions of 'at last' – when a client managed to put into words something they had struggled with for months, or when someone was leaving and they shared a touching intimacy with their peers and staff – then suddenly, quite out of the blue, it would all fall into place and we would have the extraordinary group experience of sensitivity, insight, where the distress was contained, held and shared fairly. This experience seems to be ubiquitous in therapeutic groups where the rewards seem occasional and the work continual. I think this is because coming together in groups involves conflict.

It seems that intimacy, even everyday normal intimacy, breeds conflict of one sort or another. So the very nature of our being together in a group involves conflict. This will always be exacerbated when the group is composed of people who are there because they have problems, particularly if those problems consist of difficulties of being with others, not to mention the difficulty of being with oneself. Drug users don't want to be with others, not in a real sense, that is why they numb themselves: so groups with addicts are destined to be difficult. I have often felt the urge to apologise to a new member of a group. I might say: 'Welcome to the group, I am sorry you are here, this is not going to be easy for you. It would have been hard enough just talking to one person, but here you are with fifteen others'. This may sound a bit pessimistic, and I am not critical of optimistic group members when they cheerily welcome a new client to the group because it is a big step for someone to accept treatment, and because they know just how scary thinking about themselves and being with others can be. But I read between the lines when a group says: 'We are glad you've made it here'. I hear them saying: 'We're glad you're here because together perhaps we can survive the fear of being together'.

I think we do a client a disservice if we do not point out just how bumpy the road is to recovery. I remember a colleague saying to a client who had complained of feeling 'shitty' in a group: 'Well, that's what this group is for, better to feel shitty here than to feel shitty elsewhere!' The temptation is always to try and make things better, but it is better not to do so. It is better to model a survival of the 'shittiness'.

We need to ask, what is it that makes working in groups with drug users so difficult? By identifying these difficulties, it hopefully will take us a step closer to identifying what are the curative factors in the group experience – because I'm convinced there are curative factors. My memory of different groups is most often a fond one, even though the occasions of triumph were few and far between. After months 'pushing the group like a tractor around a treacle field', as one colleague put it, we would 'get there' (to use Narcotics Anonymous speak). These were the groups where I would be drawn to tears – the point where joy touches sadness. In the next session it would be back to the treacle field.

I sometimes wonder if clients survive groups in spite of the staff rather than because of them. In my experience, I recall we muddled through on our ward: learning on our feet, making sweeping interpretations at inopportune times, pointing out mother transferences when the clients just wanted to be loved, or interpreting their need for nurture when they complained about the heating, at a time when it was freezing cold! Yet some of the clients managed to get through. And sometimes very successfully ... some are now counsellors at other agencies, one ex-resident is managing a citizens' advice bureau. Looking at these examples, it is tempting to think that we must have been doing something right. On the other hand, it could be that the clients who observed us muddling through what we described as 'therapy' in the groups and individual sessions, thought: 'If they can do this then I'm sure I can too'. So it may not be so much that we got it 'right' with these clients; it is possible that what was most helpful was that we were prepared to try, admitting that we did not have the answers and indeed we might even be wrong. Winnicott (1965) has talked much about the value of being wrong where the client and the therapist can exist in a real world and the client's image of the therapist as the all-knowledgeable being who will save them is confronted. I want to bear this in mind as I postulate here about some of my observations of group work with addicts, that it is perhaps of less importance whether or not my formulations are correct but rather what might be important is that I and others took the time to make the observations, remaining interested and keen enough to want to understand. If this is the only thing to have rubbed off on the clients, then that is enough: if their experience showed them that they could give time to themselves, to understand why they had troubles and distress in their lives, and that through giving meaningful attention to the distress, resolution and reparation were possible.

Why has group therapy been found to be useful in the treatment of addiction? In particular, the longevity of Alcoholics Anonymous (AA) and Narcotics Anonymous (NA) is testimony to the success of a group-oriented approach to treating drug addiction. Both AA and NA place emphasis on the role of group support for recovering users. Both organisations have a wide reaching international network of group meetings where the central therapeutic experience is that of 'sharing'. The group meetings begin with the allocated chairperson telling their 'story'. This story involves describing past experiences, including the circumstances of the person's first encounter with drugs. Life events, relationships and environmental influences are all included, among which are the factors which may have led to addiction in the first place. This story might last up to half an hour. Afterwards, others are invited to share their own experiences, and in particular those experiences which may have similarities with the chairperson's story.

These meetings are for people who are 'clean' (drug-free) and in recovery. In the early stages of being clean, new NA members are advised to undertake ninety meetings in ninety days. But NA also offers primary treatment programmes such as detoxification and residential treatment. These programmes are sometimes referred to as 'twelve step' or the 'Minnesota Model'. As part of the philosophy of the NA group approach, whether in the early or later stages of recovery, addicts are advised not to form individual relationships. Instead it is recommended that the person form a relationship with the group as a whole. The early steps of the NA twelve step programme necessitate the addict making a commitment to the group, in which the group is conceived to represent a higher power. For some this higher power might also come to mean God in more Christian oriented programmes. For others who are less comfortable with the concept of God, it is recommended that they perceive the group as their higher power. Whether it is God or the group, the concept has the same texture of belief, faith and trust in something external.

Group therapy is also pivotal in other models, such as the 'Concept House' approach of places like Phoenix House, where there is a group emphasis on peer feedback and working in a group or team. The development of the therapeutic community (TC) movement has been synonymous with addiction treatment since the late 1950s, particularly in the US where the TC approach to working with addicts continues to thrive (Heit 1993). The inception of the TC approach was closely linked with the early group experiments of Wilfred Bion at Northfield Hospital in 1942 (Bleandonu 1994). So the principles and practice of group therapy in the TC have emerged out of an ethos whereby group relations theory has been applied to the whole treatment milieu and not been limited in its application to formal group sessions. For instance, in the TC, there are clearly group dynamics apparent in the interaction of the participants in the experience of working as part of a group allocated to ensure that the environment is maintained cleanly and safely. The same applies to a group allocated to kitchen duties or those responsible for maintaining the garden. Group theory is a worthwhile framework with which to explore the organisational tasks of a treatment setting where leadership and followership issues are apparent at different levels in both the patient and staff hierarchy (see Bion 1961). For instance, the group that is allocated to kitchen duties needs to be creative in organising how the task can be completed efficiently. Each member of the team needs to function with some degree of autonomy. Reliance on a leader who will tell everyone what to do is a false assumption. The development of addiction treatment settings has consistently sought to confront this leader–dependence basic assumption. Most settings attempt to organise the treatment in order to empower the client to achieve their optimum level of responsibility. For instance, residents cook their own food, do their own washing and in the later stages of their treatment programme are involved in decision-making processes and running groups themselves. Thus in a residential community there are group dynamic events throughout the day, a twenty-four hour group setting (Winship and Firmin 1993). I am describing here a notion that the treatment of addiction has at its core a variety of therapeutic group experiences but these may not necessarily always be described as group therapy. So defining a group therapeutic experience and thus group theory should not be limited in its definition only to formal group therapy.

Why is group work so central to the treatment of addiction? I believe that the nature of group therapy as a social solution is an indication that drug addiction is fundamentally a social problem. The concept of a 'social' problem I suggest refers to the interpersonal field of human relationships that underpins the cause of addiction. A social problem then breeds a social treatment tool, hence group therapy has evolved as the core treatment intervention. The social context of addiction does not so much preclude the constellation of biological and cognitive factors, which are important to consider, such as genetic disposition and disease concept (Milkman 1991), rather a social approach embraces these associated factors in the aetiology of addiction. The causes of addiction should always be considered as multi-layered, that is to say, ranging from formative experiences in infancy to later life experiences and environmental factors, such as poverty (Wurmser 1974). If we conceive addiction from a social perspective, then the fundamental principle of treatment should emphasise an understanding of the importance of the relationship between the addict and other people – their peers, their therapist or counsellor (Kaufman 1991; Winick 1991). Broadly speaking, this is the basis of a psychodynamic approach where there needs to be a willingness to explore in depth the relationship between the addict, their family and environmental relationships through the transference experience of working with a counsellor or therapist. I have yet to work with a problem drug user who does not have in-depth inter-relational problems. It is clear that their drug use did not arise out of nothing. It is not a case of a recreational pursuit that has gone wrong. Consistently clients present difficulties they have had with their families and most notably with their parents. Over recent years we have noticed an increase in our clients reporting incidents of past abuse, often dating from childhood. I am not suggesting that there has been an increase in child abuse which has led to addiction, more realistically I think we have become more sensitive to developmental issues and the impact that formative experiences might have on later life. I am suggesting a model of understanding addiction from both a psycho-dynamic and social perspective and, below, would like to outline a psychodynamic theory of addiction.

Addiction and the manic defensive state

Rosenfeld (1965) outlines a theory relating addiction to a manic defensive state. According to Rosenfeld the pharmacotoxic effect of the drug creates an idealised experience for the drug user. The drug then comes to represent an idealised object. The drug and its effect acts as a defence against anxiety or persecutory feelings by creating a 'high' – a chemically heightened hallucinatory state that is split off from reality. Rosenfeld describes the intoxicated state as reinforcing the omnipotence of the mechanisms of splitting and denial. These mechanisms of splitting are primitive and are formed during the earliest months of our lives. The split refers to a process of sepa-rating the good experiences such as feeding, nurturing and so forth, from the bad experiences such as hunger and loneliness. Rosenfeld compared the experience of the intoxicated state of hallucination from drug use with the experience in infancy of sucking the finger or thumb in an attempt to hallucinate the ideal feeding breast. In others the heightened experience of using a drug defends against the experience of depression. Rosenfeld saw that the continued use of a drug meant that the good internal sense of self became increas-ingly dominated by destructive drives (Joseph 1982).

Rosenfeld's theory stresses the importance of early experiences and most notably the primary relationships. Formative relationships are of key importance and Rosenfeld suggests that if there has been a disturbance in the capacity to inter-relate to the primary care givers, this might manifest itself in addiction in later life. We might see drug use as a solution to a relationship hunger where the capacity to tolerate a 'real' (non-intoxicated state) has been deeply affected. Thus, in the same way that the experience of frustration and pain in infancy is defended against by the creation of idealized fantasies, a thumb-sucking fantasy for instance, the same system of defence can be mobilised in adulthood by the use of drugs. The source of this defensive system is, at a depth level, a disturbance in the 'social' experience, a problem with inter-relatedness. Michael Rustin (1991) has been helpful in drawing together the discourse of social development within a psychoanalytic framework. He has described individuality not as the starting point of life but as emerging out of an intricate experience of dependency on another.

This emergent model of individuation is therefore likely to feature in the treatment of addiction where the dependence on a drug is shifted to a dependency on others. It has often been interesting to note how clients during treatment shift their attachment/dependency from drugs on to the staff. Balint (1968) talks of how the therapeutic relationship has the potential to engender an addiction like dependency in the patient. The following case illustrates this.

Michael

Michael, a heroin addict in his early thirties, underwent quite a difficult withdrawal. The symptoms were exacerbated by severe headaches. Attempts to control the headaches using hot baths, herbal teas and tiger balm, were all unsuccessful. As a last resort, Michael was prescribed paracetamol. Several weeks into the treatment programme, Michael was doing well and had progressed on to a day pass. While out on this pass, he craved drugs. When he returned to the Unit, he reported that when he craved drugs he had an image of his keyworker rushing down the ward, carrying two paracetamol in a beaker to give to him. This image was a reference to his early experience when he was detoxifying and indeed his keyworker had dispensed paracetamol, although she did not report having rushed down the corridor to do so. The image in Michael's mind was significant insofar as it appeared to represent how he internalised his keyworker. There appeared to be an inter-relationship between the objects of the beaker, the drugs and the keyworker. This vignette seems to illustrate something of the transition between relating to drugs and shifting the dependence to the staff. It appears that Michael had internalised his experience of the caring keyworker which had helped him to deal with his feelings of craving and enabled him not to succumb to using. It also highlights how, when we conceive of addiction to painkillers, we are in the realms of mind of pain-physical disturbance, and how pivotal the inter-personal relationship between the therapist and the client is during the process of treatment.

To return now to the concept of a group, how can this psychoanalytic object relations theory be applied to a group setting? First, the object relations model is a model of social development as described by Rustin (1991) mentioned earlier. A group setting is primarily a social experience by virtue of its interpersonal affiliations. Balint (1950) has asserted that object relations theory is the basis for exploration of group relations. In the group, transference and counter-transference take place from member to member – for instance, one member may identify a peer as reminding them of their mother or father, or similarly a member of staff may remind them of a sibling, school teacher, etc. From an object relations perspective, transference and counter-transference can be understood as the externalization of internal object relations (Ogden 1982). The splitting off of experiences into good and bad – the idealisation process that Rosenfeld describes – might occur in a group where one member of the group is perceived as bad and is the recipient of hostile projections and another member of the group is experienced as good. Transference and counter-transference can take place from member to member in a group, thus part and whole object relationships may be expressed through the group interactions (Lagache 1953). A group experience then could be said to represent an amplified experience of inter-relatedness that reminds us of early experiences. The past is a template for experiences in the here and now. If addiction has its roots in problems with inter-relatedness, as outlined earlier, then group therapy represents a useful medium with which to explore these relational problems. The following two examples show how some of the dynamics are expressed in a group. In particular I shall play close attention to aspects of *splitting*.

Seven brides

It was common practice that the staff would co-ordinate the preparation of the lounge area on the ward for the small group sessions.

This involved ensuring that there were the correct number of chairs available in a circle and that the room was sufficiently prepared – windows were open, lights were on, telephone calls were transferred, and that a 'group in progress' sign was placed on the door to prevent interruptions. On this occasion there were fourteen people expected in the group. Everybody was in attendance on time and so the converging into group room and taking seats was for the most part a random process in the chaotic few minutes before the start of the session. This in itself was not unusual; the group rarely failed to start on time and people often converged at the same time. What was unusual on this occasion was that the group was perfectly divided with the seven men sitting in one half of the circle and the seven women in the other.

For the first ten minutes the group discussed the tension on the ward between two members of the community who had seemingly paired off. There was also some discussion about how the residents were angry with the staff. It appeared that attempts were being made to locate the difficulties, first in the pair and then in the staff. I pointed out that clearly there was an atmosphere of Us and Them, and that the split was apparent in the way that they had ended up sitting. I suggested that the difficulties in the group belonged neither to individual members, nor solely to the staff. It seemed clear that they belonged to everybody. The group looked around and observed the male–female split. One other person had noticed this too. At first the group found this amusing. One staff member commented: 'It reminds me of seven brides for seven brothers'. Someone later referred to this as 'seven brothers for seven sisters'. As the discussion inevitably focused on the difference between men and women, the atmosphere became quite heated as the tension between the men and the women became the focus of the group conflict.

The wasp

At the beginning of one group session, a wasp became the focus of attention. It is quite probable that the wasp had been there prior to the start of the group, as it had been a hot summer day and the windows had been open since early morning. Some members were frightened of wasps. The situation was further compounded by the wasp's behaviour. It appeared agitated: it did not settle or stay by the window which is the usual behaviour of a wasp. It flew around the room and caused much unsettlement, which in turn probably agitated the wasp further. One or two members, including a member of staff, wanted to leave the group until the wasp had gone. There was some talk of killing it. At this point there was a humanitarian reaction from some people: 'the wasp is harmless', they said. There was talk about whether it would sting anyone. 'If we ignore it, it won't bother us'.

The window was opened wider to allow room for the wasp to fly out, although there was concern lest more wasps might fly in. There followed a discussion about phobias, first wasp phobia and then spiders. The discussion was interloped with further cogitation about the wasp's behaviour, and several periods of silence. Almost three quarters of the session continued in this manner. Later a parallel was drawn between the fear of pain from the wasp and the work of the group in giving up 'pain killers'. At the time many members of the group were having difficulty staying in treatment. I pointed out that despite the unsettlement during the group, no one had left the room. The group finished with some discussion of the need to stay in the group (staying in treatment). At ten o'clock, just as someone announced that that it was time to finish, much to everyone's bewilderment, the wasp flew out of the window!

Each of these two vignettes illustrate something of the phenomenon of 'splitting' in the group (see Richards 1983: Chapter 7). In the 'Seven brides', the split was enacted in the seating arrangements where the males and females were separated. The initial discussion where the group focused on two of the clients who had paired off seemed on the surface to be legitimate, certainly in terms of confronting the emergence of a 'couple' which contravened the house rules. To an extent, the confrontation of the pairing and the criticism of the staff were legitimate and not necessarily a defensive response. But on another level, the material also indicated that there were splits below the surface relating to individual experience. The inter-relationship between men and women is a universal phenomenon.

In 'The wasp' story, the pain and distress of the group were split off and projected on to the wasp. Returning momentarily to the psychoanalytic model of Rosenfeld, the process of splitting is the mechanism whereby the idealised perception of the self can be established and maintained through the projection of the unwanted aspects of the self. This was apparently the case in the wasp group, where initially it was perceived as a sadistic, attacking object. The distress of the group was split off and placed into the wasp, meaning the group was able to avoid dealing with the very real distress, the psychical pain so to speak.

So what is the process of therapy that may emerge from these group experiences?

Therapy with drug users is about helping the recreation of a 'reality capability' of the self. By this I mean the reality of human emotions. Most drug users struggle to deal with negative emotional states, feelings of sadness, loss and separation. Research has shown that it is a negative emotional state that is the most likely cause of a relapse following treatment (Marlatt and Gordon 1985). The process of therapy therefore involves a rehabilitation of the experience of these negative emotions. I have often found myself thinking, 'welcome to the real world', when a resident expresses sadness about an event like the meal they were cooking for everyone going wrong. These are opportunities for therapeutic encounters, like real life in small doses, as Winnicott (1965) calls it. Disappointment and sadness are not usually faced by most drug users. The process of group therapy therefore offers a kind of reality confrontation. In the crucible of group dynamics there is an aggregate experience that seems to amplify the tensions and conflicts that might otherwise remain unseen. The 'Seven brides' case study is a prime example. The group also becomes a training ground for establishing the 'reality capability' in which the splits are inevitably experienced. The group enables the conflict to be shared collectively. The bad, unwanted aspects that are usually projected are then contained, first within the group and then within the individual. 'If others can sit here and bear the unpleasant experience of being in the same room as a wasp, then maybe I can'. At the end: 'I survived the wasp, and look – it leaves the room, it no longer persecutes me'. Or: 'The staff are different, I feel hostile towards them but I feel hostile about many things. They are not so bad. Even the bad parts sit there, unified together, and they too are happy with that'.

In the context of a social relationship it could be said that during the earliest experiences in infancy there is little differentiation between an idea of the self and the external world. Object relations theory and particularly the work of Klein (1940) offer an explanation of these early experiences. Klein found that the earliest experiences of infancy were dominated by 'part objects'. She saw these 'part objects' – nipple and breast, for instance – as being continuously split in the infant's mind. The process of splitting being an attempt to maintain a good, pleasurable state separate from a bad, unpleasurable one. The bad experiences were therefore split off and projected outwards. Hostility or hate, then, in Klein's model, is directed at the part objects that are perceived as causing the bad experiences. Love is directed at the good objects. Eventually there is a realisation that the good and bad feeding experience is the result of one and the same object. That is to say, the mother that was perceived as bad and depriving was the same mother that was nurturing. The realisation that these separate experiences are part objects are dependent on a single person, is the beginning of a recognition of whole object, that is to say, the mother is perceived as a whole person.

Conclusion

In this chapter, I have tried to present a psychodynamically informed picture of the potential of group work. I would like to reiterate that, although I have examined material primarily from a small group psychotherapy perspective, I believe the theoretical framework outlined to be applicable to other group settings, including arts therapy groups. I have personally observed a great deal of therapeutic group work happening in pottery workshops, cooking and cleaning groups and these are not always cohesive or supportive interchanges. There is much that can be learnt through the *dialogue* of conflict. Too often there is an overemphasis on the idealised perception of treatment. Therapeutic group phenomena are not the sole property of therapists, and NA itself is a testimony to this.

Bibliography

Balint, M. (1950) 'Changing Therapeutical Aims and Techniques in Psychoanalysis', *International Journal of Psychoanalysis*, 31: 117–22.
——(1968) *The Basic Fault*, London: Tavistock.
Bion, W.R. (1961) *Experiences in Groups*, London: Tavistock.
Bleandonu, G. (1994) *Wilfred Bion: His Life and Works 1897–1979*, London: Free Association Books.
Foulkes, S.H. (1964) *Therapeutic Group Analysis*, London: Allen & Unwin.
Heit, D.S. (1993) 'Therapeutic Communities for Drug Abuse. The Contemporary Scene in the USA', *Therapeutic Communities*, 14, 3: 151–63.

Hinshelwood, R.D. (1991) *Dictionary of Kleinian Thought*, London: Free Association Books.

Joseph, B. (1982) 'Addiction to Near Death', *International Journal of Psychoanalysis*, 63: 449–56.

Kaufman, E. (1991) 'Critical Aspects of the Psychodynamics of Substance Abuse and the Evaluation of their Application to a Psychotherapeutic Approach', *The International Journal of Addictions*, 25, 2A: 97–116.

Klein, M. (1940) 'Mourning and its Relation to Manic Depressive States', in *Contributions to Psycho-Analysis*, 1921–1945 (1948), London: Hogarth.

Kohut, H. (1971) *The Analysis of the Self*, New York: International Universities Press.

Ogden, T. (1982) *Projective Identification and Psychotherapeutic Technique*, New York: Jason Aronson.

Marlatt, G.A. and Gordon, J.R. (1985), *Relapse Prevention*, New York: Guildford Press.

Milkman, H. (1991) 'Remedies for Alcoholism and Substance Abuse: An Overview', *Drug and Alcohol Review*, 10: 63–74.

Lagache, D. (1953) 'Some Aspects of Transference', *International Journal of Psychoanalysis*, 34: 1–10.

Richards, B. (1983) 'Psychoanalysis in Reverse' in *Crises of the Self*, London: Free Association Books, pp. 41–7.

Rosenfeld, H. (1965) *Psychotic States*, London: Hogarth Press.

Rustin, M. (1991) *The Good Society and the Inner World*, London: Verso.

Winick, C. (1991) 'The Counsellor in Drug User Treatment', *The International Journal of Addictions*, 25, 12A: 1479–502.

Winnicott, D.W. (1965) *Maturational Processes and the Facilitating Environment*, London: Hogarth.

Winship, G. and Firmin, F. (1993) 'Evolution in the Psychiatric Ward Community', paper given at the Tuesday Seminar, Bethlem Royal Hospital.

Wurmser, L. (1974) 'Psychoanalytic Considerations of the Etiology of Compulsive Drug Use', *The Journal of American Psychoanalytic Association*, 22: 820–43.

Chapter 4

Introducing new psychosocial elements into already functioning systems

The case of art psychotherapy, dance movement therapy and psychodrama at the Centro Italiano di Solidarieta

Diane Waller, Marcia Pleven and Angelika Groterath

Introduction

During a period of transition at the Centro Italiano di Solidarieta (CEIS), from the late 1980s to mid-1990s, art and dance movement therapy and psychodrama were introduced to the organisation. This chapter is the result of the three 'protagonists' of these interventions reflecting on their experiences and the outcome of some of their work. It was only in 1997 when we had each written papers in preparation for this book, that all three authors met together and found that we had shared many of the same feelings of excitement and frustrations when introducing our disciplines. We thus decided to join the individual papers together to form one chapter in three sections.

The orientation of each author reflects our different backgrounds and training – in the UK, USA/Italy and Germany – and the roles we held within CEIS. We have in common the psychodramatist Jakob Moreno's (and CEIS') basic philosophy, a shared experience of living and working abroad, and a strong desire to continue to work in a multicultural and multidisciplinary system.

The Centro Italiano di Solidarieta

The Centro Italiano di Solidarieta started life in the early 1960s as a small project for the rehabilitation of Rome's street drug users, thanks to the energy and initiative of Fr. Mario Picchi. Today, CEIS, under the presidency of Fr. Picchi, is a non-governmental organisation, a co-ordinating and consultancy centre for the United Nations (UN), which has a complex network of treatment, rehabilitation and staff training programmes focusing until recently almost exclusively on problems of substance abuse. It has a multidisciplinary, multicultural population of staff and clients. During the 1970s, CEIS had learnt how to create a therapeutic community (TC) using an American model (De Domenicis 1997: 55–104), based on 'Concept' or 'Daytop' principles. This model gave important input and support but it was far from being a real translation of CEIS philosophy into practice. During the 1980s, CEIS went through a considerable transition period. In response to changes in public and governmental attitudes towards treatment and rehabilitation of drug abuse in Italy, and in the role of the Italian family, CEIS moved away from these somewhat authoritarian models and from the structured residential programmes which were the norm, towards a more 'open' approach. As Angelika Groterath points out, although in the late 1980s CEIS was mixing and sometimes confusing many therapeutic approaches and specific TC tools, it shared the psychodramatist Jakob Moreno's basic philosophy, which is that every human being is creative and the protagonist of his or her own life.

The evolution of CEIS owes much to visiting specialists from abroad, and in its formative years Maxwell Jones was a regular visitor. In 1978 and 1984, CEIS hosted the Third World Conference of Therapeutic Communities. The latter conference was preceded by a working institute to discuss theories and practice within communities, to which many distinguished specialists – including Jones, Louis Yablonsky, Don Ottenberg and Harold Bridger – contributed. Of the sixty-four contributors, fifteen were from the US.

Several projects were established in the latter part of the 1980s, funded by UN and other agencies. One such project was Progetto Uomo, 'Project Man' (Picchi: 1988), and of particular importance to the art psychotherapy programme described in this chapter was Project Koine, which was concerned with the treatment and rehabilitation of young addicts. This project had a substantial commitment to work with schools in the Lazio region, in particular to sensitise and support teachers in their counselling role.

The prevailing view of CEIS staff today is that drug taking is an indication of an existential crisis for the individual concerned; that drug addiction is the result of economic, political and social problems, requiring the assistance of UN agencies and similar bodies in attending to the economic base of the countries supplying drugs, and on a re-education of drug users with the support of the community and above all, their families. In the past few years CEIS has entered into partnership with many European universities, designing projects not only in the field of rehabilitation of drug users but also for community welfare, vocational training, youth employment and supporting inner-city regeneration programmes in Italy and elsewhere. The partnership of Fr. Picchi and his vice-president, Juan Corelli, a former dancer, choreographer and film director, and their multicultural, multidisciplinary team, has stimulated a very dynamic and creative network, and as Harold Bridger of Tavistock Institute has put it, a complex and open system (Bridger 1997: 4).

I ART PSYCHOTHERAPY AT CEIS

Diane Waller

Diane Waller, an art psychotherapist and group analyst, worked for over ten years at CEIS in a collaborative project with the Art Psychotherapy Unit at Goldsmiths College in London. She focuses here on the effects of art therapy training on a group of CEIS staff and how the staff integrated art therapy into their work with drug addicts.

Traditionally, art psychotherapy (AT) does not appear to have been greatly used or valued in communities involved specifically in the treatment of addiction. This is partly to do with the Concept model, discussed in the introduction to this chapter, which does not support the more indirect, seemingly 'gentle' approach of AT. Research by Mahony (1992) in the UK which focused on alcohol treatment centres, revealed a lack of knowledge about the function of AT. This is surprising to say the least given that the profession has existed (in the UK and the US) for at least forty years.

There are now indications of a move towards a more holistic approach to people with 'drug problems' which incorporate psychotherapy and 'alternative' therapies, but these are few and far between. In Italy changes in attitude towards the treatment of addiction have been evident for several years, reflected in the role of CEIS. In 1988, I led an intensive training week for permanent and visiting staff at CEIS, involving theoretical and experiential workshops based on a combination of art therapy and group analytic/interactive therapy. This highlighted many issues of differences in models, but above all showed to the participants that AT is a powerful, dynamic force, capable of getting underneath the verbal defences and intellectualisation so typical of drug dependent clients, while at the same time enhancing their creativity. It was not, as had been fantasised, a gentle relaxing pastime, nor an opportunity to dissect the art work of one another. The composition of this group was challenging in that it was multicultural, multidisciplinary, with professionally trained participants as well as *operatori*, or 'social therapists' (who themselves had been addicts and had been treated within the structured Daytop model).

This training was followed by two further intensive blocks in 1990, in which staff and residents were mixed, and in 1991 for a group of staff from CEIS and other communities in Italy. An ongoing training for staff from the new adolescent project 'Koine' and the 'out-patient' project 'Ecco' was planned after these workshops and was begun in 1993.

In this section I will discuss the effects of the training, paying attention to issues such as transferring models of training and treatment from one culture to another (UK university to Rome TC), problems of working with an interpreter, containing the participants between blocks and facilitating actual practice of AT within the communities of CEIS. I have also included an example of how the art therapy experiential groups in which the students participated enabled them to have greater insight into and understanding of the ambivalence or 'resistance' of their clients. Likely outcomes of this first ongoing training are also discussed.

A brief history of art psychotherapy at CEIS

Between 1988 and 1991, at the invitation of Juan Corelli, the vice-president of CEIS, I conducted several intensive introductory workshops for staff of CEIS and trainee operators (in the UK we might call these 'group workers' or 'social therapists') from Italy, South America, Spain and Mauritius. The aim was to give participants an idea of how art psychotherapy might be used in various treatment situations; an insight into the power of images; and to stress the need for caution when introducing image-making into a therapeutic procedure. The aim was not to provide professional art therapy training. Participants learnt that art therapy was not a recreational activity or a tool for diagnosing psychopathology. I used a group interactive model (Waller 1993, 1995) to underpin the art therapy workshop sessions, so that participants acquired an understanding of group dynamics as well as art therapy. A wider aim was to insinuate art therapy into 'the system' of CEIS, which at that time, like many therapeutic communities, was suspicious of anything resembling elite professionalism or psychoanalysis.

With such a complex organisation, it was hard to see how and where art therapy training could be established, but it was clear that it had to be relevant to the needs of staff who could be working in remote places with minimal resources. Training had to be practical yet grounded in enough theory so that participants could fully understand the process.

In 1991 an opportunity for ongoing training presented itself in the form of project 'Koine', working with young drug addicts and seeking liaison with schools in the Lazio region; and project 'Ecco', in which staff work with adults at risk but not necessarily addicted, in the community. It was decided to include two staff members from the Koine project, and two from Ecco in a three-year continuous training course, conducted in blocks. Of the other participants, one was an 'assistant' in the art and craft workshop of Koine, four were operators within other CEIS communities, and one had worked voluntarily in CEIS for some years. Several staff had attended previous workshops and were in key positions in the organisation – a deliberate policy in order to 'sensitize the system' to this new approach.

Although there were other long-term trainings in CEIS, notably logotherapy, New Identity Process (NIP) person-centred (Rogerian) therapy, and both dance/movement therapy and psychodrama, offering an image based therapy was a radical move in an organisation which had mainly relied on verbal psychotherapy throughout all its communities.

Art psychotherapy and the therapeutic community

Before designing the training – which was to be tailor-made for CEIS – I re-read the literature on therapeutic communities and specifically that dealing with art therapy in the TC. A few UK authors have written about their experiences of working as art therapists within a TC (Cole 1975; Maclagan 1985; McNeilly 1989; Schaverien 1985, 1987; Mahony 1992). TCs seem to pose particular problems for art therapists whose working methods encourage the production of images which often contain pre-verbal material and whose references may be to the unconscious and dream world, all within a defined and apparently exclusive relationship. This may be seen as threatening to the prevailing verbal, intellectual and often confrontational culture of many TCs, especially those concerned with treating substance abuse.

To give some idea of the issues: Maclagan (1985) noted the tension which arose between the verbal emphasis in groups and the non-verbal imagery of art therapy in a community where verbal group psychotherapy was the norm. He felt that there were advantages in using art therapy in such settings as its ability to penetrate verbal defences enabled members to get to the root of their difficulties and find expression and containment for them through the creating of images. However, he acknowledged that there could be problems for a community concerning the 'specialness' of art therapy: the fact that specific conditions are necessary to carry it out effectively, such as access to water, a room which can be made messy without provoking too many difficulties, a private space in which apparently regressive activity takes place, and in which strange objects and paintings and bulky materials have to be stored. Mahony (1992) identified similar issues in her work at the Henderson Hospital. On the other hand, some communities, notably those with a Jungian orientation, appear to have integrated art therapy fully into the system (Schaverien 1985; Stevens 1986; Nowell Hall 1987), demonstrating that it is indeed possible to do so given goodwill and openness on all sides. When this is absent, art therapists may become scapegoats by being perceived as outsiders, and thus provide an easy target when a community has a crisis.

The fact that art therapists (in the UK, at least) usually have an art background followed by a psychodynamically oriented training and that they make use of art processes in their work, places them in a useful position to engage clients at a different level, perhaps in a more 'indirect' way than through verbal psychotherapy: that is to say, the image may act as mediator or object of transference. As Angelika Groterath has suggested in Chapter 1, in the case of drug addicts such an indirect, playful, and non-judgemental approach could be particularly useful. The complexities of this three-way transaction are often not understood: sometimes the production of images is seen as a diversion or a soft option.

Mahony's (1992) research on the use of art therapy within alcohol treatment centres in two large regions of the UK, which is discussed in Chapter 5, revealed a lack of insight on behalf of staff respondents about its nature and function, with only two centres considering its introduction. Such ignorance makes a mockery of the notion of 'client choice' for this particular group of clients. We can conclude that art therapy, with its 'non-directive' and generally client-led ethos would fit uneasily, or not at all, into such systems unless much preparatory work was done and some common fundamental attitudes were agreed. The literature on art therapy in relation to substance abusers is sparse (hence the motivation for this book) in both the UK and US and emphasises highly structured methods which tend to fit into the 'Concept' model of treatment (see Mahony and Waller 1992). Notable exceptions include the work of Luzzatto (1989) and Springham (1994) and in this book in Chapter 6, which, although using short term models, operate within a psychodynamic framework and in the context of the National Health Service (NHS) drug dependency units.

In brief, there wasn't much help to be found in the available literature for establishing an art therapy service within CEIS, so a collaborative, 'action research' approach to this venture seemed to be appropriate and containing for myself and the participants.

Devising a syllabus

In devising and conducting a training for CEIS staff, in which I remain grateful for the help of the late Dan Lumley, a specialist art educator experienced in work with adolescents, we had to address issues to do with working cross-culturally, working with people with little or no art experience, and with diverse occupational backgrounds. Our aim was modest: to give the participants an opportunity to experience art therapy for themselves, to present them with a range of visual art experiences, to introduce them to basic theories and professional issues and to enable them to integrate art therapy practice into the programmes of CEIS. At that point we did not intend to train them to work as professional art therapists but to add some skills to their existing competencies.

Bearing in mind the difficulties experienced by art therapists which I mentioned earlier on, it was essential that art therapy was well understood and taken seriously by participants and their colleagues.

Thinking about the elements needed for such a training threw up many questions for us: when a new procedure is, so to speak, transferred from one country to another, there are particular issues which need to be addressed. For example, in the case of CEIS:

- The structure and function of CEIS itself as a co-ordinating centre and one which is constantly evolving
- The structure and function of its therapeutic communities and its various projects
- The Centre's philosophy concerning substance abuse and its philosophy of treatment
- The Centre's multicultural population of staff and residents
- Language: staff and residents are expected to speak Italian, but their first language might be Spanish, Portuguese or French. The trainers spoke English – thus it would be necessary to work through an interpreter
- The physical resources available – i.e., rooms and materials
- The participants themselves: what kind of educational, social, ethnic backgrounds would they come from; did they have any experience of art, psychotherapy, art therapy? What were their expectations? And what were the expectations of management and other staff in CEIS?

Conducting the training

At the start, in 1991, we planned six blocks of sixteen hours each and one week's intensive training each year. This was extended in 1995 to once monthly blocks and an intensive week as there was an increasing need for supervision of art therapy practice. As a result of the continuous monitoring, and the wish of participants and the management of CEIS to bring this to the same level as art therapy training in the UK and US, the training was extended for a fourth year, and included a week's Spring School in the UK.

Ten participants were registered and six remained as committed members. Of the ones who left, one took up a high-level post in the States, one returned to a previous job as an actor and two decided the training was not for them. Each block consisted of some art therapy theory, practical art or art therapy workshops, art history and study of group and institutional dynamics. In the final year systems theory and supervision of art therapy practice was included, and participants met regularly between blocks for peer group supervision.

Discussion

Most of the problems described in the literature about art therapy and therapeutic communities arose during the training. It proved a difficult task for participants to introduce art therapy. The first and most commonly mentioned problem in the literature had to do with timetable arrangements and altering existing structures which had to be dealt with promptly. This happened early on in the training, when participants were relatively insecure about their art therapy practice. In order to overcome problems to do with timetable arrangements, participants ran one-off groups for clients, using themes experienced in the training workshops. It quickly became apparent that, though these were successful in their aims, and a great deal of material came out of them, it was necessary to conduct continuous groups or individual sessions at regular times and in the same place each week, so that the powerful material could be contained and processed. Related to this was the urgent need for participants to provide feedback to their colleagues, so that art therapy became integrated into each project. This was important in overcoming the myth that art therapy could work magic in just one session.

As the trainees became more confident in their own creative and psychotherapeutic abilities during the training sessions, they extended their practice, sometimes working together and going out of CEIS into schools to run groups for teachers and students.

It is essential that any new intervention is seen to be supported by the management so that it is taken seriously. The fact that the training happened in blocks with a course coordinator abroad meant that it tended, in the first two years especially, to be regarded as on the margins of CEIS. It was therefore more difficult for liaison to take place between the coordinator and the management of CEIS when difficulties arose, leaving the participants with a lot of responsibility at a vulnerable stage. This was particularly acute due to the 'role change' they were experiencing, which I discuss further on in this chapter. This situation eased when participants became more secure.

The question of having an art background, or the lack of one, was adequately compensated for by intensive involvement in experiential materials workshops and exposure to the major movements in art history throughout the period of training. For example, in June 1994, we ran a workshop focussing on Dada and Surrealism to coincide with a major exhibition taking place in Rome which we all visited. We studied the Italian futurists, and experimented with their visual ideas; the Impressionists, Expressionists, Pop Art and so on. In the third year we devised a project based on Fellini's *Roma* which involved watching the film together and making a visual response in the studio, then taking a walk around Rome with the images from the film and the art objects in our minds. The ensuing discussion raised many important questions about the cultural context of images. The importance of film is often overlooked in art therapy practice but can provide a valuable creative stimulus (see Gary Winship, Chapter 5). We took account of the fact that this training was happening in Italy and more specifically, in Rome, and used visual references which might be meaningful to trainees and their clients.

The participants had experience of working therapeutically in CEIS. We took this experience as a starting point and built on it, using the trainees' groups to help them understand basic group dynamics, strengthening the practical experience with theoretical seminars, videos and presentations about work with different client groups (for example, autistic, psychotic, the mentally handicapped). This meant that the trainees were always actively involved in their own learning.

The problem of language proved not too daunting. It was necessary to work through an interpreter and initially this made for rather cautious interventions on all our parts. However, the interpreter gradually became a full member of the trainees' group. She held a lot of power for without her we were obliged to communicate at a basic level, or hardly at all. Over time, we improved our Italian and the trainees their English so that we could get by if necessary. I felt as if the interpreter were a co-therapist and we were devastated when she had to miss one week's block and we had to get used to someone else very quickly.

We feel it is *essential* that trainees are able to communicate in their own language as the expression of deep emotions in a foreign language, unless one is very fluent, is extremely difficult.

Physical resources presented several problems: it was hard to find a suitable room despite the spacious buildings of CEIS. Our allotted space became smaller as the group developed, which placed constraints on us at a time when we needed to expand. There may have been something 'unconscious' in the system which had to limit the influence of art therapy and this was played out through room difficulties: a problem common to art therapists working in public institutions in the UK. The fact is, art therapy is messy, uses strange materials and produces often disturbing images which can have impact on the immediate environment. It has connotations of child-ishness in that it can be playful and perceived as 'not real work'. Careful renegotiation eventually secured a large space within the central administrative area which was good for morale as well as creative activity.

Questions of professional status

The participants' increased confidence in the value of art therapy – which was also perceived by their colleagues – caused them to feel dissatisfied with the limited time they had to practise it. When we started the training, it was not intended to qualify the trainees as art therapists but to enable them to incorporate the therapy within their existing professional work. However, as time went on they began to identify themselves as art therapists. They no longer saw art therapy as an adjunct to their other work. They had undergone a major *role change*.

It is hard for a trainee to change their role in a setting where they are already considered as an operator, teacher or coordinator, and begin to introduce something new about which there is understand-ably ambivalence. Other staff member's perceptions and expectations have to be understood. Inevitably, through lack of understanding of the new intervention, there are timetable clashes, conflicts about frequency and length of time of groups and so on. These factors are usually encountered when introducing any new element into a functioning system (see Waller and Gheorghieva 1990). Much emphasis has therefore had to be placed on analysing and understanding the structures within each project, and in helping the trainees to explain the function of art therapy to colleagues: that is to become more articulate about their aims, objectives and needs for the benefit of clients.

Observed benefits to clients

The groups and individual sessions of art therapy offered by the trainees appeared to be useful in containing the ambivalent feelings of the clients towards the institution and towards their rehabilitation from drug use. Many clients were verbally articulate and tended to over-intellectualise their feelings. Images can have many different layers of meaning and can communicate directly by getting underneath such defences. The art therapy sessions gave a legitimate opportunity to play, to get in touch with and to understand child-like feelings of dependence, as well as feelings of loss and fear – painful feelings which had been annihilated by drugs. The images produced contained turbulence, despair and chaos as well as order and joy – even sometimes within the same picture or object.

Engaging with materials also provided an outlet for anger and frustration, in that the process could be active, and required physical exertion (such as in pounding clay or the building of three-dimensional models). Participants were able to use some of the theme-centred approaches that they had used themselves during the workshops, adapting them to the needs of the clients.

The difficulties

The overwhelming difficulty experienced was one of ambivalence: of staff and, initially, of trainees and of clients. CEIS itself was in a period of transition, moving towards treatment philosophies which could more easily embrace art therapy and other psychosocial models. These models, which imply responsibility and choice, can pose problems: the conflicts that young people experience while trying to overcome their dependence on drugs are often terrifying, not least in that they have to reject a peer culture which has been familiar and in many ways 'safe', for an unknown 'drug-free' one. Within the hierarchical 'Daytop' model it was clear what one's plan of action had to be: there was no choice but to fulfil the duties assigned. During the period of the training, we spent many sessions discussing the pros and cons of both 'closed' and 'open' systems. The notion of 'personal autonomy' rooted in humanist tradition, while seen as desirable, was felt to be hard to achieve, especially when for so many people their lives had revolved around drugs and a lack of choice. Being told what to do, and how to live one's life could seem attractive. It was not surprising that many recovered addicts returned to work in the closed communities which had 'cured' them. In one of the pre-training weeks (in 1990), on the only occasion when I worked with a mix of staff and residents, I learnt how difficult it was to experience feeling caught between different possibilities and how dangerous it felt to choose one over the other.

There had been a tendency for the group to split into two parts, with images representing opposites predominating (for example, heaven and hell, black and white, virgin and whore, priest and sinner). The trainees discovered that some clients found it almost impossible to choose their own materials or methods of working and wanted to be told what to do. Also, it was painful for them to be faced with the images of others, made when defences were lowered and with results which were raw and harrowing. This exposure to others' pain caused a certain amount of ambivalence about art therapy and despite efforts to contain this pain, some clients found it too upsetting to continue.

As for the institution itself, which had sponsored the training and supported it at the highest level, it also took an ambivalent attitude to what we were trying to achieve. On the one hand staff seemed welcoming, but on the other there was a curious 'shutting of doors': an agreement on one day could be followed by a denial the next.

It felt as if the dynamics of addiction combined with the dynamics of institutional and social change had to be faced along with the client's own ambivalence. In this system, art therapy acted as a catalyst in the process of change.

Conclusion

Of the four participants who completed the training, which included a substantial amount of written work, all are continuing to run groups or to see individual clients within CEIS, but only one remains in her original post (as a teacher) while substantially engaged in practising art therapy. Two people have left, but have returned to provide art therapy sessions, and one has a different role within CEIS and can only manage a small amount of art therapy practice. Two other participants completed most of the programme: one had a baby and the other is currently finishing her written

Figure 4.1 Making the models

Figure 4.2 First model, 'Primavera' ('Spring')

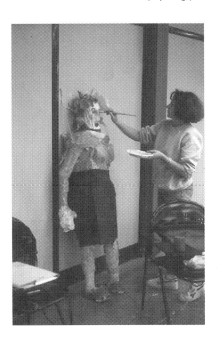

Figure 4.3 Transforming 'Primavera' two months later

work. Plans were made to continue with another training block, with the intention this time to train professional art therapists from the outset, taking participants from outside as well as inside CEIS who could be partially taught by the CEIS trained staff and supervised by myself or other qualified art therapists. Time will tell whether this as yet fledgling art therapy can be integrated into the system, or whether the 'old' culture will prevail.

A story from an art therapy training group

During a week's block training, as part of the three-year programme, the group were engaged in making three-dimensional life-sized models. In the early part of the week they had learnt how to make masks out of papier mâché and mudroc, had studied the sculptures of Kienholz and Oldenburg, and worked intensely on colour mixing through focusing on face colours. Their task in the second half of the week was to make a human figure in any way they wished: it could represent themselves or another character. The aims were: to give trainees confidence in constructing objects from everyday material, such as cardboard, cardboard rolls, tape, parcel paper and old clothes; to enable them to create a figure and to 'own' this figure, which could be from their imagination or a direct representation; to help each other in the process of making by working in pairs.

By the end of the week each person had made a figure and discussed it with the group. Some people had not completed their figure, finding the task difficult despite help. At the close of the week, the figures were transported to another part of CEIS where they were placed in a storeroom. Two months later we met again, in the same place, at CEIS' training centre in Castel Gandolfo in the mountains near Rome. This time it was exceptionally cold, dark and the atmosphere was gloomy in contrast to the summer sunshine of the previous meeting. The agreement had been for the group to arrange to bring the figures back to Castel Gandolfo in preparation for the next course meeting. I reminded them of this but was met with a negative response – that 'they didn't want to do this again'. I pointed out that the work had not been completed and that we had agreed to continue. There was considerable resistance to the idea of

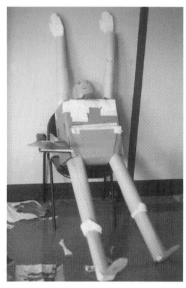

Figure 4.4 'Primavera' becomes a working woman

Figure 4.5 A stage in making a figure

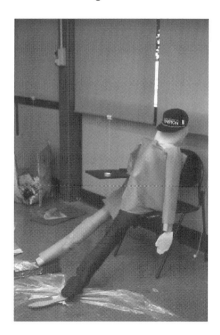

Figure 4.6 Sporty figure with Benetton cap (belonging to the author)

fetching the figures, and as it indeed was unrealistic to try to collect them that evening, I asked the group how we should resolve the problem. Some said 'let's forget it' but others were disturbed by the unfinished business and wanted to continue, but without the figures. We spent three hours that evening partially discussing the figures *in absentia*, and then moving into an active phase whereby everyone wanted to paint something individually, to break up the chilly, depressing atmosphere. (It was literally cold as the heating had failed and the theme was one of feeling rejected and abandoned – 'out in the cold' like the figures left in the storeroom in Rome.) The group felt adolescent, although two or three members were trying to resist this behaviour. I felt cold, isolated and irritated with the group and with CEIS (as the parent figure) – counter-transference and reality feelings! The lake, which I usually find splendid in its dramatic mountainous surroundings, looked forbidding and I wished we could return to Rome which for me represented warmth and security. During the somewhat desultory discussion, doubts were expressed about the use of art therapy with clients and the frustration at trying to establish group and individual sessions.

Eventually a solution was found to the issue of the models – two members, including our interpreter, Sandra, agreed to collect them the following morning and bring them back. The next morning they delivered the models and everyone helped to bring them in. One member was upset by what they had found: the models, which had been placed carefully in the storeroom, during the period between courses had been knocked over, damaged, and in the words of one person: 'looked like victims of a concentration camp'. This was a powerful, awful comparison and made everyone shiver. The dismembered limbs and tatty clothing were piled on the floor and everyone started to identify their figure, and those of the two absent members. The general mood was that the group did not want to work on them any more. With the various figures identified and lying around the room, we sat down and began to talk about the experience. The theme of frustration, damage, rescue and repair emerged, which was indeed a common theme experienced in the group's own work with drug addicts. There had been a strong group wish to leave the figures, which they had not been satisfied with, lying isolated and damaged while they escaped into a fantasy world of bright

Figure 4.8 Student re-making first model

Figure 4.7 Student with first model

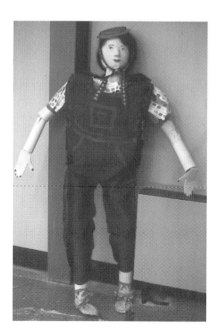

Figure 4.9 The second model: A mechanic

colours. My insistence that we face this dilemma, of 'rescuing' the figures, had been resisted, leaving me feeling isolated and useless and wondering if to carry on really was the correct thing to do. Intuitively I felt it was. By sitting down together and working through the feelings, a solution had been found to bring these damaged objects back 'into the light' from the dark store cupboard. There they were, fragmented but with the potential to be mended. One of the group said she wanted to re-make her figure – she had thought about it and had an idea. She wished to do this alone, whereas others following this idea sought help from other members. The group was not sure what to do with the figures belonging to the absent members, one of whom had actually left the course (and whose figure was unfinished). These were brought into the group space and mended and later one was amended and the other was restored to its original state. The other figures went through a transformation – sometimes quite remarkable. Some of the figures became more active and dynamic – engineers, mechanics, soldiers – whereas others had their characteristics emphasised. Only one person was unable to complete a figure, but this person ended up helping the others with their models.

When the task was finished, everyone discussed the figures and their feelings about the process. When thinking about how to continue, someone suggested a 'play': something like Pirandello's *Six Characters in Search of an Author*, and spontaneously, the group made up a story about the characters which involved a long train journey, espionage and love affairs, and in which each character had his or her own part to play. It was hilarious and ended up with everyone laughing and crying simultaneously.

What seemed to be particularly valuable about this experience was that symbolically the group went through frustration, despair, rage, feeling damaged and annihilated, but found the resources to repair and transform. Most people chose to be photographed with their figures and the figures themselves felt like a solid presence, remaining in the room until the end of the course, after which they were dismantled and the material was put aside for recycling.

I think this experience is a particularly interesting illustration – played out symbolically through the images – of the kind of trauma that drug addicts go through. Drug addicts, however, often get stuck at the despair or escape stage, or seek a form of rescue by taking a drug. They find it too painful to get beyond this stage, when they could use their own or other people's resources to repair their damaged objects. The group was able to take this experience into their art therapy practice with increased insight into their clients' troubled existence.

Bibliography

Bridger, H. (1997) 'Preface' in A. De Domenicis *La Comunita Terapeutica per Tossicopendenti*, Rome: Centro Italiano di Solidarieta, p.4.

Cole, P. (1975) 'Art Therapy at the Henderson Hospital', *Inscape*, 12: 6–10.

De Domenicis, A. (1997) *La Comunita Terapeutica per Tossicodipendenti*, Rome: CEIS.

Luzzatto, P. (1989) 'Drinking problems and short term therapy: Working with images of withdrawal and clinging', in A. Gilroy and T. Dalley (eds) *Pictures at an Exhibition*, London: Tavistock, pp. 207–19.

Maclagen, D. (1985) 'Art Therapy in a therapeutic community', *Inscape* Autumn: 7–8.

McNeilly, G. (1989) 'Group Analytic Art Groups', in A. Gilroy and T. Dalley (eds) *Pictures at an Exhibition*, London: Tavistock, pp.156–66.

Mahony, J. (1992) 'The Organisational Context of Art Therapy', in D. Waller and A. Gilroy (eds) *Art Therapy: A Handbook*, Buckingham: Open University Press.

Mahony, J. and Waller, D. (1992) 'Art Therapy in the treatment of alcohol and drug abuse', in D. Waller and A. Gilroy (eds) *Art Therapy: A Handbook*, Buckingham: Open University Press.

Nowell Hall, P. (1987) 'Art Therapy: A way of healing the split', in T. Dalley, C. Case, J. Schaverian, F. Weir, D. Halliday, P. Nowell Hall and D. Waller (eds) *Images of Art Therapy*, London: Routledge, pp.157–87.

Picchi, M. (1988) *Un Progetto per l'Uomo*, Rome: Centro Italiano di Solidarieta.

Schaverien, J. (1985) 'Creativity and the institution', *Inscape*, Autumn: 3–6.

——(1987) 'The scapegoat and the talisman: Transference in art therapy', in T. Dalley *et al.* (eds) *Images of Art Therapy*, London: Routledge.

Springham, N. (1994) 'Research into patients' reactions to art therapy on a drug and alcohol programme', *Inscape*, 2, 1994, BAAT, London. pp.36–40.

Stevens, A. (1986) *Withymead*, London: Coventure Ltd.

Waller, D. (1993) *Group Interactive Art Therapy: Its Use in Training and Treatment*, London: Routledge.

——(ed) (1995) *L'Uso dell' Arte Terapia nei Gruppi*, Rome: Fondazione Centro Italiano di Solidarieta.

Waller, D. and Gheorghieva, J. (1990) 'Art Therapy in Bulgaria, Part III', *Inscape*, Summer: 26–35.

II SHAPE-SHIFTING FROM ANTHROPOMORPHIC TO HUMAN FORM

Conscious body ego development in a recovering substance abuser

Marcia Plevin

Marcia Pleven, a dance/movement therapist, worked with both clients and staff at Centro Italiano di Solidarieta over several years. She has chosen to focus on the development of a young woman in a group, specifically using dance/movement therapy (DMT) and image-making.

The power of images to carry us into new spheres of understanding is part of the in-depth transformational process in psychological work. The challenge for art therapists in whatever medium is how to facilitate releasing from the unconscious these images in movement, sound, words or art. In this section I will describe how one patient's animal and nature drawings gradually changed into drawings of human body senses as she became more present in her body and more present to the group. These emerging body parts indicated her developing body consciousness, enabling her to contain emotions that began contributing to the reduction of splitting mechanisms. As a dance/movement therapist who has conducted groups for recovering substance abusers (mainly for cocaine and heroin abuse) in the therapeutic communities of CEIS, I admittedly, although unconsciously, set in motion a creative process that combined both art and movement.

I shall call the patient Pia. Responding unconsciously to my own need to take care of myself while conducting the groups, I enabled embodiment to occur, particularly for Pia. Through clinical experience I have found the phenomenon of projective identification to be powerfully present within the substance abuse population. Two counter-transference images and accompanying feelings were present in my memory from previous groups: the first that I was a circus lion tamer, brandishing a chair and flailing a whip, keeping expressed and unexpressed rage and hostility at bay; the other was that I was a member of the Mad Hatter's tea party from Alice in Wonderland, making no sense out of the nonsense flitting around my head. Verbal undercuts flew by like fast hardballs – whizzing around, under and through the ten women in the group. I had to grapple with these powerful and invasive projections and at the same time confront my own fears of rage, impotence and despair. No doubt, taking care of myself became an unconscious necessity as I approached this new group of women.

With both directive and non-directive movement therapy approaches, I introduced what I later came to realise was a co-therapist in the form of a large sheet of paper (usually 2 by 3 metres) that was accessible for every group. I presented the paper as a consistent non-interfering object in the therapeutic setting. It took on the role of diffusing the one-therapist-to-group dialectic, becoming another object in the space to use for projection. The paper had considerable influence on the development of movement vocabulary and embodiment in the group. Each sheet of paper became at one time or another the projection screen where images of pain and fear were reflected in forms that held primitive defence mechanisms particular to this population, such as splitting, fragmentation, omnipotence and ambivalence.

I did not look at the symbol through the eyes of a visual art therapist, which I am not. My own aesthetic sense and use of my body as an amplifier of emotion was the primary receptor. Bartenieff and Laban's (1980) Effort/Shape theory and Kestenberg's (1975) developmental movement profile form the theoretical framework, discriminating and distinguishing levels of communication. Fundamental to my hypothesis is Winnicott's (1971) work on transitional and transformational phenomena in the form of object, place, atmosphere and process. Connected to and supporting Winnicott's work is the concept of the mother/therapist as transformational object as defined by Bollas (1987).

The setting

I began conducting groups with recovering substance abusers within therapeutic communities in 1987. Pia's group, made up of ten women, was seen once a week for two hours for six months between 1990 and 1991. A period of residency in the community could be from seven to nine months.

Before starting the new group, I reflected on my past experience in the hope of formulating a different approach. Reflections that became significant include: identifying what in my experience was the primary fear of this client group; how to become more conscious of separating out my own feelings from the strong counter-transference reactions provoked by the client group; subsequently, in what way I could help take care of myself while also taking care of the group.

My previous experience in these groups was that substance abusers' response to sensory awareness experience reinforced their lack of, or fear of, embodiment, which underscored the major split we were confronting between the body/mind. Clearly, facilitating conscious awareness of the body was my task as a therapist. It was also the group's primary fear. How could they experience perception of sensations or movement the body provoked if they had little or no body concept? How to bring the body back? Perception is seen as the essential function of the mental apparatus that translates sensation into psychological representation (Siegal 1984). Pia's journey of shifting human attributes in animal forms to her own body (i.e., coming to her senses) can be viewed as an initial step toward retrieving body consciousness.

The most difficult counter-transference reaction was having to deny the feelings of helplessness and impotence pervading the setting in order to animate the group. With Pia's group, I was able to recognise and hold my own and their impotence. This action of staying with non-action helped them to get in touch with the underlying feelings of anger and abandonment.

Although I recognised that the inadequacy and impotence I felt were part of their own projections, I found myself looking for help. I might have limited the size of the group or found a co-therapist, but this was not possible. In hindsight I realised I elicited help in the form of a visual art process, which became the 'other' container. Its presence created an object constancy that helped to reinforce my capacity to hold projections.

Dance/movement therapy approach

In my sessions, I used a mix of directive and non-directive therapeutic approaches: modern dance warm-ups to rock, disco or ethnic music; circle dances; the use of various transitional objects, such as balls and scarves, to facilitate interaction; guided meditations to relax and visualise or simply 'be' in silence. Whatever creative process emerged was underscored by the invitation to listen to autonomous choices to move or not to move. The group's greater awareness of their bodies could provoke emotional flooding that might take the form of retreat or boisterous action that required me to place limits.

Invariably one of the women would come up to me in private or even openly declare, 'I don't want to feel today'. Behind this message I sensed both the power of dance/movement therapy and her fear/resistance of me as a person who could trigger pain or even joy, neither of which could be tolerated for more than a few minutes.

The dance/movement therapist guides people into feeling the body. I have found that silence and simply sitting with whatever came up was a powerful facilitator of perceiving sensation. The first few minutes of our work was generally dedicated to the perception of sensations the women were feeling as they walked, sauntered or ran in late to the therapy setting. This initial sense perception was referred to at the end of the session with the objective of bringing consciousness to the reality of change and transformation in the body through time.

I had to hold, counteract or work with the group's powerful induction to make me 'move them'. Not infrequently, I would work their resistance by creating an openly indulgent and holding environment. In the first two months, sleeping would often occur, which would become material for elaboration and in time a point of reference for resistance, dependence or possibly need. Allowing sleep served a variety of functions, the first of which was being able to be in a non-purposive state (Winnicott 1971). In my experience, when other members observed the sleeping or slept themselves, it served to create a similarity of experience. Having similar experiences aided their confidence in the setting and subsequently hostility, denial and resistance decreased. The creativity that slowly followed, seen in autonomous gesture, movement, word or drawing, was the doing that came out of this being. Silence, stillness, being alone with oneself are the atmospheric necessities serving action rather than reaction. Assurance of safety and mutual trust among members, including the therapist, were constantly being negotiated and renegotiated.

Setting up the work in the initial sessions of the group, I referred to whatever they did with their bodies as a dance. This became common vocabulary among the women and helped them move from concrete to symbolic thinking. If a resident repeated the 'sleep dance', individual and group consciousness of this behaviour became more pronounced. Sleeping became a witnessed and/or felt dance that could be elaborated on within the context of emerging group themes. After four or five sessions this behaviour disappeared to return in times of crisis.

After the group had completed a movement portion of the work, it was then a task to bring them from a primary non-verbal level to the possibility of associating and thinking through verbal elaboration. One technique I found useful in previous groups, especially in early sessions, was to make available paper and magic markers so that the residents might express themselves visually. They needed a bridge to anchor their experience in something concrete. It would be enough in some sessions that the participants were willing to put something on the paper since by 'making one's mark' they might be judged. Sometimes the atmosphere lent itself more to moving than drawing; at other times they had to move longer and would then spontaneously open up to speak about their feelings.

The overall response to drawing as a bridge to movement experience was positive enough for me to introduce the paper in Pia's group. Instead of having separate sheets of paper available after a movement experience, I decided to have one large sheet present at the beginning of each session. Why collective paper? My unconscious motive was to create, perhaps, a large enough concrete co-therapist. The group's response to the paper was that it became an object on which to express themselves and to practise adjusting to a collective space. How would they use the paper if it was present all the time?

The paper

The paper was the still, quiet, ever-present object that asked nothing, whereas I proposed, acted, reacted, set time limits, danced with them or sat still. I could become the indulging mother figure or turn into the more limiting rational father figure. As I write about the paper as object, I am also referring to the role of therapist in the same terms. One could substitute the word 'paper' for 'therapist'. Our duo held different roles for the group but can be viewed in similar ways.

The paper and I became both transitional phenomenon and transitional object, creating an intermediate area of experiencing to expose the inner from the outer, the me from that which is not me. We became area/object that allowed for both rest and/or action when need be. At times we were used symbolically as caressing arms of the mother or as objects that could be hit or damaged and yet still survive. This was not so much about the object used as the use of the object (Winnicott 1971).

Bollas has written about the mother as not yet fully identified as Other but as a process of transformation. Using a concept similar to that of Winnicott's holding environment, Bollas stated that this

> feature of early existence lives on in certain forms of object seeking in later life, when the object is sought for its function as a signifier of transformation. The adult patient can surrender to it (the therapist) as a medium that alters the self, because there is an atmosphere of enviro-somatic caring.
>
> (Bollas 1987: 14)

Walking into the dance/movement therapy setting was entering into a transitional environment that held the possibility of transformation. Pia and the group members (their ages ranging from 22 to 36 years) could begin retrieving, re-working, re-creating growth experiences that had been missed along the way. But what use would they make of the environment presented to them?

Certain distinctions need to be made with regard to how I applied these concepts in the context of this particular group. First, the object was not physically found; I made it available to be found. Although it could be used in any way during the dance therapy session, it was not carried away by the group. It was also a collective object reinforcing both a social and individual organisation. Because it was a collective object it also gave room for the women to discover differences and similarities among themselves. The paper was simply presented as being always there – to be used or not as they wished. I actually referred to it infrequently or attention was turned to it because the members wanted to talk about it. It was not used specifically for elaboration. They knew I took the paper with me and they could ask to see it at any time.

Parameters found in both Laban's Effort/Shape theories (Bartenieff and Laban 1980) and Kestenberg's movement profile (1975) suggest that the paper served a principal role in facilitating regression. It was always found on the floor in the horizontal position, which opened a potential space for communication in what Kestenberg identified as the task in the oral phase of development. A duet would form between patient and paper that would always implicate some form of spatial and boundary consideration as other members used, were using or could use the paper at any time.

Choosing to go to the paper became an autonomous movement toward the object, which implied direct contact and focusing of attention. A continual refrain at the beginning of the session was, 'I'm in pieces', 'My head feels like a fog', 'I'm not really here'. These utterances – usually made under the person's breath – along with a fear of the body, made movements alone for some of the women too abstract a notion. The paper served the function of putting the mind and body together in service of some sort of expression and certainly exposure of themselves. What was perhaps not yet able to come out in movement or verbal expression would find itself revealed on the paper. Their movements toward or away from the paper and their body positions for drawing and how they drew became part of the total movement observation in the session. At times, going to the paper would serve to separate themselves from the group and myself. However, within the parameters of movement analysis, it was elaborated in consideration with what needs were being met in the moment. It could be that a woman simply needed to be alone and play by herself with colour, shape and form. The mosaic of movement to drawing, drawing to movement was interwoven in the setting. No specific attempt was made to demarcate cause and effect. Both experiences were open to the ever-changing feeling tone of the atmosphere in the room. My own observation and analysis were definitely more on the side of movement elaboration. In a way, I left the drawings alone. The point of it (transitional object) is not its symbolic value as much as its actuality (Winnicott 1971).

The paper and I worked in tandem: in the same way that the paper could be ignored, found, drawn on or left, I too could be ignored, found, projected on with abuse in one session and lovingly embraced in the next. The dance/movement therapy process privileges listening to the body. I believe a holding atmosphere was created in which I also became, to quote Bollas, 'less significant and identifiable as an object than as a process that is identified with cumulative internal and external transformation' (1987). Dance therapy techniques enlarged Pia's movement vocabulary; the paper served to move her along visually in a different but similar self-directed process. The paper, as part of the therapeutic process, facilitated the individual and group work as transitional phenomena and object. The women found 'us' in the way developing infants find themselves in a particular environment or surrounded by particular objects. In Pia's case I would like to advance that the paper became a transformative medium on which emerging images that appeared toward the end of the group became internalised as mental concepts. Both movement and drawing worked to transform the animal and nature me/not me projections into 'me' internal objects containing recognised senses and feelings.

I will now outline Pia's progress in dance/movement therapy, from animal/instinct to consciously sensing/feeling to thinking.

Pia: A case study

Pia was 27 years old when we met; a tall, very thin woman with short cropped hair and an attractive pixie-like face. Her uncoordinated way of moving and her height gave the impression of a gangly teenager. Frequently she would cross her long arms on her chest and hold the group with a contemptuous icy stare.

During the initial sessions, beginning in 1990, Pia was a willing if hesitant participator in movement. Although in the early sessions different group members would fall asleep, this never happened to Pia. In moments of anxiety she would go to the paper and draw. She had skill and could draw very precise and clear shapes that were always representations of animals or nature. Her movements were awkward and stiff, holding in what I sensed was a fear of falling from a great height. And this she did – falling and fracturing her right wrist (the hand she used for drawing) in the sixth session. This splitting of the bone, which can be seen as a dismemberment, became, paradoxically, the beginning of Pia's opening to her senses. She could no longer draw and was more than ever hesitant in moving. She sat quietly and observed. This fear of moving (both before and immediately after the fall) was accentuated through what Laban (Bartenieff and Laban 1980) has described as a near-reach kinesphere. Her long body folded like an accordion onto itself. Yet when she began to draw again, her long arms, hands and tapered fingers began to 'dance' on the paper.

Pia was usually silent, and showed a reluctance to speak about herself except by making short ironic wisecracks full of self-deprecating humour. Her initial animal figures seemed to hold both the longing and desire for that which she could not feel, and they showed, quite literally, her splitting mechanisms and ambivalence. Figure 4.10 (drawn before her fracture) shows two animals that speak about their wish for what is opposite. The elephant says:

'I wish for the poetic lightness of the butterfly,' and the butterfly says: 'I wish for the likeable heaviness of the elephant'.

These figures gave Pia both a voice and a psychic and physical volume she could not express with her body. In another drawing she paired a large scaly dinosaur with a tiny ant. Spatially her drawing style was expansive. Compared to other members of the group, she usually would use up large sections of the paper, which I sensed was a request for space. It also indicated her fear of intimacy. During a difficult and emotionally sad moment, Pia was lying close to my body. I was moved to touch her calf lightly. The touch, meant as comfort, was perceived as such but could not be tolerated. Pia did not know how to receive touch that was consoling. It was a risk for her to feel touch that was both positive yet emotionally painful.

Figure 4.11, also drawn just before she fractured her wrist, shows a tree split down the middle representing life and death. Proportionally, there is more life in the brown colour and leaves than the side in black which is labelled 'death'. Other tree images would emerge later, holding eyes for leaves that dripped tears and blood.

The drawing surprised her. She had not done anything like this for at least two years since she said she had become incapacitated

Figure 4.10 Pia's elephant and butterfly picture

Figure 4.11 Split tree illustration

through her drug addiction. Her comment was that her hand trembled and she was too much of a perfectionist to tolerate the wavy lines. She was also afraid that she had lost the ability to draw through her addiction.

Holding to her near-reach kinesphere, Pia had a limited range of movement possibilities and would move through space only when directed or guided by me. Her stiffly held knees and back spoke to me of control, her eyes would become wary and frightened by anyone or anything that came within her physical boundaries. She wouldn't move away, just close in a little bit more. Pia's body message seemed to say: 'Keep your distance…Danger!' And in fact there was danger. During a movement experience she attempted to move out in space to dance with another woman. She tripped and fell over a person lying on the floor, fracturing her wrist. Pia's body consciousness was beginning to open, yet she was still held within a very rigidly controlled body 'container'. My reflection was that she did not know how to surrender and fall to the earth, instead she tried to hold herself up with her hand. Pia's split became symbolically that which we were trying to heal – the splitting mechanisms that lay under the psychic and physical skin of the recovering substance abuser.

As therapist I needed to confront the very real and potential dangers that lurk within the setting of dance/movement therapy and to confront the symbolic meaning of the fall which split her bone. The group became immediately aware of the physical levels of working in the session. During DMT, some people may be on the floor while others are up and moving. Spatial awareness, in terms of where one places one's feet and body, became important. We all, including myself, became more sensitised to where bodies were in space. After only two sessions of sitting quietly and observing, Pia began to draw with her left hand and to move her trunk and legs. Not being able to move fully began to bear fruit in her listening more deeply to her sensations. She watched herself and watched the others and began introducing a small black cat in her drawings (see Fig. 4.12).

The black cat, sitting toward the centre of the page with its back turned, seemed a strangely out-of-place animal in Pia's landscape of elephants, butterflies, bees and various insects. Full, round and cosy looking, it emanated the feeling that it could be touched. The fourth and fifth month of our work saw Pia using the paper less and

Figure 4.12 Black cat illustration

spending more time moving. She began to locate pain in her body, be able to move with it and speak about its shape, feeling and sometimes meaning. The cat was a more reachable animal, whereas it was difficult imagining the other animals being touched or held. It was also a domesticated animal. With reflection, it seems that the black cat could be viewed as a metaphor for flexibility, which helped Pia's transition out into space with the wariness of the species but with a decidedly less rigid body.

In the sixth month, Pia introduced human shapes in the form of the senses. They first appeared in a drawing that included her black cat (Fig. 4.13). The cat sits watching a hand that holds a placard on which are drawn the shapes of a human ear, mouth and eye. Arrows indicate how she experienced each sense. Underneath the placard is written: 'I in the group', defined in strong red colour. The words, smaller in size, are also written close to the black cat. This could be considered a crossover drawing during a period in which Pia's movement vocabulary began to change. During this time she moved through space more freely, dancing hand in hand with other members of the group and enjoying playing with transitional objects in the space, such as balls and scarves. She showed a more conscious interest and curiosity about her own movements toward and away from me and others.

The last two months saw Pia and the group become courageous and trusting enough to move/dance for each other. The group was approaching separation and their eventual move toward the final phase of recovery/re-entry, during which time they move back into the outside world. After almost seven months of work, Pia was able to embody her ambivalence and to deal with the emotional flooding that could occur by consciously feeling and staying with it.

Standing sideways to the group, she planted her right leg forward and left leg behind with the right arm reaching forward, leading the body toward where she was going. Her left hand touched her chest, the left elbow leading backwards toward her leg. With pain in her heart she was going forward, leaving the group, out of the residential community to the next phase of recovery – still caught in the ambivalence of her feelings. This extraordinary movement of being able to perform solo in front of the group capped what was a very difficult journey of accepting her body.

Figure 4.14 is the last drawing Pia made in the group. All the senses, including the heart, have wings and are seen flying above the water. Tears from her eye and blood from her heart are dripping

Figure 4.13 The introduction of human shapes to the pictures

into the sea. My interpretation is that the sun could represent the symbolic physical sensation of heat that we sense through the skin. After she finished the drawing she was very present in her body, with her back softly curved and sitting with her legs loosely crossed. Although she was crying and obviously in pain, Pia's body and picture were holding the flood. She spoke quietly and softly about the imminent separation and what the group had meant for her. This was a big step away from her wisecrack responses seven months earlier.

Conclusion

I believe that Pia's last drawing (see Fig. 4.14) was an initial attempt to come to her senses in the only way possible at the time. One could also view this drawing in other terms, such as the separation of the senses or fragmentation felt in the body. However, I feel that

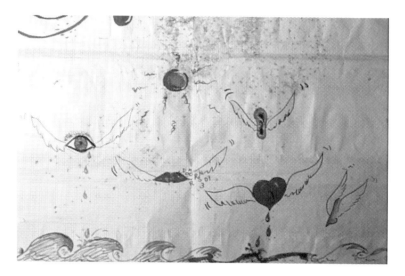

Figure 4.14 Pia's last drawing made within the group

simply acquiring sense consciousness brought about the forming of a body ego. Conspicuous in its absence is the background for the senses, the connector, that makes us whole – the skin. This could signify the body itself as a container of the senses. It was coherent, however, with Pia's use of distance and feeling uncomfortable with physical closeness or touching. It seems she wasn't ready yet for 'skin'. The visual work reflected back to her and the group that she was receptive to emotion, conscious of sensory information and able to translate this into the reality of her pain. Along with accepting her senses came rudimentary attempts to retrieve projections that were revealed in how she spoke about herself in the group and in her movement choices. Pia's seven month odyssey was reflected in the transformations shown in the table.

Curiously enough, about ten months after our last session, we bumped into each other. Pia was working as a graphic designer and wanted to make an appointment to show me something. What Pia showed me (Fig. 4.15) made me gasp. It had been drawn about eight months after she had left the group. Significantly, she wanted me to see it, to share in the experience of looking at it. The senses seem older, more developed. They are larger, fuller, more embodied. The open mouth indicates speech. The ear is listening to music. The eye

Table 4.1 Pia's progress and transformation over a seven-month
period

Therapy phase	Movement process	Visual process
Initial three months	Near reach kinesphere bound tension; a tendency to hold body high in the vertical plane; small, jerky, peripheral gestures. Mainly silent except for ironic or self-deprecatory remarks.	Animal and nature drawings show strong opposition, polarity ambivalence.
	Fractures right wrist in sixth session. Imposed immobility, stillness. Observation of self and group. Attempts to move cautiously.	Observes group movement work with concentration. Tries to draw with left hand. Speaks about wanting to move more.
Fourth to seventh month	Initiates playing with transitional objects (balls, scarves, etc.) and with therapist. Actively initiates and participates in group work. Space range increases, moves with more free-flow tension. Moves alone in front of group. Speaks about her own sadness and anger.	Less drawing, more movement. A black cat appears in several drawings. Appearance of the senses in drawings in the fifth month. An image of a heart in the last drawing.

is rimmed with a light flesh tone. The larger heart is still bleeding. Both the tears and the blood dripping from the heart now have wings. She titled the work: 'My essence, my absence'. We did not comment on the title. My own feeling was that there was an awareness that she had been absent from herself for a long time. Recovering the senses gave her back essence and presence. What seemed a striking change was the addition of a swirling background. More formless than any of her previous work, it showed a sense of fluidity and movement. As background for her senses it seemed to indicate the formation of what was perhaps 'skin'. The swirling colours suggested that something was moving differently inside Pia. Based on what I had seen her draw, this was the first drawing that contained an expression that was not literal or representational. Pia's interaction with me held colour and tone changes. Her eyes lit up as we laughed together and we both found ourselves more close to the earth talking about the still bleeding heart. Pia, little by little, was bringing her body back.

The experience of using a constant visual art process within the dance/movement therapy sessions was a positive one. The combination of the two art forms could be seen on one level as active/therapist to passive/paper. Yet the paper activated the group's movements at times, whereas I was still and held the space. Although theoretically the group was led by movement, observation and analysis, the paper enabled and enlarged visual expression and also became the other container for group and individual projections. The paper's silent, non-active presence facilitated both reactive and impulse moving. In order to be and to have the feeling that one 'is' one must have a predominance of impulse doing over reactive doing (Winnicott 1971).

The last drawing (Fig. 4.15) suggests that there was an internal tether that held in memory what had developed through both the movement and visual processes in the group. It indicated that a

Figure 4.15 Pia's drawing made after having left the group

mental concept of the transitional and transformational object had internalised within her body/psyche. Pia looked content and well. Clearly, then, she was in the process of using her senses.

Bibliography

Bartenieff, I. and Laban, R. (1980) *Body Movement: Coping with the Environment*, New York: Gordon Breach.

Bollas, C. (1987) *The Shadow of the Object: Psychoanalysis of the Unthought Known*, New York: Columbia University Press.

Kestenberg, J. (1975) *Children and Parents: The Development of the Young Child From Birth to Latency As Seen Through Body Movement (vol. 2)*, New York: Jason Aronson.

Siegal, E. (1984) *Dance/Movement Therapy: Mirror of Ourselves*, New York: Human Sciences Press.

Winnicott, D.W. (1971) *Playing and Reality*, London: Tavistock.

Note

Acknowledgement is made to *The Arts in Psychotherapy*, which published a substantial amount of material from this paper in vol. 23, no. 2, pp.121–9 in 1996.

III PSYCHODRAMA IN THE CENTRO ITALIANO DI SOLIDARIETA

Angelika Groterath

In this section Angelika Groterath discusses some of the experiences that she had when introducing psychodrama to CEIS, and how her own practice and approach changed during the period 1990–1997, a period which reflected major changes in the institution itself.

A note on psychodrama

Psychodrama was 'invented' and developed in the early part of the twentieth century by the psychiatrist Jakob Levy Moreno. It is known in particular for its wide variety of group techniques and role-play skills which are in use today within various therapeutic schools. As Zerka Moreno, Moreno's wife and herself a distinguished psychodramatist, said in an interview: 'Moreno has been absorbed by the therapeutic culture' (Moreno, Z. 1988: 4).

Psychodrama can take many forms: these include systemic, analytic, behavioural versions, and even some forms of 'classical' or 'Morenian' psychodrama – this is maybe because 'as a thinker Moreno is often declared to be unclear' (Moreno, Z. 1994: xi).

In my own work as a psychodramatist, I refer directly to Moreno – or at least I try to – not only to his techniques, theories and skills, but also to his moral philosophy and basic ideas about humankind. In describing this philosophy, Moreno's son, Jonathan Moreno, a professor of bioethics, has written of a 'general orientation towards the good' (Moreno, J. 1994: 97). Although Moreno lived in Vienna at the beginning of this century, at the same time as Freud, he was not a student or follower of Freud, and he did not consider human nature to be dominated by instinct. His ideas about people were of a more philosophic, even religious nature.

He believed deeply in the creative resources of people and their ability to interact with each other. His methods – group psychotherapy, psychodrama and sociometry – were designed to enable people to discover their creative resources and to learn how to use them during interaction with others. Indeed, Moreno was the first psychotherapist to break with the 'holy principle of individualism' (Groterath 1995). Moreno's concept of group psychotherapy does not involve the therapy of individuals in a group, but instead, is the therapy of a group as a whole, or even the whole of humankind (Moreno, J.L. 1996: 3).

Zerka Moreno, who for many years worked alongside her husband, recalled three key points about Moreno's ideas and methods:

> First, that a truly therapeutic procedure.cannot have less an objective than the whole of mankind. Second, his definition of group psychotherapy: one person the therapeutic agent of the other. Third, that psychodrama is the exploration of the subjective truth of the protagonist by methods of spontaneous dramatic improvisation.
>
> (Moreno, Z. 1994: xii)

Moreno frequently expressed doubts about how psychodrama could work when, as was increasingly the case, it became detached from its theoretical and philosophical ideas – for example, when it was used as a technique or auxiliary method by other therapists. Indeed, many Moreno or psychodrama institutes gave up their attempts to retain the strong social concepts of psychodrama, and instead tried to adapt the philosophy so that it conformed to various national laws concerning the practice of psychotherapy which favoured a concentration on the individual.

In the winter of 1989/1990, I found myself on the verge of giving up after a long period of working in clinical and educational settings in which I had often used psychodrama. I had never really had the chance to translate Moreno's ideas into practice, mainly because I moved in the professional environment of clinical psychology and psychotherapy (and even German psychodrama) where psychoanalytic terms were used continuously. For example, terms such as 'counter-transference', 'resistance' and 'defence mechanisms' seemed to be perceived as a reality of human nature and not as they really are: constructs of a strictly defined theory. It wasn't until 1990 that I finally had an opportunity to use Moreno's (sometimes magical and often sensational) methods of psychodrama, combined with some of my own ideas, at the Centro Italiano di Solidarieta, which I later describe in this section.

CEIS as an institution shared Moreno's main assumptions and affirmed his basic premise that human beings are creative protagonists of their own lives, free, independent and responsible for their own decisions. They are also only small elements in a complex social network, in 'a world with others' (Moreno, J.L. 1991: 35) for which they have also to assume responsibility. I began my collaboration with CEIS when the institute was making a transition from a closed to an open system, thus giving me an excellent opportunity to participate in this process by attempting to put into practice Moreno's philosophy. In the following section (see pp.99–103) I outline two examples to illustrate this transition process. I must stress that I did not work regularly with clients of the therapeutic community, but rather used psychodrama in training sessions with the staff. This was intentional, since to mix different therapies within a therapeutic community – which in itself is a powerful therapeutic instrument – is very difficult. CEIS was interested in growing as an institution, and thus benefiting the clients, rather than just bringing in 'a doctor from the outside'. As a result I worked with staff who on a daily basis have to deal with the problems of drug addicted clients, including the many emergencies and crises, and in particular the effects brought about by the 'slow suicide' of heroin addicts. On the rare occasions when I worked with clients, I made only single interventions with a well-defined focus, for example, with a group who had been involved, both actively and passively, in homicides (Groterath 1993: 249–69). Sometimes I made interventions with clients at the request of staff, and sometimes so as to train my students in a real working situation. All these actions were embedded in the complete therapeutic programme and were thoroughly discussed with staff who had to deal with the effects brought to the programme by 'a doctor from the outside'.

The early 1990s

In this period CEIS needed the staff to have solid professional training. Many staff members were ex-users who lacked professional qualifications, and who were trained mainly in classical therapeutic community (TC) tools, such as encounter group techniques. A few had some limited psychodrama experience, gained during short periods of work with internationally-known psychodramatists who had visited CEIS – in particular the American criminologist, L. Yablonsky, who followed the 'Synanon' approach (Yablonsky 1995), in which participants enacted real 'dramas', with sensational or even cathartic outcomes. Because these powerful dramas took place within a closed and contained system which worked as a whole, they could be absorbed. However, sometimes they produced just a 'good show' – one of the many that drug addicts had been used to staging throughout their lives. Because of their short period of training, staff were unable to go to any depth in the psychodrama process. However they often handled group situations better than qualified psychotherapists. Perhaps because of their belief in the creative resources of human beings, these staff members were able sometimes to conduct more effective psychodramas than certified, individual-centred psychodramatists (Groterath 1990: 276–82).

During 1990–1994 I conducted three training programmes at CEIS, each running for a period of two years. Participants were drawn from CEIS staff as well as from other similar centres in Italy; many of whom were psychologists and not engaged in work with addicts. These heterogeneous groups had a high conflict potential: the ex-users had no theoretical preparation, but in contrast to the professionals experienced no problems with group work. They were used to being members of a group and were able to act as leaders. The professionals, on the other hand, had a good theoretical grounding, but this was mainly in psychoanalysis. The professionals tended to want to identify and diagnose individual 'cases', and they experienced a lot of problems in understanding and accepting the psychodramatic theory of groups. In hindsight, I can interpret this situation as follows: the ex-users were the 'slaves of the we' (the big 'we' of the TC) and the professionals were not so much slaves, but more the 'despots of the I' (Groterath 1997: 5).

I had several tasks to perform in these training sessions: to help the ex-users to grow personally and to find some security within themselves (the TC gave them a form of security from the outside, but even so, they remained dependent); to halt the professionals from using their theoretical knowledge as a defence mechanism and to prevent them from 'closing up' in a group situation; and to make it clear that the training was not intended as a professional course which would lead to qualifications, but was designed to help participants use psychodrama in their workplace. Furthermore, I had to do what every psychodramatist has to do: create a group which could serve as a laboratory for personal experiences during this training, in which people could trust each other and me. This was not easy, and it was one of the greatest challenges in my professional life.

As an example, I will describe an incident from the first group I conducted in the 1990–91 period. This was a special group in so far that I only worked with them in their second year. All the participants, both professionals and ex-users, had assessed themselves as 'advanced students' because they had participated in several week-long psychodrama workshops conducted by visiting psychodramatists at CEIS. Many of them had already been using psychodrama in their work and even defined themselves as 'psychodramatists'. Although they were united in this belief, they were not united as a group: the ex-users, who knew each other well, formed a sub-group – the strong one – whereas the professionals, who did not know each other, formed another sub-group – the weak one. These two sub-groups immediately united in a strong but not explicit opposition against me when I tried to focus on the group's sociometry and personal issues. My efforts to convince them that nothing dangerous happens when one admits to one's weaknesses were not successful. Evidently, they all thought they had to demonstrate to me, and to the other members of the group, that they were 'perfect psychodramatists', in a way that was comprehensible in the atmosphere of hierarchy and competition of the 'old' TC model.

After several unsuccessful attempts, I finally understood what I had to do: I had to treat them as colleagues rather than as students and to 'fail' myself so as to give them the opportunity to help me. I realised that this was not something which I could enact artificially, and luckily the dilemma I found myself in was resolved by 'destiny', as the following example shows.

I had agreed to take part in a psychodrama session in the TC, with the students acting as colleagues or assistant directors. During work with one of the clients he enacted in a psychodramatic scene a traumatic childhood incident: as all the other boys watch, an elderly female teacher hits a kneeling twelve-year-old boy on the bottom. It was clear that this was a real-life event in the client's life and, as an experienced director, if I had been alone I would have continued with this psychodrama since the client group was warmed up and I could have contained the situation. However, my intuition told me that it was doubtful that this client would have remembered and enacted this situation if my students had not been present. Could it be that he had recalled the incident 'for them'? And did they perhaps feel the same way with me as he had felt a long time ago with his teacher? Were they not afraid of what would happen if they now, in the TC, were not able to deal with this situation, if they did not behave like 'perfect' psychodramatists? Perhaps something similar would happen to them as had happened to the poor boy – with everybody watching. Although I don't know the answers to these questions, I do know that a psychodramatist should never use his or her client to enact their own psychodrama; and certainly this client could not continue to be the focus of a conflict between myself and my students. Psychodrama is a powerful instrument, and one needs to be aware of the ethical issues so as to avoid doing harm. I teach my students that if there is any doubt about what is happening in a session then they should stop; and I certainly have to practise the same methods.

I finished work with the client, softly, but without leading him into any 'catharsis'. The 'show' which I had given as a psychodrama director was neither 'splendid' nor 'sensational'. People who have seen a complete psychodrama enacted – with its many scenes, actors and catharsis – would not have considered my effort a masterpiece. But, on the contrary, I consider this to be one of the masterpieces in my psychodramatic career – and, ironically, it was at this moment that my students were given the opportunity to help me. I had 'fallen' – they said, 'Don't worry, Angelika, we'll think of a way to carry on'. This event served to unite the group. Professionals and ex-users, now side-by-side, worked together. They became active, and helped each other in the work that was still left to do with the client group.

I no longer run groups such as this one at CEIS: I perform this kind of work only in institutions which are trying to evolve in a similar way to CEIS, institutions that are going through transition processes and using the CEIS methodology of an open system as a model. Some of my former students have now become effective psychodramatists who develop and direct projects in CEIS programmes and outside. I provide supervision if asked, but mostly we work together as colleagues.

The late 1990s

A more recent example of a psychodramatic intervention shows how times and the method have changed. During the 1990s, CEIS put a lot of effort into training staff in different therapeutic approaches, and ex-users were given the opportunity to acquire professional qualifications. Many of them now are educators, some are psychologists and sociologists and are not dependent on CEIS: if they wish they can leave, they have the opportunity to work elsewhere whereas their previous lack of qualifications bound them to the TC.

The following example is from December 1996. A staff team in one of the TCs was actively involved in questioning its working methods, reflecting in particular on the characteristics of the client group – which had changed a lot over the past years – and the interventions of the TC. The team were used to asking for help when they needed it. In this case the staff asked for help because they felt that they had become alienated from their clients. The consequences of this 'distance' between staff and clients could be observed at many levels throughout the TC: there was little trust, a lot of deceit, hidden game-playing between men and women and so on. 'It seems as if they don't know us as human beings', was one comment expressed during our preparation meeting. It was not clear whether this was due to an exaggerated professionalism in the staff or to changes in the user population, or for another reason. At this stage, however, the reasons were secondary to what was important, which was that the team felt the need for an intervention which would allow them to take a fresh approach to their clients.

The intervention I proposed after evaluating the situation was not so much a psychodramatic one as a sociodramatic approach. For the 'evolvement day', as I called the intervention, I took the key sentence: 'They don't know us as human beings' as a point of reference and asked staff members what they liked to do outside of their working lives, and whether they were ready to share this information with their clients. I started the day 'alone', that is without the staff, in the auditorium of the TC with all the clients – approximately sixty-five people. I introduced myself and explained what we were going to do and the reasons behind it, mentioning the alienation problem and noticing from the nodding heads that the diagnosis of the staff was correct, or at least their perception was shared by the residents. I then asked the staff members (who had dressed up) to come in. They came in a variety of costumes: a hairdresser, a cook, a clown, a musician, a waiter, and even one woman was dressed as a book. They presented themselves and what they had to offer – which included working groups lasting for about three hours: a 'beauty' group, a 'theatre' group and so on. The residents could choose which group to join and each group ended up with similar numbers. They then went off to different rooms, with each group working on a production to present to the others.

The outcome was a lunch that, as one woman described it, was the 'lunch of a fairy-tale'. The presentation of the beauty group, all of whom sauntered down the steps in the TC garden as if they were models on a catwalk, resembled a haute couture show; the book group had written an adventure story which they recited; the music group involved the audience in its work; and the theatre group developed two pieces of drama. The atmosphere after the presentations was animated. At the close of day in the auditorium, I asked the residents whether they had discovered something new about the staff and to return to their activity groups for fifteen minutes without the staff member. I asked them to discuss how they had perceived the staff member who had been in their group and to develop a sketch around this experience. The subsequent five sketches were amusing and well prepared. Several groups re-enacted some aspect of their working group, but they also referred to how they normally saw staff, focusing on the contrast between this 'normality' and the behaviour of the staff members during the day of evolvement. I then asked the staff to improvise a sketch whereby they took the residents' roles. They spontaneously enacted a meeting of six residents after the day of evolvement and, while still in these roles, commented on how the day had progressed. They received a lot of applause – and the six clients recognised themselves immediately.

I want to emphasise that in these last activities one psychodramatic technique in particular was the most important and effective: role reversal. In their sketches the clients had to examine the role of a staff member, and at least one of them had to take on this role for a period of time. In addition, all staff members had to perform a role reversal. There are different indications for the use of this technique: in the case of work with the whole TC it should facilitate a mutual approach between the client group and the staff group. Since communication processes are always mutual, the 'they don't know us' attitude of the staff certainly implies the question, 'but do we know them?' Indeed, in one preparation meeting in which I asked staff members to perform a role reversal with one of their clients and to try and see the problems in the TC through the client's eyes, not all felt able to do so, and this was not because they were unfamiliar with psychodramatic techniques. Those involved declared that they did not know what to say in the role of a client. This can be interpreted in several different ways: for example, that the representation of the internal object was missing or that staff members were resistant in a psychoanalytic sense. I don't wish to make these interpretations because as a psychodramatist I feel it is not my job to do so. Instead I process the information which is offered and deal with it simply as a problem of communication and interaction. I then continue using concrete techniques and my own trained and developed creativity on the stage to try to prepare this stage so that what before seemed impossible becomes possible in this instance, a role reversal, a sympathetic understanding of each other's problems – not empathy in the sense of a one-way feeling, but a two-way feeling, or 'tele' as Moreno called this phenomenon.

The day of evolvement did not finish at this point: we had another meeting the next day all together where we continued to use psychodramatic techniques. This was designed to 'normalise' the situation in the TC, a process that is important when working with a whole social system. The direction needed to be given back to the director and the team of the TC, and it was my role to facilitate this handing over process. Furthermore, together we evaluated what had happened and how it could be contained.

Conclusion

As is by now probably evident, at CEIS I said a final farewell to any kind of psychoanalytic orientation I might have had, and this is at least in part due to the experience I gained in international and intercultural work from 1990 to the present time (Groterath 1994). But my personal farewell to psychoanalysis and similar approaches does not mean that I do not appreciate this theory and some of its practice. I am used to working alongside therapists and professional staff from other therapeutic schools and would never insist that 'my' psychodrama is the only one, or even the right way to resolve problems. I try to devise a plan with colleagues of how we can combine our methods for the benefit of the clients. Psychodrama is only one element in the complex treatment system of CEIS and other institutions' treatment programmes. What is important, in my experience, is that those who work together in complex treatment programmes should share a common system of basic values and ethical standards, and should be aware of the fact that, in the words of Moreno to one of his students: '[a psychotherapist is] only a tiny element in the cosmos of human nature, but tends to attribute to himself an enormous importance' (Blomkvist 1991: 131).

Bibliography

Blomkvist, L. (1991) 'Das therapeutische Agens und der Psychodrama-Regisseur in der Gruppentherapie', in M. Vorwerg and T. Alberg (eds) *Psychodrama, Psychotherapie und Grenzgebiete*, PG Leipzig-Heidelberg: J.A. Barth.

Bridger, H. (1997) 'Preface' to A. De Domenicis, *La Comunita Terapeutica per Tossicopendenti*, Rome: Centro Italiano di Solidarieta.

De Domenicis (1997) *La Comunita Terapeutica per Tossicopendenti*, Rome: Centro Italiano di Solidarieta.

Groterath, A. (1990) 'Una favola. Zu Gast im Centro Italiano di Solidarieta, Rome', in *Psychodrama*, 3, 2: 276–82.

——(1993) 'Und wenn sie non doch nicht krank sind? Psychodrama als Probe dur das Leben im CEIS, Rome', in *Psychodrama*, 6, 2: 246–249.

——(1994) *An der Sprache liegt es nicht. Interkulturelle Erfahrungen in der Therapie*, Mainz: Mathias Grunewald.

——(1995) 'It shouldn't always be a Drama. The Use of Psychodrama in Therapeutic Communities', unpublished conference paper, Europe Against Drug Abuse, EFTC, 28 May 1995–2 June 1995, Thessaloniki, Greece.

——(1997) 'Lo psicodramma come strumento di formazione degli educa-tori delle Comunita terapeutische del CEIS', unpublished conference paper, Vent'Anni di Psicologie di Comunita in Italia (1977–97), University of Trieste, Department of Psychology, 14 February 1997.

Moreno, J. (1994) 'Of Morals, Ethics and Encounters: Psychodramatic Moral Philosophy and Ethics', in P. Holmes, M. Karp and M. Watson (eds) *Psychodrama Since Moreno*, London: Routledge.

Moreno, J.L. (1988) *Gruppenpsychotherapie und Psychodrama*, Stuttgart and New York: Georg Thieme.

——(1991) 'Globale Psychotherapie und Aussichten einer therapeutischen Weltordnung', in F. Buer (ed.) *Jahrbuch fur Psychodrama, psychosoziale Praxiz und Gesellschaftspolitik, 1991*, Oplanden: Leske und Budrich.

——(1996) *Die Grundlagen der Soziometrie, Wege zur Neuordnung der Gesellschaft*, Opladen: Leske und Budrich.

Moreno, Z. (1988) 'Moreno has been absorbed by the therapeutic culture', *Psychodrama*, Sept l988: 4–12.

——(1994) 'Foreword', in P. Holmes, M. Karp and M. Watson (eds), *Psychodrama Since Moreno*, London: Routledge.

Picchi, M. (1994) *Un Progetto per l'Uomo*, Rome: Centro Italiano di Solida-rieta.

Yablonsky, L. (1995) *Synanon*, Stuttgart: Ernst Klett.

Chapter 5

'Screen memories'

The role of film in the therapeutic milieu

Gary Winship

Introduction

The day-to-day experience of the therapeutic milieu is imbued with encounters with the arts in the general exchange of daily living. The aim of this chapter is to expand the conception of engagement with the arts in the therapeutic milieu with regard to the role of film as a therapeutic medium. This chapter's title, 'screen memories', is an intentional play on Freud's (1899) paper about amnesia and recollection, and is discussed in the context of watching films about drugs with addicted patients.

Film watching: A group dynamic

In the history of the Therapeutic Community (TC) movement, the hospital cinema carries a certain notoriety. When Wilfred Bion's patients at Northfield Hospital (*circa* 1944) destroyed their ward during the first week of his psychiatric ward leaderless group experiment, the hospital authorities turned a blind eye. However, when the patients wrecked the cinema a few weeks later, it was felt that Bion had overstepped the mark. The cinema became the public setting for the collective expression of discontent. Affronted by the anti-authoritarian impact Bion was having on his patients, the authorities sacked him. The fear was that he would incite insubordination which would filter through the hospital which was in the business of preparing soldiers to return to active duty.

Bion's sacking, however, was delayed long enough for the fruits of his experiment to become apparent. As we now know, after six weeks his ward was the cleanest and most disciplined in the hospital. Michael Foulkes, who replaced Bion, was more successful at hierarchical relations, convincing the authorities about the virtues of patient empowerment.

Foulkes went on to develop the philosophy of treating the hospital as a therapeutic whole and this ideology shaped the work of many psychiatric hospitals during the 1950s and 1960s which established TCs, including Warlingham Park, Fulbourne, Belmont (later to become the Henderson) and the Cassel. At the Bethlem Royal and Maudsley Hospital, where Foulkes worked towards the end of his career, a 'community centre' was opened in 1965 which was intended to be a communal meeting area for the whole hospital. The centre housed a cafeteria, library, hairdressing salon, a small swimming pool and a large function hall. It was in this hall that films were screened on the back wall from a small projector room high above the stage.

Part of the hospital-as-community ideology at the Bethlem included the weekly screening of a film. The audience consisted of up to sixty patients and staff, including patients from the geriatric and adolescent units. From the age of eight years, I would go along with my father who worked as the projectionist. I was rather better behaved than Toto, the little boy in the film *Cinema Paradiso*, and I remember being charged with the thrilling responsibility of dimming the lights. The 35mm projector was occasionally faulty and my father would have to use a pencil to create the necessary tension in the spool to ensure the film ran smoothly. The regular slippage of the film reel became a much anticipated part of the proceedings. The amused audience would remonstrate by stamping their feet, a welcome opportunity to join in the noise of collective protest integral to the cinema event for an audience of patients who were unwitting guinea pigs in experiments with the latest in chemical cures.

Films such as *The Italian Job*, starring Michael Caine, and James Bond movies were shown and – in spite of the occasional technical hitches – there was no shortage of popular quality movies. However, the timing of the weekly screening clashed with the change over of staff shifts; this meant that the numbers of patients attending gradually dwindled as staff enthusiasm waned. Community enthusiasm suffered a fatal blow during the 'winter of discontent' in 1972, and soon the only person who was turning up regularly was Fred, a cleaner from the kitchen. The film night at the Bethlem saw its finale in 1973 and the projector was put away to gather dust.

The late 1970s saw the advent of video technology and by the

1980s momentum was such that every unit was able to have its own potential mini-cinema. The difference between watching a film on video in a small group setting compared to the large group of a picture hall is noteworthy. It could be argued that a cinema setting evokes a greater degree of regression. The filial experience of watching larger than life figures returns us to the point when our parents were larger than us. At an unconscious level the experience of watching a larger than life performance may evoke a primal scene phantasy (Klein 1923). From a large group dynamic perspective the larger than life regressive experience of the cinema may resonate with the primitive feelings that are often experienced in large groups. Turquet (1975) noted that people were more likely to wish to see sacrifice and blood in a large group, and this may account for the popularity of the horror genre in the cinema. Feelings of paranoia are exacerbated by the alienation that is felt when one becomes part of a crowd, the darkness accentuating the disappearance into anonymity.

However, in the cinema one is able to be with and be without people simultaneously when watching a film. An audience can gasp or cry together or laugh in unison, the affiliation of shared experience is part of the agenda. During a horror film, one may grab the hand of a partner as reassurance that one is not alone. The experience of surviving a horror film evokes a collective triumph and even after a gruesome film, the audience will leave the cinema happily conversing.

Yet a cinema audience is shrouded in darkness and silence, both of which help to create a level of anxiety and anticipation. This all adds to the enigma of the film. Any noise – be it the rustling of a sweet wrapper or whispering to the person beside you – is met with a stern 'shush' from other members of the audience. The silence during a film is a public experience; one which finds its equivalent in funerals, prayer services, memorials and libraries. Cinemagoers talk about 'losing oneself in the film', meaning that they enjoy a personal experience where they may laugh or cry without anyone knowing. Overall, the cinema audience could be seen as oscillating between an experience of disappearance into the self on the one hand, and feeling part of a shared exchange on the other; a tension between a private and public experience.[1]

Television, however, occupies a different location and space in the experience of watching a film. The television screen is small enough to only take up the space normally occupied by one other person. In the small group setting of a family, the television is viewed often by a maximum of four or five people and can appear to take on the role of an extra family member. It has an incessant narrative, not only entertaining, but provoking discussion and providing information.

At other times its presence may be intrusive and obscuring. Compared to cinema, there are less taboos regarding noise when watching television. Whereas silence is revered at the cinema, at home participant observation with the television is not only permissible but often desirable, especially with the increase in interactive television – game shows, discussion programmes, talent shows – all of which involve telephone voting.

What is constant in the move between television and cinema is the content of the experience. Rarely does a film's structure and narrative change when a film is screened on television or is released on video. The film story appeals to a childhood capacity to play, to be entertained, to fantasise and experience a leap of imagination. Bettleheim's (1976) discussion about the educational role of fairy-tales in children's lives is well known. Winnicott (1971) expressed it as 'life in small doses'. Cinema is like a fairy-tale for grown-ups, except in larger doses.

Yet it would be misleading to say that films deal with adult issues. For the most part, films are involved with the primitive struggles of infancy. For instance, in embarking on a thematical meta-analysis of films, one does not need to be a Kleinian doyen to see that most films work with issues pertaining to a paranoid/schizoid balancing act of the triumph of good over evil. And in the more recent history of the cinema an increasing number of films have been able to embrace a complexity signifying the move from the paranoid schizoid to the depressive position (Segal 1991). In psychoanalytic terms these are both emotional states pertaining to the first year of life.

Watching films with patients

Before discussing some of my experiences of watching films with patients, I shall begin with a brief reflection on the innovative experiment carried out by Will Self and Phil Robson at the Oxfordshire Regional Drug Dependency Unit (DDU) where they watched the film *Naked Lunch*, directed by David Cronenberg, with a group of drug addicted patients.

The film is loosely based on the William Burroughs' (1959) novel of the same name. Cronenberg claimed that the film was 'in the spirit' of Burroughs rather than an attempt at faithful reproduction. Reading Burroughs' drug-hazed book is like trying to listen to a disconnected, over-sexed beatnik schizophrenic conversing with himself in an ethereal void. To return from such a tortured twilight interzone to recount the experience might well lend itself to poetry, even prose (indeed *Naked Lunch* has some purple patches), and this might be of some interest when processed for the rest of us. But one has the feeling that Burroughs never came back. His writings are dense and inaccessible. The vintage trace of outwardness and the capacity to communicate is the hallmark of classical writing. The poet Samuel Taylor Coleridge fell into a laudanum haze (opium mixed with alcohol) and had a vision of 'Kubla Khan', an experience which was the source of his great poem. But it was on his *return* to sensibility that he began to compose his poem. Moderation was something which Burroughs didn't have in order to strike a balance between being 'inside' drugs and yet far enough removed so as to give the impression that he was still a functioning member of the human race.

Cronenberg's creepy-crawly film is as elliptical as Burroughs' book. That Self and Robson hoped to generate coherent data from such a film was, to say the least, ambitious. The focus group discussion after the film is recounted in Self's (1995) collection of writings about drug use, titled *Junk Mail*. The patients and Phil Robson were disappointed about the depiction of drug use in Cronenberg's film. None of the addicts had experienced a hallucination of a cockroach typewriter, and one addict felt that the film would give people the wrong idea about what it was like to use heroin. There followed a discussion about unlocking the creative muse through drug use, for which there were voices for and against Burroughs as a spokesman for a generation. Self had begun the experiment optimistically but at the end of the discussion had to admit that he felt confused by the experiment; 'It's as if having enacted a Burroughsian conceit, I have become subject to one of its own fictional methods' (Self 1995: 56). Self began with the Burroughsian ideal that drugs generate creativity, but in the end he was disappointed. His starting point, however, was hardly conducive to group interaction.

My experience of watching films with drug addicted patients dates back to 1981. Although not conducted in the same spirit of research as Self and Robson, in the milieu of a residential DDU, I have always regarded the experience as a window of therapeutic opportunity. Many addicted patients in recovery might see a film sober for the first time in many years.

In 1981, I and several in-patients from the DDU at the Bethelem Royal Hospital went to see *Christiane F* (1981) when it first came out on general release. The patients were blasé about seeing a film about drugs, yet they found it more alarming and evocative than they expected. *Christiane F* made earlier films about drug use, such as *The Man with the Golden Arm* (1955) and *Easy Rider* (1969), seem gentle in comparison. Its style is quasi-documentary, with a title suggestive of an anonymous case study, and the film was allegedly based on the true story of the death of Babbette, a 14-year-old girl.

The film charts Christiane's plummet into depravity, a bleak portrait of youth culture strung out against the backdrop of the seedy underworld of drugs and prostitution. From Christiane's first snort of heroin, which makes her violently sick, to her switch from smoking to injecting, we see her desperate hunger for heroin spiral until she finally turns to prostitution to fund her habit. There are explicit scenes of injecting, from cooking up to hitting the vein, and it was the first general release film to show a needle penetrating the flesh, hitting a vein and blood being drawn back into the syringe (confirming that the needle is correctly *in situ*).

The film, arguably, has one of the most disgusting scenes in cinema history: Christiane, desperate for a hit, borrows a syringe from another addict still filled with blood. She rushes into a public toilet cubicle and flushes out the syringe down a filthy pan. She draws her heroin up into the syringe and injects herself. Her degradation seems complete. When one considers that this is a pre-AIDS film, this scene today delivers an even greater impact. The deterioration of Christiane is agonising to observe and it is a relief when she and her friend detoxify. The cold turkey scenes are equally explicit, as Christiane writhes and twitches in pain reaching a – literally – sickening climax as she projectile vomits.

Most of the drama takes place at night, sequestered in toilets, nightclubs, subways, underground stations. The soundtrack marries the bleak narrative and is taken from the David Bowie album 'Station to Station'. Bowie makes a cameo appearance as himself performing 'The Return of the Thin White Duke' at a pop concert. The song is a reference to his own drug use, and with his gaunt pallor and heavy dark eye make-up he looks like an archetypal addict, 'a walking dead'. Christiane attends the concert and stands gazing emptily at Bowie as he performs and at one point their eyes meet. The feeling one has is that this is a mirroring of nihilism and the absence of the good paternal object is inculcated. The ironic strains of Bowie's classic song, 'We Can Be Heroes', is used as a backdrop against which we come to realise that Christiane is the archetypal anti-heroin(e).

After seeing the film, one of the patients, Mark, described how he had experienced a 'buzz' from watching the drugs being ingested. He said he felt like it was he who had used. In the scenes in which Christiane is seen withdrawing, both Mark and Martin experienced stomach cramps and sweats. Simon also reported experiencing a bizarre spontaneous 'cold turkey' when watching the harrowing scenes of using and withdrawal. They all agreed that it was a close study of drug using, well researched, including the inevitable throwing up after the first hit of heroin. On the way back to the tube station two of the patients were craving so much that it took some persuading from the others to get them to return to the Bethlem rather than going down the 'Dilly' (Picadilly Circus), at the time the scoring centre of London. The film and the experience afterwards was for me a baptism of fire; fresh out of school, I began to understand the gravity of undertaking work with drug users.

In 1989, another film prompted heightened levels of craving among some of my patients. We had watched Alan Parker's film of Pink Floyd's *The Wall* (1983) on video at the unit. I had reservations about watching the film, not because of any drug scenes but because I remembered my experience of going to see it at Leceister Square when it was first released. I attended the evening screening and as the afternoon matinee crowd spilled out, they looked like they had witnessed an accident: no-one was speaking, no-one was smiling, everyone looked as if they had seen something shocking. And so they had. The film is about a father who is killed during the Second World War and his son who grows up to become a fascistic, chemically-addicted pop star with a failed marriage and a suicidal temper. The soundtrack is haunting and is matched in parts of the film by horrific scenes of war, madness and some of the most blood-curdling and sexually explicit animated sequences to be seen in a film (courtesy of the animator/cartoonist, Gerald Scarfe). Bob Geldof, who played the lead role, described afterwards how he had been traumatised by the demands of his part which involved enacting paranoia, morbid jealousy, self-harm, drug taking, as well as shaving off his body hair (and his eyebrows) and smashing up a hotel room.

When we watched the film on the unit, several of the patients reported afterwards that they were particularly excited by the scene in which Geldof/Pink rolls a joint (a cannabis cigarette) from a huge lump of resin. The lump of resin was felt to be unrealistically large but was clearly jealously desired by the patients. The other drug scenes in the film, for example when Pink is injected with speed in order to do a performance, occupied most of the early discussion. As the group began to talk about the narrative the atmosphere became heavy. One of the patients considered the film to be exploitative, gratuitously violent and overly pessimistic. He was furious with the film and felt that the staff should have thought more carefully about allowing it to be screened. The general response was mostly one of disturbance, a resonance of the violence and madness depicted in the film that was felt within the group.

The negative feelings evoked by the film were apparent the next day when two of the patients discharged themselves. It is not feasible to locate this entirely with the film, but it certainly did act as an unsettling catalyst. My feeling is that the much talked about cannabis scene was a welcome relief from the rest of the film, and that it was not the cannabis that had caused the craving and the patients to leave, but rather the bleakness and sense of loss embodied in the rest of the film

In 1990, *Rebel Without a Cause* (1955) was screened on the unit to a particularly rebellious group of young patients. This film had been at the vanguard of a new film genre that emerged in the 1950s, dealing directly with adolescence and the generation gap, and I thought it would be a pertinent commentary on the group's progress. Beginning with an intoxicated James Dean in a tussle with the local police, we discover that Dean and his family have just moved into the area. Dean rebels against his parents by getting drunk, getting into knife fights, and risking his life in a brinkmanship game of 'chicken' (driving a car towards a cliff edge and jumping out at the last minute). The film is underpinned by a classical Oedipal struggle that reaches a climax when Dean and his father fall tumbling to the ground with Dean strangling his father. Among the cacophony, Dean's mother who witnesses the event, screams, 'are you trying to kill your father?'

My feeling that the film might refract the group's difficulties with authority was not borne out. Although the patients were keen to see a James Dean film – he was in vogue at the time and some of the patients had posters of him on their wall – only one of the group of ten had seen a James Dean film. His attractiveness was the quasi-mythological resonance of his live-hard-die-young life and there was much anticipation about the screening. The curtains were closed and the chairs were positioned to ensure maximum viewing for all, creating a cosy mini-cinema in the lounge of the unit.

However, after ten minutes or so the group became unsettled. A few patients were in the uncomfortable early stages of detoxification which accounted for some of the unrest, but the main reason was that the film was less than riveting for the group. Only two out of ten patients watched the film all the way through. The others drifted off to play snooker and drink tea. When the group came back together for a discussion afterwards, the major complaint was that it did not relate to their experiences, that it was old and out-of-date.

Screen therapy: A working hypothesis

Clarke's (1994) start point for a psychoanalysis of the cinema experience is that the 'silver screen' excites in us aspects of ourselves, that the dramas of the film resonate with our unconscious. He regards the underlying mechanism that accounts for this resonance as projection and identification, that is to say, we invest our emotions into the characters on the screen, thereby collapsing the distance between us and them.

In the vignettes I have just described the identification was a close one for the patients in so far as their own desperation, greed and criminality were depicted. This identification was so strong in some patients that they experienced strong somatic responses such as craving and withdrawing. The identification in this sense was mostly unwanted. The potency of the cravings, indeed so strong that a couple of the patients wanted to score following *Christiane F* and it may have accounted for the two patients who discharged themselves after *The Wall*, suggests that the desire to use drugs was repressed and the film served to catalyse these feelings.

In considering this unconscious process of repression Freud's (1899) notion of screen memories would seem apposite here. First, Freud identified that memories, like dreams, were usually visual. But he found that memories or dream images owed their value to not only that which was remembered, but also to that which was forgotten or suppressed. In his clinical work he found that amnesia occurred commonly where there was a repression of bad and painful memories, always associated with displeasure. He found that the memory or dream was a screen on which the real meaning might be concealed; the riddle of memory was not only the mentation of forgetting but also how remembering might occur. The task of understanding screen memories began with the process of deciphering the riddle. The analyst and patient worked jointly to disentangle the contiguous concealment, a technique of interpretation which Freud (1900) initially honed in his book, *The Interpretation of Dreams.*

Addiction films would appear to be a reminder of a screen or surface memory which evokes memories and feelings. For the patients in the examples I have given, the films had the capacity to evoke feelings of craving, in a sense the film acted as a mirror. In my experience, many clients in the early stages of recovery have a rather idealised view of being drug free. In the confines and safety of a residential unit they talk about having 'kicked it' or 'got the monkey off their back for ever'. Being drug free and believing that there will be no urge to use again is an unrealistically resilient position. The vast majority are caught out and find themselves unsettled by situations which trigger strong cravings. The triggers are varied: emotional states, set-backs, bad news and so on. It is always useful in the milieu to seize opportunities to explore with a patient what it is that prompts them to crave. An experience of watching a powerfully evocative film, such as the examples above, represents an opportunity for exploration. Far from being undesirable, when a patient experiences strong feelings of craving the realistic task of remaining drug free and dealing with the urge to use can be explored. The group's affiliation is always a useful tool in this task and this is the case where a film, having been viewed by several patients, becomes integral to the group matrix and a common reference point for interchange.

I would like to make one final point about the process of identification. I believe it is too simplistic to say that the craving caused by the films described above was solely associated with the desire aroused by the drug content of the film. In each of the films there was a bleak narrative of loss, the death of a father, divorce, family conflict, loneliness, isolation and so on. These deeper levels may have been equally resonant. The drug content was the upper layer of identification that was a screen for other more interpersonal identifications. I have watched many more films where there has been no drug use and yet the film has still caused unsettlement in the group. In terms of the film as 'screen memory', to use Freud's term, the patients are reminded of aspects of their own lives which may have been suppressed and forgotten. The task of working with the film would seem to be of a psychoanalytic nature in so far as the facilitator (in a post-film group discussion) might try to make conscious those identifications which are unconsciously felt. The interpretation of the film, by the group, may be a useful start which might lead to the more rudimentary task of therapy of deciphering what lies behind the screen memory for the individual and the group.

Note

1   Much needed further research into this arena of audience response to the film is currently being planned by the psychoanalytic group psychotherapist David Glyn.

References

Bettleheim, B. (1976) *The Uses of Enchantment*, Harmondsworth: Penguin.

Burroughs, W. (1959) *Naked Lunch*, Paris: Olympia Press.

Clarke, G. S. (1994) 'Notes Towards an Object–Relations View of Cinema', *Free Associations*, 4, 3; 369–90.

Freud, S. (1899) *Screen Memories*, SE III, 307.

——(1900) *The Interpretation of Dreams*, SE IV.

Klein, M. (1923) 'Infant Analysis', in *International Journal of Psycho-Analysis*, 7:31–63.

Segal, H. (1991) *Dream, Phantasy and Art*, London: Tavistock/Routledge.

Self, W.W. (1995) *Junk Mail*, London: Bloomsbury.

Turquet, P. (1975) 'Threats to Identity in the Large Group', in Kreeger, L. (ed.) *Large Groups*, London: Tavistock.

Winnicott, D.W. (1971) *Playing and Reality*, London: Tavistock.

Chapter 6

Art therapy and art activities in alcohol services

A research project

Jacky Mahony

In this chapter I will outline a research project that I carried out into an area which is of particular interest to me: the use of art therapy in the treatment of alcohol related problems. During my research, I was surprised by some of the things which I found; including the fact that as many as half the alcohol projects I looked at used art activities. However, I also had my suspicions confirmed – that there was almost no art therapy in use. Even more disturbingly, it emerged that there was a certain amount of confusion about the actual term 'art therapy'. One aspect of this confusion has very serious implications in so far as in some cases clients were misled about the treatment that was provided for them. Other arts therapists may have come across similar experiences in other fields – I certainly have during my work in the mental health field: on introducing myself to a colleague recently, the reply I received was, 'Oh, I do art therapy. ... I did think about doing the training – why *is* it so long?' My initial amusement regarding this comment has probably more to do with displacement of anxiety since sober consideration of the implications, which I outline in this chapter, produces a less comfortable response.

The way in which my research developed was all-absorbing, and at times it almost seemed to take on a life of its own – a trait that seems indicative of a creative process, and one which I have experienced before with a painting, pot or sculpture, or, for that matter, in the therapeutic process of art therapy (see Gilroy 1992). Although my research was not initially about clinical practice, some of the results produced information relating to theoretical issues in art therapy – in particular, regarding treatment approaches, models and methods – in fact, highlighting the essential attributes of art therapy that distinguish it from art activities used for therapeutic purposes. I believe that there are significant implications revealed in the results of the study, both for the profession and for individual practitioners when thinking about our clinical practice, and most importantly for the clients who are not receiving access to a treatment that could be beneficial. I begin by describing the study and include an outline of the process.

A review of the literature

The benefits and relevance of art therapy in the treatment of alcohol problems

Both British and American authors writing on the subject of art therapy consider there to be distinct therapeutic advantages provided by art therapy in the treatment of drug and alcohol related problems. As an art therapist, I find this of particular interest as it is in marked contrast to the significant treatment difficulties found by other disciplines. For example, in her review of substance abuse literature, Moore (1983) provides a detailed account of addiction related problems which are addressed in art therapy, and considers that certain characteristics found in addicts make it a particularly appropriate form of treatment. She points out an interesting feature of art therapy treatment which forms a contrast to the experience of other disciplines: that is, art therapists consistently feel their work to be therapeutically effective. The frustration and disappointment reported so frequently by other workers in the field is an interesting and significant counterpoint. Although in some cases, in the extensive literature on the dislike and ambivalence felt by professionals towards alcoholics, this has been explained by prejudice and stereotyping (for example, Beckman 1975; Fisher et al. 1975), a more rational argument has been put forward by, for instance, Strong (1980), Knauss and Freund (1985) and Farrell and Lewis (1990), who report therapeutic pessimism based on the difficulties of treatment.

There are several themes to be found in the art therapy literature regarding the particular relevance of art therapy in the treatment of this client group. Briefly, these relate to facilitating the expression and communication of emotion (Adelman and Castricone 1986; Head 1975; Kaufman 1981; Moore 1983; Wadeson 1980;), in particular by serving to protect defences (Albert-Puleo 1980; Mahony and Waller 1992; Springham 1992) and with the artwork providing a form of containment (Donnenberg 1978; Foulke and Keller 1976; Johnson 1990; Potocek and Wilder 1989). The characteristic fear of being overwhelmed by painful and confusing emotions is seen to be addressed by developing a sense of control through distancing (Head 1975), experimentation and redirecting of impulses (Albert-Puleo 1980; Adelman and Castricone 1986; Foulke and Keller 1976; Head 1975; Mahony and Waller 1992; Moore 1983; Spring 1985; Ulman 1953). Low self-esteem is enhanced by developing and building on resources (Albert-Puleo 1980; Foulke and Keller 1976; Head 1975; Johnson 1990; Kaufman 1981; Mahony and Waller 1992). Communicating and reducing isolation is described either through the actual making of the artwork (Allen 1985; Potocek and Wilder 1989) or as a basis for sharing experiences (Foulke and Keller 1976; Head 1975; Springham 1992; Ulman 1953), or purely through symbolic expression (Adelman and Castricone 1986; Luzzatto 1989). The specific and unique advantages offered by art therapy with this client group are seen as stemming from it being a predominantly non-verbal medium combined with the concrete and tangible nature of the work – these characteristics allow access to early experience which can then be worked on at that level, bringing about change (for a more detailed discussion of this last aspect, see this volume Chapters 7 and 8).

My review of the available art therapy literature revealed intriguing issues that subsequently led to my research. What was striking was the lack of literature on the subject by British authors, and the predominance of structured and didactic approaches used by the authors with their clients even when this was seemingly unrelated to theoretical approach (see Mahony and Waller 1992). My own experience of working with such clients has shown art therapy to be particularly relevant as a treatment approach, so I was curious about these findings and why there appeared to be so few art therapists working in the field in the UK. In deciding to look deeper into these issues and in order to narrow the focus, I limited the study to art therapy in alcohol services.

Further discrepancies emerged. There is a conspicuous absence of references to the use of art therapy in the general literature on alcoholism, both in books and journals. A major study of Alcoholism Treatment Units (Ettorre 1984 and 1985) fails to mention art therapy in its examination of treatment activities, even though it finds what are described as eight 'art/music therapists' (Ettorre 1985). A follow-up study in 1984–85 suggests, with regard to staffing, that there may be a decrease in the employment of art therapists and a large increase in community psychiatric nurses (Ettorre 1988). In the 1991–92 Alcohol Services Directory (Alcohol Concern 1991), only five services offer art therapy to clients or have an art therapist on the staff team, and in some cases report having art therapy but no art therapist and vice versa. There is almost no mention of art activities, as distinct from art therapy, being made available to clients.

Organisational considerations

Possible reasons for the situation could include problems in integrating art therapy into the services – as reported by numerous art therapists (see, for instance, Edwards 1986, 1989; Maclagan 1985; McClean, this volume, Chapter 8; Waller and Gheorghieva 1990). Perhaps differing cultural or philosophical approaches to treatment cause conflicting therapeutic models and ideologies (for a discussion of the literature, see Mahony 1992). Art therapy may not be seen to be a viable or complementary partner in the light of an alcohol service's treatment policy and values.

In addition, the profession is comparatively new (in the UK it was recognised by the Department of Health in 1982; the National Joint Council in 1990; and became state registered only in 1997) and some workers may know little about it. A British survey on attitudes of psychiatric nursing staff towards art therapy (Richardson and Gnanapragasam 1979) found that only 65 per cent of nurses and nursing students considered art therapy to be a form of treatment and many saw it to be an ancillary service 'similar to occupational therapy'. This is despite the fact that the study took place in an institution where art therapy had been established for ten years. If there are difficulties in integrating a different treatment approach, art therapists may consciously or unconsciously try to fit their model to the institution, even if there are very different ideologies. Ettorre (1984) looks at treatment policies in Alcohol Treatment Units and past and present influences on current thinking and finds that psychoanalytic theory has a continuing but lessening influence – an indication of less than favourable conditions for a psychoanalytically informed modality. Allen (1985) describes how staff where she worked were concerned about art therapy as they considered it psychoanalytic and therefore potentially detrimental to the organisation's view that drinking is the primary problem.

Treatment approaches in art therapy

Another area to consider is the response of workers to the client group and the institution and how this could affect therapeutic models and attitudes to treatment. Moore (1983) finds that assignments and special art techniques dominate therapeutic approaches in the US. Similarly, here in Britain, when reviewing the literature, Diane Waller and I found an emphasis on structure and control in the methods applied by art therapists in the treatment of this client group and cited the prevalent 'Concept model' as a particularly harsh example of the treatment approaches to be found in the field of substance abuse (Mahony and Waller 1992). That these approaches are so widely used could indicate a response to either the client group and/or the institution.

Several art therapists highlight the benefits of using art therapy in the treatment of narcissistic disorders such as are found in alcohol dependence (see, especially, Albert-Puleo 1980; Lachman-Chapin 1979; Springham, 1992 and this volume, Chapter 7). Narcissistic traits are commonly seen as, at an irrational level with judgemental attitudes, being self-centred, self-indulgent and immoral and sometimes evoking punitive reactions. Discussion of counter-transference responses to the client group (Mahony and Waller 1992) suggest that these may find their way into the model that is used. However, it seems important that art therapy is clearly seen to be informed by psychoanalytic and psychodynamic theory – such views deliberately take a more neutral and less judgemental attitude to the client and guard against counter-transference responses. In this way, one can effectively respond to narcissistic disorders and provide an appropriate treatment approach. McClean's case study (see Chapter 8) is an example of the therapist critically examining her counter-transference responses, particularly bearing in mind projective identification.

The study

Looking at the literature enabled hunches and half formed ideas to eventually become defined into the key areas for further investigation regarding therapeutic models and attitudes to treatment. The main research questions had to be extracted before going any further.

From the literature, there appeared to be hardly any art therapy being provided for people with alcohol related difficulties. The intention of the study was to clarify if this was indeed the case, and if so, explore what such an absence might mean. By using a representative sample, my aim was to gather information which could be critically examined with a view to discovering patterns and links that might help to explain if and why art therapy was being used so infrequently in these services. I also wanted to look at attitudes towards art therapy in order to explore the relationship between therapeutic models and assumptions behind treatment approaches. How did staff in alcohol services view the relevance of art therapy to the treatment of alcohol associated problems? And how would these views relate to the reported use or non-use of art therapy in these particular services?

The method

A questionnaire survey of one large health region was chosen to carry out the research after a pilot study. This region was picked because there was no reported art therapy, art activities or art therapists. The questionnaire offered multiple-choice and fixed-alternative questions to provide quantitative data to establish, for instance, exactly how much art therapy input there was to a service. Bearing in mind relevant literature (in particular, Mahony and Waller 1992 and Moore 1983, who speculate on whether the emphasis on structured approaches is in response to the client group), I intended open-ended questions to produce text which could then be interpreted to identify assumptions behind treatment methods, attitudes towards art therapy and the aims of the institution. The method of analysis is described in the following section, 'Analysis of qualitative data' (p. 123). It was hoped that the interpretation of the qualitative data would substantiate and illuminate the 'hard' evidence provided by the quantitative data.

The questionnaire design divided respondents into those projects which had the input of an art therapist and those without an art therapist. The two categories were then subdivided into those projects which had some form of art activity other than art therapy and those which did not. The aim was to see how and if projects differentiated between the use of *art activities* as distinct from *art therapy*. It was hoped that certain patterns might then come to light.

Analysis of qualitative data

What follows is a summary of the findings: I have described the analysis in detail in a previous paper (see Mahony 1994).

I was excited and relieved to find that the bulky envelopes coming through the letterbox contained considerable descriptive material from respondents relating to their beliefs, opinions and attitudes surrounding the use of art activities and art therapy in their services. After lengthy perusal of the information, it soon became apparent that it could be divided into three distinct ways of viewing the use of art as a therapeutic medium. In order to define these views, I drew on previous work by Diane Waller (for a more detailed discussion see, in particular, Waller 1991 and 1992) which examined the influences on the development of art therapy as a profession. The three major themes which emerged can be described as: art which is used for *educative*, *healing*, or *psychotherapeutic* purposes.

The concept of analysing the use of language in order to extract underlying beliefs is helpful to my thinking as an art therapist; not only about how others see art therapy but also in considering my own work. For instance, what aspects of the therapeutic process or art-making are particularly helpful to a client in their therapy, or even in one session? Obviously each case can and does vary enormously, but I find it helpful to critically examine my practice, including the appropriateness of styles and techniques which I may adopt. For the study I was about to undertake, it proved to be very revealing.

In order to illustrate my method of analysis, the following three examples of respondents' statements typify the major themes:

Art as education

> (The project's art activities are ...) very beneficial – increase confidence, motivation, leisure interests, link to adult education, help to express emotions, learn to be creative in a constructive way.
>
> (Respondent no. 4)

Within this view is contained the notion that art can be used to promote *development*. The emphasis is on educating and enriching the person so that they become an active, participating member of society – art is seen to have a beneficial effect on everyday life. In the example there is an implicit reference to the constructive aspects of creativity implying these need to be controlled. Waller (1991) refers to the continuing influence of Read (1943) and Lowenfeld (1947) on the theories of art education which were prevalent in the 1930s, and still exist today, and which were a logical development of the ideas of the early twentieth-century American educational philosopher, John Dewey.

Art as healing

(Art therapy has relevance in alcohol services because it can ...) channel pent-up feelings creatively. Realise creative potential. Use colour, movement, posture, expression to release suppressed feeling. Provide safe channel for expression.

(Respondent no. 3)

This view acknowledges that the person's inner state of mind needs addressing. Here it relates to emotions that are 'pent up' and 'suppressed' and an implicit assumption is that the feelings might be dangerous in some way. This falls into the category of 'Therapeutic Art' (see Waller 1991) as perceived by Hill (1951) and Petrie (1946). The emphasis is on the making of the image as being therapeutic with some implication of distracting the patient from their difficulties. In using this interpretation, art can be seen as offering the opportunity for *regeneration* as put forward by Petrie (1946).

Art as psychotherapy

(Art therapy is ...) the non verbal expression of conscious and unconscious thoughts and feeling, with professional assistance to help unravel their meaning and significance, and to start to resolve any emotional/psychological conflicts expressed in the artwork.

(Respondent no. 6)

The view expressed here describes different layers or levels of meaning held within the artwork which can be explored and integrated in the context of a relationship with a professionally trained person. The experience is set apart from everyday life. The emphasis is on the art object itself being *integrative* and as being part of a therapeutic transaction between therapist and client (see Waller 1991) as perceived by Naumberg (1966) and Champernowne (1969). This view involves concepts such as the unconscious, transference and counter-transference.

The results of the study

The overall picture presented by the Alcohol Services Directory (Alcohol Concern 1991) was supported by the study's results. I was not surprised to discover that there was hardly any art therapy available. Out of the twenty-eight questionnaires which were sent out, sixteen replied – making a total of 57 per cent. Only one of the projects employed a registered art therapist (see Table 6.1) – and even then, only for a two-hour weekly session.

Table 6.1 Employment of art therapists

Cases	Yes	No
16	1	15

No art therapists had been employed previously. However, as noted, I was surprised at the widespread use of art activities by staff other than art therapists (see Table 6.2).

Table 6.2 Projects with and without some form of art

Cases	Art therapy	Art activities	No art
16	1	8	7

The nature of alcohol services

From the information given by respondents about their projects, it was possible to form a profile of services. Table 6.3 shows that only four out of the sixteen alcohol services are in the UK's National Health Service (NHS); additionally, one of these four projects is jointly funded with Social Services.

Table 6.3 Status of responding projects

NHS	Non-NHS	Total
4	12	16

Projects outside of the NHS are described as charitable (five), voluntary (four) and private (three); with six of these projects having sub-centres. Eight of the sixteen facilities are described as advice/counselling agencies and six as residential. Four projects are described as Alcohol Treatment Units, two as hostels, one as a Drugs and Alcohol Treatment Centre, and one as a Community Alcohol Service. I compared the projects with and without art activities, and Table 6.4 shows that the majority of art activities take place in non-NHS facilities. The project with art therapy is the jointly funded Drug and Alcohol Treatment Centre referred to previously.

Table 6.4 Status of projects with and without some form of art

	Cases	Art therapy	Art activities	No art
NHS	4	1	1	2
Non-NHS	12	0	7	5
Total	16	1	8	7

Facilities which have some form of art are described predominantly as Alcohol Treatment Units and as residential.

Size

Art mainly occurs in the bigger institutions: for example, a larger institution *with art* is described as: 'a psychiatric hospital which has two residential homes, two psychiatric units in general hospitals and one other hospital' (Respondent no. 16). Whereas a larger organisation with *no art* is described as: 'advice/counselling agency with a hostel for recovering alcoholics' (Respondent no. 7).

Staffing

Table 6.5 presents the overall picture for reported staffing of the sixteen projects. Even though there are 168 staff working at the sixteen projects, there are only two hours per week input by an art therapist. (The art therapist does not appear in these figures as they were not included in the responses to the questions on staffing but in response to specific questions about art therapy.) Nursing staff and 'other' staff far outweigh the other designations. Although I expected to see far more, only one CPN (Community Psychiatric Nurse) is referred to directly by a respondent: 'there is some CPN intervention when required' (Respondent no. 4).

Table 6.5 Reported employment of staff by designation

	NHS	Non-NHS	Total	Percentage
Nursing staff	13	43	56	33
Medical staff	5	14	19	11
Social workers	3	16	19	11
Psychologists	0.5	4	4.5	3
Therapists*	2	18	20	12
Other staff**	3	47	50	30
Total	26.5	142	168.5	100

Notes:

*Therapists' designations include: seven addiction therapists; five alcohol/drug counselling therapists; three occupational therapists; two physiotherapists; and three counsellors.

**Other staff designations include: sixteen care staff; four counsellors; three administrators; one aromatherapist; two yoga teachers; one children's services worker; two out-reach workers; one training officer; and one director.

Table 6.6 shows that a far greater number of staff and range of staff designations exist where some form of art is taking place, and this is further confirmed in Table 6.7 by comparing the staffing averages.

Table 6.6 Comparison of reported staff designations

	With art (9)			No art (7)		
	NHS	Non-NHS	Total	NHS	Non-NHS	Total
Nursing staff	9	43	52	4	0	4
Medical staff	5	14	19	0	0	0
Social workers	2	16	18	1	0	1
Psychologists	0.5	4	4.5	0	0	0
Therapists	1	13	14	3	17	20
Total	17.5	120	137.5	9	22	31

Table 6.7 Average staff numbers per project

With art	Cases	No art	Cases
15.3	9	4.4	7

Thus in conclusion, the projects which incorporate some form of art are mainly larger non-NHS organisations, employing significantly more staff from a wider range of designations.

Constraints, provision and potential

Table 6.8 Respondents' opinions as to why there is no art at their project

		Cases
Deliberate choice	4	8
Never considered	2	8
Other reasons	2	8

Financial reasons were given by the majority of respondents whose projects did not have art. The four projects which had decided not to include art cited resource constraints and one who gave 'other reasons' said: 'Until recently the facilities for providing Art Therapy were not available' (Respondent no. 7). The second who gave 'other reasons' said encouragingly: 'At present, the Treatment Programme is very full of activities. In the future, art therapy could be structured into the programme' (Respondent no. 14).

Unfortunately little information was given by the respondent whose project includes art therapy. They did not answer the open-ended questions or the ones which required a descriptive answer. In part, this could be because art therapy was a recent innovation to the project. The characteristics of this project and its staffing seem in general similar to the ones where some form of art takes place, although it lacks sub-centres, therapists or 'other' staff. Group art therapy is provided: two staff are involved and it came about through the choice of clients and a decision by 'a staff member'. The respondent did not answer the question, 'In your opinion, how beneficial is art therapy to the clients attending your project?', but considered it had potential for further development and that art therapy was relevant in alcohol services. Because they answered a question aimed at those who had art activities and not art therapy, it seems as if they were unclear about the distinction between the two terms. They thought their 'art activities' were both recreational and treatment-based.

Three other respondents show quite a favourable response to the idea of providing art therapy. The most positive response from a project stated that, 'art therapy is seen as a vital component' in a Day Care programme that is planned (Respondent no. 7). By contrast with the tiny provision of art therapy and its newness, art activities used by staff who are not art therapists seem well-established – the most recent had been in place for ten months, the longest for fifteen years, and the average time-scale was about seven years. When asked how beneficial the activities are to their clients, the respondents seem fairly satisfied: three respondents think they are 'very beneficial', one 'good', and another 'useful'.

However, it becomes clear in the responses to questions about art and art therapy that there are many misconceptions about what actually constitutes art therapy as opposed to art activities used by other staff. In one instance, a respondent's understanding of art therapy is described as both: '(1) Use of art activities to help people come to terms with personal problems of an emotional or psychic nature; (2) Specific techniques used by a qualified Art Therapist to facilitate personal growth in another person' (Respondent no. 4).

At this project, art activities are used as part of a treatment process and an occupational therapist is employed. Another respondent's descriptions reveals that they make little distinction between the use of art activities and art therapy:

> (some form of art activity other than art therapy would be potentially valuable to the clients, such as:) creative writing, poetry, drama, role play – to help express feeling.
>
> Art Therapy is a medium that anyone can use to express oneself. It doesn't simply mean drawing but also language, movement, music, sound, solid material like wood, clay.
>
> (Respondent no. 3)

It can also be seen from many of the descriptions that a distinct implication of the survey is that art therapy is often considered synonymous with recreational therapy (see, for example, the quotes by Respondent no. 13, p. 130). Before going any further, it is therefore necessary to discuss the confusion surrounding the terms.

Considerable qualitative data was given by the respondents in answering the questionnaire. Although some of it reflects the confusion I have just described, the information holds the potential for insight into the respondents' views about possible uses of art and art therapy with their clients and in alcohol services generally. Some of the beliefs involved will be implicit assumptions not necessarily held at a conscious level. Defining these views was essential in order to disentangle the apparent confusion surrounding art therapy and art activities and to attempt to extract information. Without analysis of the text it would make no sense at all. The three definitions that I arrived at, as described on pp. 123–5, represent three different ways of viewing the use of art as a therapeutic medium as found in the descriptive material. To reiterate, I have labelled the three major themes: 'Art as education', 'Art as healing' and 'Art as psychotherapy'.

Confusion: Art psychotherapy versus art education

Whereas some respondents appear to have a partial understanding about the nature of art therapy, others believe that staff other than qualified art therapists can practise or are practising art therapy with clients. Three respondents state that 'art therapy' is taking place at their projects when there is no art therapist employed.

Even though for the sake of clarity the term 'Registered Art Therapist' was defined on the questionnaire, one respondent ticked both 'Yes' and 'No' when asked if one was employed and made the comment: 'An Art Teacher is employed for three hour session each week' (Respondent no. 13). It is clear from their description of what takes place that this is 'art as education' and not art therapy:

> It is not called Art Therapy, but explores creativity and teaches skills e.g. we have a lifeclass sometimes, create murals, design and experiment, posters, still lives, etc. and visit art galleries.
>
> (Respondent no. 13)

The respondent goes on to answer all the questions designed for those projects with an art therapist as well as those aimed at projects where other forms of art take place. They say that 'art therapy' is beneficial to their clients because:

All art is therapeutic and clients benefit, but we have found calling the class 'Art Therapy' puts people off – they have often had bad experience of classes in treatment centres. BUT they thoroughly enjoy art PROPER, learning new skills and reminding themselves of old skills. Absorbing and a real change from therapy in general. Several are very talented and have become Art students.' [their emphasis]

(ibid.)

Not only is art therapy seen to be a name that can be given to some kind of class which often gives people bad experiences, but it is obviously not 'proper' art, whatever that may mean (something to do with learning skills and seeming to provide some relief from therapy!). Another respondent, although not employing an art therapist, considers their project has provided art therapy for six years. Described as 'Collage masks', all staff at the project are involved in this activity (nine nurses, four doctors, one psychologist, seven addiction therapists and a psychiatrist). Although they consider what takes place to be 'useful' to their clients, they are (unsurprisingly) 'not sure' if 'art therapy' has any relevance in alcohol services, while their understanding of it is revealed to be 'art as education'.

The descriptive material reveals that, first, there are marked differences in attitudes and beliefs about the use of art as a therapeutic medium and, second, there seems to be a relationship between these attitudes and whether or not the respondent's project already has some form of art. Where there is some form of art at a project, respondents mostly see the therapeutic use of art (whether activities *or* art therapy) in terms of 'education'. Apart from the project providing 'art therapy in a gestalt way', all the art activities are described in such terms. For instance one respondent says: 'Drawing for pleasure, trying abilities. Sewing, embroidery, basket making, clay modelling, light woodwork, making stools. Basically for creativity and learning skills' (Respondent no. 16).

Another says: 'Painting, drawing, use of photographs. Visits to museums and galleries etc.' (Respondent no. 12). The benefits of these activities are also seen as 'education' – for example: 'It develops better concentration. It provides a sense of achievement' (Respondent no. 16). However, although apparently satisfied with the activities, respondents largely believe that there is room for development (see Table 6.9).

Table 6.9 Potential for further development of art activities

Yes	No	Don't know	No answer	Total
5	1	1	1	8

This could have different implications. The respondents could be less satisfied with the activities than they appear in Table 6.9, perhaps sensing that there are other benefits from art which could be tapped. In fact, one says: 'a formal art therapist' could be employed to run 'projective art groups'. On the other hand, the activities might be seen to be vital, growing and expanding.

It is in the replies to questions about opinions related to art therapy that the contrasting attitudes of respondents *without* art activities become apparent. In Table 6.10, it can be seen that they show slightly more uncertainty concerning the potential value of art therapy to their clients.

Table 6.10 The potential value of art therapy to the projects' clients

	Cases	Yes	No	Don't know	No answer
With art activities	8	5	1	1	1
No art	7	4	1	2	—
Total	15	9	2	3	1

However, the descriptive material reveals interestingly that their underlying attitudes about the possible benefits are quite different to the respondents whose projects already have art activities. The four respondents with no art who think art therapy is potentially valuable to their clients, all see the benefits in terms of 'art as psychotherapy'. For example, one says: 'My experience of art therapy in other stress-related illness – is that it is useful in uncovering inner conflicts and enables insights and lowers verbal defences' (Respondent no. 14). By contrast, the respondent whose project does have art once more sees the potential benefits as 'art as education'.

Table 6.11 The relevance of art therapy in alcohol services

	Cases	Yes	No	Don't know
With art	9	6	0	3
No art	7	4	1	2
Total	16	10	1	5

Table 6.11 shows that the majority of respondents believe art therapy has relevance in alcohol services, although the figures again point to uncertainty, this time more marked, with five who 'don't know'. The descriptive material given in answering this question underlines this uncertainty (see Table 6.12).

Table 6.12 Reasons regarding the relevance of art therapy in alcohol services

	With art	No art	Total
Art as education	3	1	4
Art as healing	—	1	1
Art as psychotherapy	1	2	3
No reason	2	—	2
Cases	6	4	10

The difference in underlying attitudes is still apparent: those with art see the relevance more as 'art as education', for example: 'Self expression/achievement' (Respondent no. 5); whereas those with no art see it more as 'psychotherapy' and 'healing', for example: 'To uncover unconscious conflicts. To develop personal insight. To find a means of self expression, particularly where verbal difficulties occur' (Respondent no. 14).

When respondents describe what they understand by 'art therapy', there is a subtle shift of emphasis (see Table 6.13). Three respondents change their type of answer: whereas Table 6.12 shows the relevance of art therapy in alcohol services is more often viewed as 'education', Table 6.13 reveals that their actual understanding of art therapy is mainly that it is 'psychotherapy'.

Table 6.13 Respondents' understanding of the term 'art therapy'

	With art	No art	Total
Art as education	3	—	3
Art as healing	—	3	3
Art as psychotherapy	3	3	6
No answer	3	1	4
Cases	9	7	16

For example, one organisation with art activities sees the relevance of art therapy in alcohol services in terms of how it 'enhances self-esteem and enjoyment in particular. Encourages creativity and new avenues to be explored so creates climate for change' (Respondent no. 13). Whereas their understanding of art therapy is as follows: 'Using images to explore feelings', adding the admonition, ' can be used patronisingly if done badly' (ibid.). Similarly a respondent with no art sees art therapy to be relevant because: 'creative expression is often absent from the lives of our clients', while succinctly describing their understanding to be:

> The non verbal expression of conscious and unconscious thoughts and feelings, with professional assistance to help unravel their meaning and significance, and to start to resolve any emotional/psychological conflicts expressed in the artwork.
> (Respondent no. 6)

Although the benefits and relevance of art therapy for clients of alcohol services are more often seen to be in the sphere of 'art as education', only three actually describe their *understanding* of art therapy in this way. Twice as many described it as 'art as psychotherapy'. However, the distribution of replies still illustrates the previously described confusion and uncertainty.

These attitudes revealed in the descriptive material point to possible explanations as to why there is so little art therapy in alcohol services. Perceptions of what art therapy *is*, differ from how its relevance to alcohol services is seen. In addition, I would suggest that the findings regarding the staffing and nature of the projects with some form of art, together with the confusion and differences in attitudes and beliefs regarding the therapeutic uses of art, indicate that social factors should also be considered. I will explore this argument further on in this chapter, but Table 6.14 highlights the marked difference between projects with and without art in the employment of professional categories of staff. It seems likely that such a high figure for professional titles among the projects with some form of art would have some bearing on the situation and influence attitudes to treatment.

Table 6.14 Reported employment of staff holding a professional title

	With art	No art
Professional titles	97.5	6
Therapists, excluding professional titles	10	5
Other staff	30	20
Total	137.5	31

Discussion

The results of the survey show that there is no art therapy available for clients attending services purely for alcohol related problems – the weekly two hours that one respondent offers is provided at a Drugs and Alcohol Treatment Unit. However, it should be pointed out that this actually represents a tiny increase in the employment of art therapists, as none had been mentioned for this region in the Alcohol Services Directory (Alcohol Concern 1991). Also, I had expected an increase in CPNs as this was suggested by Ettorre's follow-up study (1988), which I refer to at the beginning of this chapter, but they appeared to be little used.

Although in my survey resource constraints reputedly pay a major part in the lack of art therapy, the attitudes revealed by analysis of the descriptive material give some idea as to why there is so little art therapy in alcohol services generally, and why many art therapists working in this field often use structured and didactic methods in their practice. The underlying view of many respondents is that the benefits and relevance of art therapy in alcohol services are mainly 'art as education' while perceiving it to be 'art as psychotherapy'. The large number of structured approaches may be a response to such beliefs.

The art activities

I was surprised to find the widespread use of art activities by other staff which were not mentioned in the Alcohol Services Directory. Although this does not necessarily mean there will be a similar picture elsewhere in alcohol services, this particular discovery is consistent with a major survey carried out in the US by Fryear and Fleshman (1981), which found that art was widely used in mental health by staff other than arts therapists.

The projects which provide art activities differ from the ones which do not in that they are mainly larger organisations, predominantly described as Alcohol Treatment Units and/or residential facilities, and employ a greater number of staff, particularly those with professional training. Projects with no art employ no medical staff, psychologists and very few nurses and social workers.

Art as a part of everyday life

That the art activities are not reported in the Alcohol Services Directory, even though they are well established and seen as beneficial, raises questions as to how they are perceived. On the one hand they appear to be stable fixtures, but on the other they are not considered important enough to advertise: they are subsumed instead under umbrella titles and described in vague terms, such as 'crafts', 'leisure interests', 'life skills', or under the auspices of occupational therapy. Art is not directly referred to, and a specifically trained staff member is not employed – suggesting that the activities are not taken seriously as part of a treatment programme. Mahony (1992), Mahony and Waller (1992) and Waller and Dalley (1992) note that art is often seen as diversional and is not considered 'serious'. Education, social factors and home environment all have an influence on attitudes towards art. The survey shows that the activities take place where large numbers of professionally trained staff are working – those with further training, many of whom will have had a privileged education and home environment. We have seen how one project at least has visits to galleries and exhibitions – while for many people this is not an unusual experience, for some it is. Attitudes to art reflect particular social values, assumptions and beliefs which permeate the fabric of everyday life rather than being thought about at a conscious level. The projects' art activities are almost all perceived as 'art as education' or as recreational therapy – for the development of the individual and something everyone can do and benefit from. Hence a specialist is not needed – anyone can do it if they have some interest.

The confusion about the term 'art therapy'

Where there is a lack of understanding about art and art therapy, it may be seen to be a 'technique' to be employed by any professional worker, as indicated by several respondents. Respondent no. 13, for instance, in reference to their art classes, states that 'art proper' is a real change from therapy, the implication being that art therapy is not 'proper' art. Respondent no. 16 doesn't consider art therapy to be potentially valuable for their clients because their 'nurses and doctors are well trained and skilled in counselling and cognitive therapy'. Respondent no. 10 says they do not know if art therapy is potentially valuable for their clients because, 'I am not involved in counselling personally so do not feel qualified to comment'.

Waller and Dalley (1992) suggest that the term art therapy has meant and still means very different things to different people. The responses to my survey graphically illustrate the way in which there is considerable confusion surrounding the term. Respondents of three projects believe they provide art therapy to their clients although they do not employ an art therapist, and in some cases, respondents see art therapy as recreational therapy. This may say a good deal about alcohol services and attitudes to treatment, but it also raises major issues for the profession of art therapy to do with public awareness and how art therapy is being presented by practitioners to clients, colleagues and the public. Similar issues are apparent with Fryear and Fleshman's (1981) finding that the majority of mental health workers using the arts are occupational therapists, activity or recreation therapists. Waller and Dalley (1992) similarly describe how sometimes different staff believe they are 'doing art therapy' with clients.

The confusion over terms and definitions not only makes evaluating a service problematic, it also raises a serious issue. In several cases the activities are actually described as art therapy. This has major implications for the profession of art therapy and indeed for client choice. If other professionals are claiming to offer art therapy, they are in fact misleading their clients. It's like being told you will receive physiotherapy, only to be given 'music and movement'. The confusion prevents clients from gaining access to a method which if practised by trained art therapists can have benefits (as described by Mahony and Waller 1992, and McClean in Chapter 8). While this confusion continues to persist, people with alcohol related problems are not receiving an effective treatment method by a professional trained in its use.

The survey's results suggest areas for the profession to address: first, in raising public awareness of art therapy as a discrete discipline – State Registration should go a long way to helping with this; second, in clearly defining to colleagues, employers and clients the benefits and relevance of art therapy as a treatment medium; and third, ensuring a scrupulous examination by practitioners of their practice and theoretical models. There is interest shown by respondents in providing art therapy and I refer back to the encouraging statement of the project which was about to introduce art therapy as a 'vital component' in a new programme. From the other chapters in this book it can be seen that it is possible to integrate art therapy into services with a carefully considered approach and provide a unique treatment approach for people with addiction related problems. The research results have emphasised a serious lack of access to art therapy for people with alcohol related problems.

References

Adelman, E. and Castricone, L. (1986) 'An expressive arts model for substance abuse group training and treatment', *The Arts in Psychotherapy*, 13: 53–9.

Albert-Puleo, N. (1980) 'Modern psychoanalytic art therapy and its application to drug abuse', *The Arts in Psychotherapy*, 7(1): 43–52.

Alcohol Concern (1991) *Alcohol Services Directory 1991–2*, Ilkley: Owen Wells Publisher.

Allen, P.B. (1985) 'Integrating art therapy into an alcoholism treatment program', *American Journal of Art Therapy*, 24: 10–12.

Beckman, L.J. (1975) 'Women alcoholics: A review of social and psychological studies', *Journal of Studies on Alcohol*, 36: 797–824.

Champernowne, H.I. (1969) 'Art therapy as an adjunct to psychotherapy', *Inscape*, 1: 1–10.

Donnenberg, D. (1978) 'Art therapy in a Drug Community', Proceedings of the Eighth International Congress Psychopath. Expr., Jerusalem 1976, *Confinia Psychiat*, 21: 37–44.

Edwards, D. (1986) 'Three years on: Surviving the institution', *Inscape*, Summer: 3–11.

——(1989) 'Five years on: Further thoughts on the issue of surviving as an art therapist', in A. Gilroy and T. Dalley (eds) *Pictures At an Exhibition*, London: Tavistock/Routledge, 167–78.

Ettorre, E.M. (1984) 'A study of alcoholism treatment units – 1. Treatment activities and the institutional response', *Alcohol and Alcoholism*, 19(3): 243–55.

——(1985) 'A study of alcoholism treatment units – some findings on units and staff', *Alcohol and Alcoholism*, 20(4): 371–8.

——(1988) 'A follow-up study of alcoholism treatment units: Exploring consolidation and change', *British Journal of Addiction*, 83: 57–65.

Farrell, M. and Lewis, G. (1990) 'Discrimination on the grounds of diagnosis', *British Journal of Addiction*, 85: 883–90.

Fisher J., Mason, R. and Keeley. K. (1975) 'Physicians and alcoholics: The effect of medical training on attitudes towards alcoholics', *Quarterly Journal of Studies on Alcohol*, 36(7): 949–55.

Foulke, W.E. and Keller, T.W. (1976) 'The art experience in addict rehabilitation', *American Journal of Art Therapy*, 15(3): 75–80.

Fryear, J.L. and Fleshman, B. (1981) 'Career information on the arts in mental health', *The Arts in Psychotherapy*, 8: 219–44.

Gilroy, A. (1992) 'Research in art therapy', in D. Waller and A. Gilroy (eds) *Art Therapy: A Handbook*, Buckingham and Philadelphia: Open University Press, 229–47.

Head, V.B. (1975) 'Experiences with art therapy in short-term groups of day clinic addicted patients', *The Ontario Psychologist*, 7(4): 42–9.

Hill, A. (1951) *Painting Out Illness*, London: Williams and Norgate.

Johnson, L. (1990) 'Creative therapies in the treatment of addictions: the art of transforming shame', *The Arts in Psychotherapy*, 17: 299–308.

Kaufman, G.H. (1981) 'Art therapy with the addicted', *Journal of Psychoactive Drugs*, 13(4): 353–60.

Knauss, W. and Freund, H. (1985) 'Group-analytic psychotherapy with alcoholic in-patients', *Group Analysis*, XVIII(2): 124–30.

Lachman-Chapin, M. (1979) 'Kohut's theories on narcissism: Implications for art therapy', *American Journal of Art Therapy*, 19 October: 3–9.

Lowenfeld, V. (1947) *Creative and Mental Growth*, New York: Macmillan.

Luzzatto, P. (1989) 'Drinking problems and short-term art therapy: Working with images of withdrawal and clinging' in A. Gilroy and T. Dalley (eds) *Pictures At an Exhibition*, London: Tavistock/Routledge, 207–19.

Maclagan, D. (1985) 'Art therapy in a therapeutic community', *Inscape*, 1: 7–8.

Mahony, J. (1992) 'The organizational context of art therapy', in D. Waller and A. Gilroy (eds) *Art Therapy: A Handbook*, Buckingham and Philadelphia: Open University Press.

——(1994) 'Perceptions of art therapy and its absence in alcohol services', *Inscape*, 1: 15–18,

Mahony, J. and Waller, D. (1992) 'Art therapy in the treatment of alcohol and drug abuse', in D. Waller and A. Gilroy (eds) *Art Therapy: A Handbook*, Buckingham and Philadelphia: Open University Press.

Moore, R.W. (1983) 'Art therapy with substance abusers: A review of the literature', *The Arts in Psychotherapy*, 10: 251–60.

Naumberg, M. (1966) *Dynamically Oriented Art Therapy: Its Principles and Practice*, New York: Grune & Stratton, 85–127.

Petrie, M. (1946) *Art and Regeneration*, London: Elek.

Potocek, J. and Wilder, V.N. (1989) 'Art/movement psychotherapy in the treatment of the chemically dependent patient', *The Arts in Pychotherapy*, 16: 99–103.

Read, H. (1943) *Education Through Art*, New York: Pantheon.

Richardson, J.T.E. and Gnanapragasam, G.R. (1979) 'Attitudes of nursing staff towards art therapy', *British Journal of Psychiatry*, 134: 221–2.

Spring, D. (1985) 'Sexually abused, chemically dependent women', *American Journal of Art Therapy*, 24: 13–21.

Springham, N. (1992) 'Short term group processes in art therapy for people with substance misuse problems', *Inscape*, Spring: 8–16.

Strong, P.M. (1980) 'Doctors and dirty work – the case of alcoholism', *Sociology and Health and Illness*, 2(1): 24–47.

Ulman, E. (1953) 'Art therapy at an outpatient clinic', *Psychiatry*, 16: 55–64.

Wadeson, H. (1980) *Art Psychotherapy* (Chapter 18), Wiley: Interscience Publications.

Waller, D. (1991) *Becoming a Profession: The History of Art Therapy in Britain 1940–82*, London and NewYork: Tavistock/Routledge.

——(1992) 'The training of art therapists: past, present and future issues', in D. Waller and A. Gilroy (eds) *Art Therapy: A Handbook*, Buckingham and Philadelphia: Open University Press.

Waller, D. and Dalley, T. (1992) 'Art therapy: a theoretical perspective', in D. Waller and A. Gilroy (eds) *Art Therapy: A Handbook*, Buckingham and Philadelphia: Open University Press.

Waller, D. and Gheorghieva, Z. (1990) 'Art therapy in Bulgaria, Part III', *Inscape*, Summer: 26–35.

Chapter 7

'All things very lovely'

Art therapy in a drug and alcohol treatment programme

Neil Springham

This chapter is concerned with the experience of the art therapist in offering groups to drug and alcohol patients. The theory of pathological narcissism is outlined as a frame of reference and the concepts of the ideal object and entitlement are explored in relation to this. It is proposed that art therapy is particularly suited to addressing narcissistic issues within the individual. Emphasis is placed on the visual expressions of unacknowledged entitlement which appear despite otherwise apparent positive motivation. I begin the piece with a theoretical discussion followed by a case study which explores how these issues manifest in the art therapy setting.

Introduction

The art therapy that I describe in this chapter, occurs in the context of a drug and alcohol service designed solely for patients whose primary problem is substance misuse. Patients who have a mental illness with secondary drug and alcohol dependency problems are treated elsewhere, and I don't intend to address in this essay the issues involved in treating patients who have dual diagnoses. Although a great deal of the service's work is out-reach based, the art therapy described here occurs within a separate group therapy programme for patients who need more help than can be offered in the community, but whose cases are not so severe that they would be unlikely to use the therapy offered. These patients typically present long-standing substance misuse problems which have resulted in substantial losses of property, unemployment and the break-down of relationships. Their childhood histories are characterised by severe emotional deprivation and a high incidence of abuse. Attending our service often represents the first stage in the process of their treatment.

The programme has a capacity to treat a maximum of ten patients for a period of six weeks, some of whom are resident on the ward for part of this time. All patients are medically detoxified at the start of the programme and have input from a full range of disciplines. The programme offers a broad mix of groups, ranging from skills-based to psychodynamically-orientated groups. All patients are admitted for treatment on a voluntary basis, but once on the programme they are obliged by contract to attend all groups. As an art therapist there are opportunities for me to follow up a number of these patients once they have completed their programme. Although my primary is aim to explore treatment in this type of group programme setting, I have found many of the concepts described here are equally applicable to longer term work.

Orford (1985) describes the contemporary view of addictions as being multi-influenced by social, psychological and physical factors. While my aim is to describe art therapy's particular benefits in the psychological area – with an emphasis on the psychodynamic – I hope not to give the impression that this approach is offered as an independent and comprehensive treatment. At this first stage in the treatment of addictions, art therapy firmly exists within a multidisciplinary milieu which continuously aims to address these other important factors.

To aid my exploration of the psychological aspects, I will use the theory of pathological narcissism as a frame of reference; and so, as a first step, it is necessary to define the term and its relation to addictions. I hasten to add, that in doing so I concentrate on pathological narcissistic defences which tend to be anti-social. While this description may appear to be rather unmitigated, I would stress that these must always be seen as understandable attempts to deal with basic psychic pain. Moreover, narcissism, like most disorders, must be considered as existing on a spectrum of severity, and my description emphasises the more severe manifestations for the sake of clarity. Where the term 'mother' is used, I am not referring to a specific person or gender, but to the individual performing maternal tasks as the child's primary care-giver.

Narcissism and addiction

In examining the relevant literature from the psychodynamic-orientation, one notes a significant gap following Freud's initiatory but inconclusive work on the subject of narcissism. Freud (1913) introduced the notion of narcissism as a clinical phenomenon but did relatively little to develop its links with addictions. However, his view of the latter involved related concepts such as 'masturbation' (Strachey 1966–74, vol. 1: 272), 'undoing sublimation' (ibid., vol. 12: 64) and 'attempted regression' (ibid., vol. 21: 84). The apparent lack of further interest in addictions has been attributed by Meissner (1980) to the fact that many drug and alcohol patients were too poor or chaotic to enter the realm of private psychoanalysis where so much theory is traditionally generated. More recently the expanding interest in the subject of pathological narcissism from perspectives other than addiction has progressed our understanding (Rosenfeld 1971). While the concept of narcissism is, like the addictions field, subject to constant debate, many contemporary psychodynamic writers now place narcissism as a central concept in their thinking about drug and alcohol addiction (Tahka 1979; Meissner 1980).

In art therapy, the American literature has until recently led the field by producing the most work on addictions (Moore 1983). The interest was so great that in 1990 *The American Journal of Art Therapy* dedicated a special edition to the subject reflecting the drive to '... design new treatment approaches to match the unique needs of substance abusers' (Johnson 1990: 296). However, the American literature's broader theoretical base has not consistently reflected the same concern with pathological narcissism. This is in contrast to the more psychodynamically focussed British literature which began to emerge from the late 1980s onwards (Luzzatto 1987 and 1989; Springham 1992 and 1994; Teasdale 1993).

In order to outline a working model some preliminary definitions need to be made. Narcissism as a pathological disorder should be distinguished from the general use of the term which is derogatory and implies vanity or excessive self-interest. Pathological narcissism describes self-interest as an unconscious psychological defence. While its etiology is complex, one relevant strand of the theory suggests that it arises in sustained exposure to unmanageable levels of frustration in the infant's early maternal relationship which results in a distortion of ego-development. In order to understand the effects of this it is necessary to expand on what this process involves.

The object relations model of development suggests that initially the infant is only capable of perceiving its various interactions with the mother as if it were meeting separate objects on each occasion. This may be referred to as functioning on a part-object level (Rycroft 1968: 101). For example, when at first the mother responds instantly to her infant's demands, the child perceives her as an exclusively good object, meaning her actions are ego-syntonic. When in the course of time she responds less instantly, the child then perceives this frustration as coming from a different, bad object. This absolutist framework makes it difficult for the undeveloped ego to regulate ambivalence and the infant tends to only experience the poles of either elation or catastrophe.

Yet moving on from this stage of development does involve disincentives for the infant. There is a certain freedom from responsibility in relating to a totally bad object which may be attacked without guilt. Equally, the hope of meeting an all good object which promises a paradise of needs satisfaction, which may be received without reciprocity, is a source of euphoria. To some degree we all maintain a regressive longing to return to this state, but in narcissism this return is actively sought as an unquestioned entitlement.

In health the mother facilitates the gradual loss of these hopes by gradually responding less instantly to the child's non-reciprocal demands while maintaining empathy in the face of the child's resulting hate. As her idealness deflates, her responding in this way inhibits the perception of her as totally bad. If these conditions of optimal frustration prevail her various aspects may more readily become integrated into a whole, mixed object which is perceived as neither solely good or bad, but 'good enough' (Winnicott 1970), thereby maintaining the child's attachment. The hypothesis is that the ego can be viewed as developing in the struggle to accommodate the loss of her idealness and the ensuing ambivalence. How this process is negotiated may be considered as a blueprint for future, adult, object relations. Without the ability to cope with loss – for example, mourn – the individual is inflexible and vulnerable. He/she finds it difficult to adapt to change or explore Otherness with any creativity. The successful mourning of the idealness of the good object, and mitigation of the bad, facilitates the realistic acceptance of one's encounters as predominantly a mixture of good and bad which yield their best if engaged on a reciprocal basis.

If the balance of frustration versus gratification is not optimal, distortions at this phase of development can occur which dispose the individual to adopt narcissistic defences. If the child experiences the mother as not 'good enough' it detaches from her, thereby discontinuing this essential developmental task of decentring. The individual then becomes stuck in part-object functioning. To paraphrase Freud (1913): if the child cannot find a mother to love, it can only turn to love itself.

A hypothetical example of this type of pathogenic interaction might be as follows: a child cries for a mother who does not appear. The child's frustration escalates and it screams more for her until it eventually feels overwhelmed and at this point falls asleep. This sleep is not born out of satisfaction, but is an evasive withdrawal into narcissistic euphoria as a defence against intolerable ambivalence. Such withdrawal into falsified pleasurable states as a means of negating ambivalence has been likened by Albert-Puleo (1980) to the withdrawal of the addict into intoxication during frustration.

The euphoria of omnipotence itself may eclipse any sense of, need for, or loss of the mother. This apparent triumph over needs can lead to a grandiose perception of self-sufficiency and this has serious consequences for ego-development. Where the untraumatised infant may still attach to 'good enough' objects, the infant who has experienced the idealness of this withdrawal finds 'good enough' is just not good enough. This absolutist infant takes up a position of 'non-communication' (Winnicott 1986) and by disengaging from the process of optimal frustration, while continuing to develop physically and mentally, it cannot mature emotionally. Here the mother as a 'good enough' object has been superseded by the new fantasy of an ideal object (the narcissistic process of withdrawal). Hinshelwood describes the principle thus:

> When an object is conceived as primordially good then it is said to be 'idealized'; good aspects of the object have been separated off, by splitting, followed by the annihilation (denial) of the bad aspects, and this gives the illusion of perfection.
>
> (Hinshelwood 1989: 318–19).

This ideal object must be understood as existing in reference to narcissistic entitlement. It is not some beautiful, separate, thing to be marvelled at, but an object which solely exists to gratify and substantiate the narcissism of the infant. The process of narcissism may be understood as a preoccupation with constantly seeking gratification from ideal objects in order to '…avoid the experience of self wanting, or needing, or desiring and of the other as free to respond in a gratifying or frustrating manner' (Belcher 1987: 245).

This splitting not only concerns external objects but also the sense of self. To this end the narcissistic individual unconsciously operates on two discrete levels. First, a 'true self' which houses the needs and affective responses which remain at an infantile state and second, a 'false self' (Winnicott 1986) which rests on a foundation of denial of the former.

Narcissistic persons are so removed from their 'true self' that they often perceive their feelings and needs as being external to them. Because they are untended, these needs accumulate and are then subject to eruption. It is common for our drug and alcohol patients to describe themselves as experiencing being taken over by an unrecognised force which makes them drink – a description which resembles the concept of 'possession'.

This distance from one's true feelings and needs is purposive inasmuch as the false self aims to perpetuate an illusion of functioning without needs. When relationships are entered into they are only partially engaged. Only those areas which are agreeable are admitted and gratification is sought regardless of personal costs. Many of our patients are highly susceptible to peer pressure in this way because they are desperate to fit in. But while the observer can notice rapid changes in their persona which are clearly contextually determined, the individuals themselves are generally unaware of this inconstancy because they identify with each 'false self' as it is constructed.

Because most of life's encounters are mixed in their value, the narcissistic individual is continuously dissatisfied. Kernberg (1975) suggests adult narcissists simply lack the emotional depth to perceive other people as anything other than potential sources of gratification. Many of our patients have entered relationships with unrealistically high expectations but when they inevitably encounter aspects of the person that they find less appealing, the relationship immediately loses all value. When the relationship turns bad, the drive is then to invest the next relationship with the same idealistic expectations.

The superficiality in relationships is coupled with a constant threat of emptiness and boredom which perpetuates the need to seek gratification by other means. In this way the addict's substance of choice has a particular appeal and may be considered as the ideal object par excellence. It qualifies for this because it is perceived as offering gratifying properties of instant comfort in a relationship that does not demand reciprocity. The initial effects of intoxication are very effective in aiding the process denial. One consumes and feels better while nothing is required in return and this, combined with the individual's pre-existing part-object functioning, inhibits the linking of cause and effect. In this way its negative effects of excessive substance consumption may be split off and the drug of choice has the allure that beats all competition.

Idealisation is evident even in the original Arabic meaning of the word alcohol, which translates as 'all things very lovely'. It was first considered to be a medical panacea (Cantopher 1996: 4) and for the modern addict its consumption may still be viewed as an attempt to administer a self-medicated cure-all.

To summarise then, the psychology of narcissism offers an understanding of how the substance has an effect both chemically and psychologically and how the removal of the chemical is clearly not the removal of the problem. The problem itself can be conceived of in circular causation: the availability of such ideal substances compounds narcissistic omnipotence and entitlement; the substances physically transform bad feelings so efficiently that the need to negotiate optimal frustration in the environment becomes obsolete; sub-optimal frustration results in a further diminishment of the ego thereby increasing the need for more substances. In the words of the old adage, for those with narcissist tendencies to encounter the substance as an ideal object means 'a taste of honey (will be) worse than none'.

This concept of the substance being an ideal object as a defence against ambivalence begins to frame the dilemmas that confront a narcissistic patient entering a treatment programme. I wish to focus on this next because it has a bearing on what the art therapist will encounter in offering treatment within this setting.

Entering a treatment programme

On entering the treatment programme our patients claim, in desperation, to recognise just how much damage has resulted from their use of substances. They are confronted with the fact that if they continue to consume substances in this way then it is likely they will lose their life. This alone is a powerful motivation for building a life without drink or drugs. However, if these were the only imperatives then abstinence would be both easy and probably already achieved. Contrasting with this is the evidence that immediately prior to their admission all our patients do everything in their power to consume their substances. The first point only offers a partial understanding of the situation. I am not suggesting that any conscious lie has occurred. Indeed this process of partial conception is deeply unconscious and this in itself is the problem. It is essential that if the substance is to be resisted then its attraction must be understood. Clearly its attractions are great, as all other concerns are ultimately given lower priority by the addict. Such ruthlessness of pursuit is really a measure of the substance's value as an ideal object.

However, in treatment the narcissistic patient must eventually confront the validity of their pursuit of the ideal object as a long-term venture. As Miller suggests, the ultimate prospect of the treatment of narcissistic disorders is to realise this conclusion:

> The paradise of preambivalent harmony, for which so many patients hope is unattainable. But the experience of one's own truth and the post-ambivalent knowledge of it, makes it possible to return to one's own world of feelings at an adult level – without paradise, but with the ability to mourn.
>
> (Miller 1979: 51)

It is treatment itself then that presents the narcissistic patient with a dilemma. Most wish to abstain from the substances because of their negative side effects, but it cannot be assumed that they have reached a point where they realise that they must give up their substance as an ideal object. In this sense, attempts to give up drink or drug taking may in themselves be attempts to split off the bad aspects to preserve the object's idealness. The primary aim for the therapist is to try to help the patient conceive of both good and bad aspects of the substance. The second is to support ambivalence in the therapy in order for it to be experienced less catastrophically. This is validated in the apparent paradox of it being those patients who resolve never again to touch the 'demon brew' tending to be the ones to relapse quickly after treatment, whereas those who remain ambivalent towards giving up, tend to be more successful. The hope of recovering from addiction without ambivalence is just another ideal object.

Just as the substance becomes denigrated, and so apparently rejected, one often notices how recovery comes to be described in the identical ideal terms that previously pertained to the substance. The patient may show sudden bursts of positivity about their recovery which appear to be an increase of motivation, but may merely be an 'idle interval' phase in the larger narcissistic project. As Svrakic (1985) points out, in periods of narcissistic deprivation, these patients resort to living in an expectant mode. This position is characterised by an euphoric sense of 'becoming', as if one is moving to a future which will promise a resolution of conflicts, thereby leaving narcissistic entitlement unchallenged. The 'idle interval' is the principle that it is better to travel in hope than to arrive, taken to the extreme.

In offering treatment then, the art therapist is destined to encounter the patient's rather confusing expressions of the 'idle interval' phase. The illusion of motivation represents an unconscious process which merely aids withdrawal and so inhibits engagement in the therapy offered. It is essential that this is brought into consciousness and explored in the therapy. If it is not, the patient will merely continue to be confounded at how they themselves continually sabotage their own progress, despite feeling positively motivated.

It is clear that to lose the substance as an ideal object would constitute a major bereavement. Recovery from this would require the individual to go through the processes of mourning, yet narcissism is itself an attempt to bypass mourning. This conflict implies any change would require a substantial transitionary phase, between letting go of gratification from the substance as an ideal object and the gaining of satisfaction and containment from more fulfilling relationships. The problem highlighted by most therapists is how to help patients tolerate the transition.

Belcher suggests that the therapist and the patient should collaborate in the aim of defining the object which is to be surrendered. 'Certainly, this [surrendering] is a process that must take place. But often, an intermediate step of clarifying desire is called for, so that spurious and substitutive claims can be discarded. Then, if limitations must be accepted, they are much easier to tolerate' (Belcher 1987: 251). I have found that in the consideration of the shortness of time on such a programme, work at this cognitive level is an appropriate first aim.

To support tolerance, Winnicott (1971) suggests that there must be flexibility or environmental adaptation in the therapy. To some extent the patient's sense of entitlement must be gratified in order to realistically create an optimal level of frustration acceptable to the narcissistic patient. The difficulty is knowing how to pitch the therapy between the two poles of frustration and gratification. I feel that it is in this area that art therapy has a particular contribution to make.

Art therapy treatment

Environmental adaptation is an issue which runs like a thread through a substantial body of art therapy theory. Lachman-Chapin, extending the work of Kohut, suggests that using art-making within a therapeutic context offers the narcissistic person a palatable relationship because:

> We become narcissistically invested in what we produce, reaching through it for that aesthetic perfection that is like the idealised parental imago. So we end up retaining some of the exhibitionism and grandiosity, finding a way to express it in adult life without the shame that might attach to an attempt made in other areas of our lives.
>
> (Lachman-Chapin 1979: 15)

Here idealness is kept alive as an element in the art work, rather than acted out in more dangerous narcissistic pursuits. She also suggests that the self-absorption involved in producing the image approximates narcissistic withdrawal, consequently making the experience of therapy more tolerable. Image production offers alternatives to the disincentives involved in trying to invest solely in a relationship with a therapist whose otherness threatens potential frustration. As the patient's relationship with their image is relatively non-reciprocal, it helps to set the frustration at the therapy as a whole to a level which the patient can find more optimal. Being omnipotent over the image the patient may get beyond their 'false self' defences and explore what gratifies them. This information is not lost, as it is in fantasy, but remains encapsulated in the image in a concretised form. This in turn is available to be reintegrated into the therapeutic relationship in a manageable way. The use of art in therapy therefore allows access to narcissistic self-interest which is otherwise not available in the therapeutic relationship.

This suggests that art-making alone is enough to help the patient. In art therapy the image making exists firmly within the therapeutic relationship and must be viewed within that context. Likewise, Albert-Puleo (1980) asserts that the art object acts to allow the patient to regulate the distance between themselves and the therapist, thereby decreasing the need for 'false self' defences. Albert-Puleo has found that efforts to bring the patient into true object relations prematurely merely exacerbates their narcissism. In art therapy the therapist's presence may be considered as background during image production and his or her role is to 'be there' for the moments when the patient emerges from 'non-communication' under their own omnipotence.

In my experience, I have found that these patients find it difficult to leave the art-making process and to make the transition to the discussion part of the therapy, and this in itself often provides valuable material to focus on therapeutically. Art therapy then, may be distinguished from other forms of verbal therapy because the dual activities of making art and talking expose different material in each of the respective relationships involved. My interest in this hypothesis was such that I conducted research into the operation of this process during an art therapy group run for drug and alcohol patients (Springham 1994).

The method I adopted was as follows. I sampled all the programme's patients on their first attendance in art therapy over a period of six weeks, which at the close of the study totalled eleven patients. I asked the patients to describe their experience of the group on questionnaires filled out privately immediately before and after the group. I later combined this with my observations made while acting as the group's therapist, without knowledge of the content of their questionnaires. As there are no other suitable measures of narcissistic processes, I relied on clinical observation and made a brief assessment of the level of narcissism that I felt I was encountering, again without having seen the questionnaires. I anticipated that there would be some discrepancy between what patients said in the group and what they were able to disclose privately via questionnaires. I also wanted to evaluate whether the content of the privately disclosed material would be at all available to me while in the therapist's position.

I found that the seven patients who appeared be the most narcissistic in the group tended to have a greater degree of incongruity
between their public and private disclosures. I also discovered that it
was difficult to anticipate the content of their questionnaires,
whereas those who appeared less narcissistic had more compatible
disclosures in both the questionnaires and the group. I was
surprised to find, as a by-product of this process, that the material
missing in the public discussions (as identified in the questionnaires)
was hinted at most strongly in the images that were produced. In
other words, it appeared to have been possible for these patients to
articulate certain material only in the comparative privacy of the
relationship with the image. This relates to Winnicott's (1971)
notion that art-making represents a wish to be seen and to hide at
the same time.

I examined in some detail one respondent from the research who
particularly exemplified this process. This individual presented as
being highly critical and attacking of any help or contribution
offered by the therapist. In the session, I found that her continual
aggressive rejection of my interventions and her haughty manner
made it difficult to consider her, in any whole sense, as a patient in
need of help. In contrast to her behaviour in the sessions, she said in
her questionnaire how much she yearned for approval from the
therapist – a figure who she had clearly invested with ideal
attributes – which she felt she was being denied. I was surprised by
this return. In the group she had painted a picture of Cinderella.
This image contained a communication that might have helped me
see this aspect of her personality if I had been able to hold it in
mind while under her pressure. Cinderella illustrates a deprived and
needy child who can only be validated by a prince. In this way her
attacks were a way of disguising her own need to be found by the
therapist as an ideal object. The idealisation of the therapist
matched her history of rushing into relationships only to destroy
them when they frustrated her.

In hindsight, I thought how much more containing it would have
been for me to have brought this material in via her own image. This
may have helped to move us beyond the confines of the confrontation that she had constructed. This was a useful pattern to discover.
While in the art therapist's position in the session I found it hard to
keep the images in mind, yet they often represented valuable
communications. This small piece of research forcefully confronted
me with how important the image is in this form of treatment and

yet how easily its significance can be lost under the public presentation of narcissism in the group. The therapy is reliant on bringing together the often incongruous communications of group presentation and image. This experience shaped the understanding and practice of art therapy described here. I now consider the significance of the picture to be paramount, particularly at those moments when the compelling pressure of 'false self' phenomenon in the group obliges one to overlook it, thereby mistaking the part for the whole.

Images of entitlement

It has been my experience of working in drug and alcohol teams that art therapy is particularly helpful at illuminating underlying attitudes which are often disguised under a defensive verbal rhetoric. My sense is that the art work provides the mechanics for appraising the idealness of the patient's object. If a pattern exists of how this comes to light in art therapy then it is through images which I refer to as 'paradise pictures'. I am continually struck by the volume and consistency of the highly romantic images of perfection and paradise that are drawn in these sessions. These occur with far more regularity than with other patient groups. The most commonly recurring image is that of a tropical island basking under a beneficent sun (see Fig. 7.1).

Variations on this prelapsarian image include English, or more often Irish, pastoral scenes or metaphorical landscapes such as 'the light at the end of the tunnel'. I consider the depiction of a favourite animal or a hobby (usually fishing) to fit this criterion also. These images contain no bad things, and the prospect is indeed 'all things very lovely'.

When discussed, these images are referred to in the future tense as ideal objects which are about to be possessed. These are often linked to the expectation of a life of sobriety, for instance: 'Life will be much better without drink because I can enjoy nature/fishing/my dog', and so on. These images are a profoundly useful tool in the therapeutic process. They communicate the nature of the ideal object and the unrealistic expectations that must eventually come into the therapeutic discourse. For those patients who are in 'non-communication', these pictures have the value of being 'postcards' from the idle interval available for the patient themselves to read.

Figure 7.1 A patient's tropical island picture

The suggestion is not that all images of beauty or pleasure automatically imply narcissistic processes; I would argue, however, that a distinction needs to be made between these 'paradise pictures' and those described by Case (1996) and Schaverien (1995) in their much needed explorations of the issue of beauty in art therapy.

Case (1996) outlines the therapeutic role of visual beauty for damaged children. The 'aesthetic moment' represents the integration of the object which enables the child to identify a beautiful part internally, within the whole of the self which allows the potential to feel loved 'warts and all'. The distinction here is that the 'paradise pictures' I describe only have positive attributes and so in fact are not really wholly conceived objects. Moreover, beauty – or idealness – is perceived as being both external to the individual and to be consumed at a future moment. In this sense the pictures more correctly represent a yearning for the gratification from an ideal object and as such represent an anaesthetic moment, rather than any kind of a vehicle for broadening the range of feelings in the relationship.

Schaverien (1995) describes the need for some patients to unconsciously seduce the therapist in order to create a benign preoccupation between them, and in art therapy beautiful imagery is often the currency involved. In this way beautiful imagery helps the patient to form a therapeutic attachment with the therapist. The 'paradise picture' differs here because it ultimately helps the patient to maintain their detachment from the therapist as a potentially frustrating object. No therapist can compete with the expectations of perfection disclosed in these images.

The position in time of the ideal object is an important factor in the patient's communication. Although the individual may depict ideal times from the past ('the good old days'), one often finds that there is a fantasy that these times somehow can be returned to. I am often struck by how such expression of entitlement creates a strange and pervasive nostalgia for the future in the groups. I would hasten to add that images of lost ideal objects must be considered differently. An example of this from my practice involved a patient drawing an image of a dog in his art therapy session (see Fig. 7.2).

I asked the patient to describe why the dog was so important and his reply was that the dog was always there for him; it listened to him, but asked for nothing in return and was his only true friend. These are ideal attributes, but the patient was able to accept my link of this description as being identical to the hope of alcohol being 'man's best friend'. The effect of this re-framing was that the patient made another association by adding, with sadness, that the dog had died some time ago. This added a contrasting aspect to the otherwise ideal attributes of the object. In this sense he was able to formulate a more exact nature of his loss of alcohol, not being of something purely bad, but as the loss of something which was loved. This was now an image which encapsulated 'paradise lost' and directly addressed narcissistic entitlement. It provided an intelligible form to a mourning process for the cherished notion of the ideal object.

Thus, substance misuse can be seen to be motivated by a deeper addiction to the ideal object and its promise of pre-ambivalent peace. If this deeper expectation is not addressed then the re-use of substances is more likely because it is the most efficient means, in the short term, of achieving that end. 'Paradise' holidays, fishing and dog walking cannot compete. These 'paradise pictures' represent a yearning for peace in the patient's own pictorial 'vocabulary', and in the art therapy processes this can make the likelihood of the patient deciphering their own communication more possible. The following case example is offered to illustrate how this material is both accessed and processed in art therapy groups.

Figure 7.2 A patient's drawing of his dog

The art therapy group

First of all, I will give a brief outline of each of the patients who attended this group:

Joe is a male in his early fifties who describes himself as drinking alcohol to calm his otherwise uncontrollable outbursts of violence. He has drunk for thirty years and has many convictions for actual bodily harm. He is divorced and currently lives with his common-law wife and her son.

Tracy is a female in her late thirties who grew up in a high-achieving family. She suffered a major bereavement in her late teens and has drunk alcohol heavily ever since. She works in the film industry where she has been very successful but has been unable to form any close relationships.

Jane is a female in her mid-thirties whose childhood was brutal and included verifiable sexual abuse. She has 'binged' on both drugs and alcohol for as long as she can remember. She is divorced and has had many relationships for short periods of time and these tend to end violently. She has two young children for which she is fighting for custody.

Tracy and Joe had been to a session once before, but it was Jane's first attendance. All patients arrived for this session on time. I outlined the basic principles of the group, and told them that half the session would be spent image-making and the second half would involve discussing the images. I stressed that there was no emphasis on artistic skill and that people were free to draw anything they wished.

Jane immediately looked panicked at this proposal. She said that she did not think she could cope and that she could not concentrate. I suggested that she try the materials without worrying about the results. I was a little surprised when she so readily accepted this suggestion and began work, as did the others. The next half an hour was spent in silent concentrated work. Although everyone sat together there was no talking and Jane appeared as deeply absorbed in the painting as the others.

I reminded everyone when it was time for the discussion and they returned slowly to the circle of chairs with their pictures. Jane was the last one to return in an effort to finish her picture. They seemed interested in each other's work when it was shown. I said this part of the session worked best if people either commented on their own, or other people's work, or on anything in the group that they felt was important.

Tracy sat forward and, referring to Joe's picture (see Fig. 7.3), immediately said, 'Is that your house?'

'It is,' he replied. 'I don't know why I drew it, it just came to me.' He then went on to describe the picture without any interruptions from the group: 'This is our house. It's a warm day – maybe a Sunday. This is us in the garden. Here's the dog in the shade. Here's me, my wife and the boy, maybe he's not gone out and so he's stopped out with us in the garden. We're having a break. Radio on, drinks – not alcoholic I might add [some laughter from the group at this point]. It's just a relaxing time.'

The group listened to this story with interest. Tracy asked if it was a terraced house. Joe said it was but that he did not like his

Figure 7.3 Joe's drawing of his house and garden

neighbours very much. I noted that they had faded in his image. He pointed out the high walls and bushes around the garden, and where there was a gap and only trees, he said – with a kind of spoiling relish – that he hung his bird feeders on the neighbour's overhanging branches. His attitude towards his own territory was in marked contrast to the disdain in which he held his neighbours. It seemed as though the good was in his space and the bad was outside. Tracy picked up on Joe's last comment and said: 'You certainly don't like your neighbours do you!' 'No,' he replied, 'I like my own space.' 'You haven't drawn them in have you?' said Jane. Joe shrugged his shoulders at this comment.

I found myself thinking about how Joe's wish for the neighbours not to impinge on his territory might be about his experience of this group. I was reminded of how, in the previous session, he had monopolised the conversation and how in other groups on the programme he had been asked to let others talk because of his tendency to dominate. I said his picture looked like all the good things were in his garden. He said he supposed I was right. Instead of responding to these issues exclusively with Joe, I then chose to remain silent since I was interested to see what else might come from the group. Tracy said she would talk about her image (see Fig. 7.4).

Jane made the comment that it was 'really artistic'. Tracy thanked her, but reiterated my suggestion that we should not concentrate on the artistic merits of the work. 'Good job!' said Jane laughing.

Tracy continued: 'I think this picture is about my choices. On the one hand, if I go down this road on the right (marked 'R.I.P.') I know where I'm going because I've been there'. 'I think we've all been there,' said Jane supportively and Joe agreed. Tracy continued: 'I'm interested in the other one now. I want something better for myself. When I go to AA meetings, the sponsors tell me that there is a life to be had out there. That it can be your wildest dreams come true. I want some of that.' This seemed to me to be an idealised expectation of sobriety. She went on to say: 'We've wasted a lot of our time haven't we? I've been "blotto" for so much of mine. All those wasted

Figure 7.4 Tracy's drawing of the two 'paths'

weekends alone, nothing but drinking. I was better in the week when I was working. But at weekends I would drink myself into oblivion.'

'You're lonely when you drink aren't you?' said Jane.

'I think so, I wanted to fill up the time. I used to have hobbies, I used to paint. But in the end I couldn't even be bothered with those, I just got pissed.'

I thought about how the image had depicted the good things on the side of sobriety and on the other, Hell and the bad things. I noted how the members of the group were describing how important the consumption of alcohol had been for them yet at the same time denigrating it as a wholly bad thing. I felt there was also a concern about the activity of painting, that it was perceived as being unhelpful in directly addressing the problem and this represented feelings about the effectiveness of this present art therapy group. I decided to be more direct in pointing out this split. I asked, if sobriety offered such peace, how could we understand the evident attraction of drinking?

There was a short silence. Tracy seemed puzzled and said to no-one in particular, 'It's true isn't it? Should I have put the peace on the other side of the walk?' Joe didn't appear to like this. He reminded everyone how bad alcohol was, and subsequently became more withdrawn within the group.

Jane said she drank for peace. Her anxiety would often overwhelm her and she would feel 'shitty'. She said at these times she would do anything to get a drink or drugs. Tracy said, 'It was different for me, if I could be busy I would be all right; it was when I was alone or at weekends.'

Tracy made the comment that it was an 'eye opener' for her to see that even merchant bankers went to AA meetings, and that they too could drink away everything. Joe said wealth just gave you a choice of where and what to drink – and this contribution seemed to make him feel better. Jane said, 'I used to try and hide it but in the end I didn't care, I'd just be pissed and slap anyone down who tried to stop me.'

I said that perhaps in our specific group there was a feeling that the good things seem to be somewhere else. Possibly there were feelings of envy about some other person who may have all the good things. Maybe people wonder if *I* have these good things? Jane responded by saying: 'I felt bad when I had no money and others did. I drank if I was angry, if someone wound me up. I was furious and I'd drink and feel sort of calmer.'

I noted aloud that up until this point both pictures concerned absolute states and, in particular, the pursuit of peace. I wondered if people's drinking was an attempt to get rid of the feeling that someone else had the good thing and that they did not. The group responded by laughing which seemed to be an acknowledgement, rather than a dismissal, of this suggestion.

'It's funny isn't it, the more we speak the more it seems the peace should be on the drinking side?' Tracy said. 'They are our pictures yet there seems to be something more in them.'

'Certainly at first,' said Jane, 'it's peaceful at first. Drink is my first love, drugs are a close second, but I love drinking.'

'I don't,' said Joe, with obvious alarm. 'I've nearly lost it all through drinking, I hate it. I don't ever want to touch another drop.'

I commented on this extreme reaction. I suggested that what was unpalatable about what had been said was that drink worked. It did give peace initially, it was loved and this is why it was so hard to give up. Tracy responded by saying, 'You only get that good feeling initially, though. The rest is hell.' I wondered if it was the hope of regaining the initial state that attracted people to return to drinking. I suggested that we had witnessed disclosures of that hope for peace within this very group.

There then followed a thoughtful silence, after which Tracy turned to Jane's picture (Fig 7.5) and said, 'I like that, it's very powerful'.

Jane said she hated it. I commented that she had told us that she had begun by feeling rather agitated but had seemed absorbed during the image-making. Jane said she had just felt bored. 'I can't settle to anything, my mind is just so…oh, I don't know.' Tracy said she also had the impression of her being absorbed. 'I like painting myself actually,' Tracy reminded us. 'I used to really love it and I did some good pictures, but I just can't apply myself somehow. I think yours is really powerful though.' Joe agreed with this comment.

Jane described how she felt there were always options, 'yet the grass always seems greener on the other side,' she continued. 'That's very "me". I think the grass is always greener on the other side and I leap over there and everything gets worse. A lot bloody worse. And this is me now at the crossroads and I don't know which fucking way to go. I don't want it worse again.' She was clearly upset at this point and I commented on this and reflected on the choices depicted in both of the pictures we had just looked at. Jane

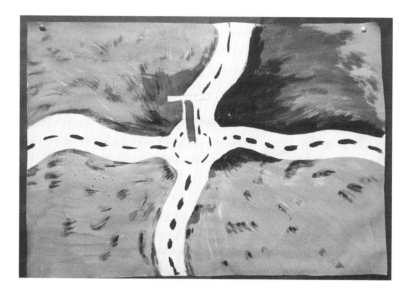

Figure 7.5 Jane's picture of a crossroads
Note: Signpost reads: 'WHICH WAY?'

pointed at both her own and Tracy's picture and said: 'I suppose we are all at the crossroads.'

This thought caught the interest of everyone in the group. Joe said, 'Wouldn't it be nice to get down that road and get away from the choice. It's like Heaven and Hell, I hope you get the right one.' This example of extreme choices put me in mind of how the group's, and particularly Joe's description of objects was consistently seen in absolute terms of either good or bad.

Jane, although still upset, responded to the idea of finality and told us how she kept going back to the choice and how it was the not knowing which road leads where that made her so tense. Tracy responded by agreeing that she hoped to be through one of the doors soon. I asked how people would know when they were through the doors. 'When you're dead,' laughed Jane. 'Look, you do get to rest in peace on this side' (and she pointed to where it said 'R.I.P.' above the drinking door). The group seemed rather taken aback at the poignancy of her black humour.

'I suppose I hope to get through this door,' said Tracy, pointing to 'Sobriety'. I questioned the group as a whole and asked if sobriety meant peace. An uneasy atmosphere fell across the group. It seemed to me that people were considering a new and alarming idea: that there might be a question over whether a future point exists where all ambivalence is resolved. It seemed as though the group had dared to take the step of examining the ideal object itself.

'Live day-by-day,' suggested Tracy, as if alarmed by the exploration of this idea. I asked how it would be if living 'day-by-day' meant staying with the discomfort of the present sense of uncertainty. 'It would be hard,' said Jane. 'Isn't that exactly what we are doing now?' I said. There seemed to be some recognition that this task which was so apprehensively viewed might actually be happening at that very moment. Moreover there was some relief that we were all apparently surviving it. I commented on this and wondered aloud how we were making this bearable now. Jane replied that it helped to have other people in the 'same boat', who had similar experiences. The other members agreed. I linked this with the solitariness of the drinking described in the session and suggesting living without everlasting peace seemed to be achieved only with support.

Joe informed me that the real therapy came from other patients, not from staff, and this was because only they knew what it was like to be an addict. I noted that my own feelings became hostile towards Joe's rejection of all staff help. I felt that his communication obliged me to carry a sense of exclusion. I was also mindful that it was very nearly the end of the session. I interpreted by saying that perhaps there was a feeling that the staff, including me at this point, had no idea of how hard it was to live without peace. There was silence at this point.

I suggested that it seemed likely to me that it was not only this group, but all of us who needed to make sure that we have empathetic relationships. 'Isn't that what makes it bearable for all of us?' I suggested. The group appeared to be a little surprised yet reassured to hear my more personal disclosure. Jane said: 'I suppose we're different, but not that different'. This was the final comment as the session came to a close.

Conclusion

The group finished with an attempt by me to normalise the task of tolerating and staying with the ambivalence and of not acting out. Given the short-term nature of this work, I find it is helpful for the therapist to be explicit about supporting patients in this task. One thing I noted was how unprepared I was, when I first began to offer my support, for the force of negative feelings which this stirred up in the patients. This group was in fact rather unusual in that they were responsive to my input. I now understand such negative responses are the result of a most precious hope which is threatened by the art therapy process and this provokes aggression and fear. I hope this description of narcissism goes some way to putting this into an understandable context. I suspect, however, that there is little one can do to prepare for such an experience, and in hindsight, my understanding as described in this chapter has developed after the experience of this group.

It is a cruel paradox that those who experience the worst aspects of life seem to possess the highest expectations. This idealism then can be a useful tool in identifying the presence of unacknowledged pain. In our society these patients' situations are weakened further by the increasing availability of substances promising the ideal. It is their hope for paradise and perfection which makes them vulnerable to these promises, and treatment must address this if they are to understand how to resist further misuse.

The process of integrating the object is essentially a mourning process and is by definition a move away from the spectacular. I consider that the therapy rests on identifying the ambivalence it produces and in trying to not react catastrophically while it is experienced. Looking at this patient group's tendency to view experience in such absolute terms, I find myself in agreement with Temple *et al.*'s (1996) notion that the group's ordinariness is its strength. As a therapist, I find it easy to get drawn into the grandiosity of these groups and to aim for too much within the sessions. Although these patients have big problems, their best solution is often to focus on small details, on the management of their own feelings stated in the moment. This seems to be best achieved in these groups by drawing on what support can be found in shared experience.

In this sense, Tracy appeared to have been helped by this group because her private hell became public through her image which then clarified the issue facing the whole group. This might be said to exemplify the art therapy process. This group showed that, although the patient has produced their own image individually, it is only through engaging with others in the group that they can discover something new about its meaning. This can be rather threatening to those patients who feel they need to have high degrees of omnipotence over their work. However, the support gained from realising that other patients have felt the same way and are struggling with similar issues is very helpful in softening the blow. The image is helpful also for the therapist who can find his or her thinking compromised by the pressure in the groups.

Joe's case is important because he is perhaps more representative of the majority of our patients who find it too painful to critically examine the idealness of the object. Joe would not accept the object becoming mixed in any way and so withdrew from the group. He based all of his motivation on denigrating the substance and denying his desire for it. Unlike the others who completed the course, Joe relapsed soon after this group.

I personally find that an understanding that it is paradise itself which is felt to be at stake puts the task into perspective and reduces my demoralisation at the low success rate of any treatment offered to this patient group. There are patients who do find that this short-term work clarifies their problem and helps them stay abstinent. Sadly, many of our patients are like Joe in that they find it impossible to live without their narcissism. I feel that in the most severe of cases, a period on the programme represents an episode of palliative care. At the very least, patients should feel that that this taste of therapy is a good enough experience to make the possibility of the necessary long-term treatment more palatable.

Bibliography

Albert-Puleo, N. (1980) 'Modern psychoanalytic art therapy and its implications to drug abuse', *The Arts in Psychotherapy*, 17: 43–52.

Belcher, M. (1987) 'Entitlement and narcissism: Paradise sought', *Contemporary Psychoanalysis* 23 (2): 40–5.

Cantopher, T. (1996) *Dying For a Drink*, Gateshead: Athenaeum Press.

Case, C. (1996) 'On the aesthetic moment in the transference', *Inscape*, 1(2): 39–45.

Freud, S. (1913) 'On Narcissism', *Collected Works*, Vol. XIV, London: Penguin.

Hinshelwood, R. (1989) *A Dictionary of Kleinian Thought*, London: Free Association Books.

Johnson, D. (1990) 'Introduction to the special issue on creative arts therapies in the treatment of substance abuse', *The Arts in Psychotherapy*, 17: 296–8.

Kernberg, O. (1975) *Borderline Conditions and Pathological Narcissism*, New York: Jason Aronson.

Lachman-Chapin, M. (1979) 'Kohut's theories on narcissism: Implications for art therapy', *American Journal of Art Therapy*, 19 (10): 3–9.

Luzzatto, P. (1989) Drinking problems and short term art therapy: Working with images of withdrawal and clinging', in A. Gilroy and T. Dalley (eds) *Pictures At an Exhibition*, London: Tavistock/Routledge, 207–19.

——(1987) 'Internal world of drug abusers', *British Journal of Projective Psychology*, 32: 22–33.

Meissner, W. (1980) 'Addiction and paranoid process', *International Journal of Psychoanalysis*, 8: 278–310.

Miller, A. (1979) 'The drama of the gifted child and the psychoanalyst's narcissistic disturbance', *International Journal of Psychoanalysis*, 60: 47–61.

Orford, J. (1985) *Excessive Appetites: A Psychological View of Addictions*, London: J. Whiley and Sons.

Moore, R. (1983) 'Art therapy with substance abusers: A review of the literature', *The Arts in Psychotherapy*, 10: 251–60.

Rosenfeld, D. (1971) 'A clinical approach to the life and death instincts: An investigation into the aggressive aspect of narcissism', *Journal of Psychoanalysis*, 52: 169–77.

Rycroft, C. (1968) *A Critical Dictionary of Psychoanalysis*, London: Penguin Books.

Schaverien, J. (1995) *Desire and the Female Therapist*, London: Routledge.

Springham, N. (1992) 'Short term group processes in art therapy for people with substance misuse problems', *Inscape*, Spring: 8–16.

——(1994) 'Research into patients' reactions to art therapy on a drug and alcohol programme', *Inscape*, 2: 36–40.

Strachey, D. (1966–74) *The Standard Edition of the Complete Psychological Works of Sigmund Freud*, London: Hogarth.

Svrakic, D. (1985) 'Emotional features of narcissistic personality disorder', *American Journal of Psychiatry*, 142 (6 June): 720–4.

Tahka, J. (1979) 'Alcoholism as a narcissistic disturbance', *Psychiatria Fennica*, Vol. 8, No. 2, 129–39.

Teasdale, C. (1993) 'Filling space and time', *Inscape*, Summer: 17–23.

Temple N., Walker J. and Evans M. (1996) 'Group psychotherapy with psychosomatic and somatising patients in a general hospital', *Psychoanalytic Psychotherapy*, 10(3): 251–68.

Winnicott, D. (1986) *The Concept of 'False Self': Home is Where We Start From*, London: Pelican Books, 65–71.

——Winnicott, D. (1971) *Playing and Reality*, London: Penguin Books.

Chapter 8

Mixed metaphors – Dependency or defence

Art therapy as an intervention within a mother–daughter relationship

Corrie McClean

In this chapter I will describe the case study of an 11-year-old girl, Christine, who began art therapy while resident at the Links Centre where her mother was undertaking a six month rehabilitation programme to overcome a dependency on crack and heroin. The study explores how the issues of dependency and defence between parent and child can become particularly problematic when parents have a history of substance misuse. It considers the defence mechanisms children may use to cope with this situation and how they can be manifest in very concrete forms which mirror those used by the parent.

Drawing on theoretical contributions from Balint (1952, 1968), Bion (1957), Klein (1940, 1957 and 1975), Ogden (1979) and Winnicott (1947, 1965 and 1971), I will reflect on the psychological and emotional factors underlying substance misuse and how these emerge within, and affect relationships between parents and children. I will mainly focus on forms of defence associated with the paranoid schizoid mode, and in doing so address: first, how those specific conflicts of dependency and defence can be re-enacted and worked through in therapy; and second, why art psychotherapy provides a particularly effective and appropriate means of treatment.

Context

The Links Centre is a residential unit for parents who have substance related problems. Part of a national charity, Phoenix House, the Links Centre is unique in that it caters for parents who remain with their children during the six month rehabilitation programme. It also accepts people before they are drug free, and the overall aim is to support residents who are working towards ending drug dependency, without the added trauma of separation from their children.

The Centre is spread out over four floors of a terraced house in the heart of the town centre; residents are accommodated in family rooms with separate facilities. There is a communal lounge and playroom on the ground floor next to the staff office, as well as two shared kitchens and smaller counselling rooms. Up to six adults and six children under the age of twelve can be housed. This includes single parents, couples and pregnant women over eighteen years.

The staff team includes a manager and team leader, three Centre workers, two child development workers and an administrator. The Centre manager has overall responsibility for decisions regarding staff and resources. She is accountable to and contributes to the management of the wider Phoenix House organisation.

Residents' children attend local schools. Their needs are assessed and monitored by the child development staff who also act as keyworkers. If considered appropriate, specialised therapeutic skills, such as art and play therapy, are bought in on an ad hoc basis, depending on the availability of funding.

My association with the Centre began when the manager, concerned about the lack of therapy for residents' children, invited me to take art therapy sessions. Since funding was limited, I could only see two children individually – a situation which gave rise to rivalry and competition among both the children and the adults. All the children had emotional difficulties and many had been in care but only those whose problems were considered extreme or particularly disruptive were referred for art therapy.

Sessions were on Saturday afternoons, which was sometimes problematic since they occasionally clashed with other activities. The playroom was, unfortunately, carpeted. I used a protective plastic sheet and screened the glass door with paper, hanging up a sign which read 'Engaged'. Some difficulties arose during sessions if residents wanted access to the washing machine in the adjoining kitchen. Passing comments were sometimes made concerning the carpet getting dirty or the lack of play space for other children while the room was being used for art therapy.

Emotional factors in substance dependency

The children and often both their parents are present during the rehabilitation programme. The children are required to cope with raw emotions unleashed by parents as they struggle to reduce their dependency on drugs. In the process some couples come to the realisation that it was their dependency which kept them together. They then embark on the painful process of separating, with the whole community becoming exposed to the subsequent tensions. Children in particular endure the agonising uncertainty when their own or other parents have doubts about continuing the programme or relapse before completing it. In addition to the common concerns around stigma and judgement, there may be legitimate fears for residents about being judged as parents and related to this, inevitable competition among children.

The behavioural model on which the programme is based and the hierarchical nature of the organisation appear to fulfil some of the complex demands for authoritative direction evident when clients have chaotic dependency related behaviour; it also provides an element of support to the staff at the Centre who constantly have to process difficult emotions, such as helplessness, anger and envy.

As a therapist I found working in this highly structured environment could evoke specific patterns of defence and dependency among staff. This was particularly the case for some members of staff who had previously recovered from drug dependency themselves. When acknowledged, these 'triggers', and the emotions they provoked were used productively to help residents work through potentially difficult issues.

On occasions, however, such counter-transferences went unrecognised, and staff resorted to unhelpful patterns of emotional defence and denial. Often these mirrored or complemented those used by residents. Sometimes this resulted in staff and residents 'unconsciously seeking gratifications and defences in their relationships' (Langs 1975: 356–9) or using distancing tactics. Much acting out could occur with a co-dependent type of existence developing between staff and client within the institution.

Aspects of defence and dependency were evident among staff at times, although often this was expressed in covert forms or 'legitimised' within the organisational framework. For example:

• Staff identifying all the 'illness' in the clients/residents which could result in a tendency for splitting, scapegoating, punitive responses or reluctance to address collusive type behaviour within the staff team.

- Being unable to tolerate or accept the emotional content of residents' concerns.
- Becoming over controlling and directive with an emphasis on 'doing' something to 'cure' the 'problem'.
- Adhering too rigidly to procedure and practical tasks or diversionary activities.
- Denial of the effects that residents' emotional concerns could have on themselves or on other staff members. This could result in neglect of debriefing, inadequate demand for provision of supervision and staff support, an inability to empathise adequately with residents and other staff and/or eventually burn-out and high levels of stress within the team.

These patterns of defence reflected and affected the overall dynamics within the institution and resonated within the therapeutic relationship.

As I introduced a more psychodynamic approach in my work with Christine, I became increasingly aware of the potential difficulties that can arise if behavioural models of treatment are exclusively used in this area of clinical practice, where clients/residents often communicate through projective identification, a particularly powerful form of defence.

I was led to conclude that when working therapeutically with this client group it is essential for the therapist and other members of the staff team to receive feedback from one another, in order to avoid 'acting into' authoritarian, punitive or similarly collusive dynamics, which can obstruct the therapeutic process.

My approach to the therapy

Fears about judgement, labelling and professional intervention were prevalent in this situation. As I was not a permanent staff member I chose to work with only the basic information given by staff and that which clients or their parents volunteered in sessions and reviews. In this way my understanding of clients' backgrounds and family dynamics grew gradually with the development of the therapeutic relationship.

Sessions were as non-directive as possible. I explained to clients that they could use the time and materials in their own way. Art-making and verbal communication was intermingled according to the needs of each client.

Theoretical considerations

When working at the Centre I took into account the following considerations:
that drugs and other substances may be used as a form of defence against anxiety or as a means of denying painful childhood feelings/experiences. The capacity to empathise and give a child appropriate emotional responses can be affected when parents use such forms of defence and denial.

The consistency and 'good enough' parenting conditions necessary for adequate ego development in childhood, are well documented (Bion 1959, 1962; Klein 1940, 1957, 1975; Winnicott 1965, 1971). These conditions and the associated processes of projection, containment, mirroring and introjection, are seriously impaired when, due to drug dependency, parents remain 'out of touch' with their own feelings and are unable to empathise or facilitate their child's emotional needs. In these circumstances children experience rejection, emotional deprivation and trauma.

Case (1990) has outlined some of the behavioural patterns commonly observed in such children, including:

1   Difficulty in the capacity to think and learn or in establishing trusting relationships.
2   An inability to symbolise, often resorting to 'safe' repetitive tasks or behaviour.
3   Re-enacting: compulsively living-out old emotional behaviour patterns in new relationships.
4   Attempts to control and/or manipulate others.
5   Denial of feelings either through developing a thick 'second skin' (Bick 1968) or by projecting unbearable feelings on to others.

These behavioural traits were certainly evident in Christine who had built-up strong defence mechanisms to cope with her situation. For the purpose of this study it is helpful to consider these defences with reference to the paranoid schizoid position traditionally described by Klein (1927, 1946) and later developed by Bion (1957) and Ogden (1979, 1982). Forms of defence associated with this position involve splitting and projection of parts of the self on to others.

In the context of drug dependency these processes are seen to occur through projection into external substances which result in a depleted sense of self, difficulties with maintaining boundaries, containment, symbolising and introjection. The incapacity to symbolise and maintain appropriate boundaries is significant in drug dependency when the substance becomes potentially life threatening while simultaneously regarded as being a 'necessity' for survival by the user. This double-bind situation, with its conflicts between dependency and defence, mirrors that experienced in early child/parent relationships.

One strand of psychoanalytic theory through which it might be helpful to view this early conflict, is that of the object relations school which developed from Klein's work (Klein 1927, 1946). Here it was believed that from a very early stage, the infant exists in relation to objects that are primitively distinguished from the ego – 'there are object relations from birth'. Put simply, Klein stipulated that in this early stage the infant cannot distinguish between the self and external objects or forces. Instinctual sensations, like hunger pangs, for example, are attributed to and perceived as motivated by objects located within the body which are intended to cause discomfort or alternatively to satisfy the infant (these are termed internal objects). The infant then experiences internal objects as good or bad according to the bodily sensations he/she feels at the time.

In this primitive state the 'object' related to has absolute qualities of 'goodness' or 'badness' and evokes from its subject (the infant) corresponding feelings of love or hate which are similarly 'split off' from an objective view. These feelings themselves are seen to be good or bad by the ego.

The infant's perceptions are based on internal states so that the feelings are not seen as being caused by an 'external mother'. Klein suggests, however, that in the infant's unconscious fantasy each impulse is felt to be separately caused or satisfied by a good or bad object (or mother/parent). They also come in pairs: those that frustrate and those that satisfy the infant. At this time the infant exists in a state of powerlessness and dependency. His/her feelings are determined by arbitrary forces from the 'object' making it seem all-powerful, something to be desired or feared according to the bodily sensations produced.

As the infant's nervous system matures and their awareness of the social and personal environment develops, they become able to recognise the external world and, if all goes well, modification of the 'object' occurs. Then, in what is termed the depressive position, the infant perceives the parent or object as encompassing both good and bad qualities. The object becomes whole and integrated.

For the purpose of this chapter it is important to emphasise that the infant can only mature to this stage where whole integrated objects are recognised, if he/she has the opportunity to experience 'contaminated' external environments and relationships. This would mean 'holding' environments and relations with parents who themselves were able to tolerate conflicting emotional states and contain the anxiety and ambiguity which they give rise to.

Throughout this chapter I will consider how drug dependant parents have difficulty in providing these emotional conditions for their children, largely because, at some level, they themselves remain in the earlier dependant stage, where internal and external forces appear merged. This gives rise to confusion over boundaries. Other people or objects can be perceived in a split way, as 'all good' or 'all bad' and tyrannical: the source of all their pain or pleasure. Communication remains at a very primitive level as objectivity is difficult to obtain.

I explore how the effect of drug dependency on the parent can result in a hostile dependant situation developing between parent and child as both attribute good and bad feelings to each other. And in conclusion, I consider how an intervention with art therapy can help in addressing and resolving the extreme issues of defence and dependency which arise between parent and child in this situation. And through the therapeutic process how their relationship can move into a more mature, less enmeshed state, where both adult and child are better able to tolerate the anxiety caused by defensive and dependent aspects within their relationship.

I wish to focus on how Christine developed similar patterns of defence to her mother (these were manifest in the parents' use of drugs). Christine used a different means of expressing them. In art therapy she made use of the art medium and therapist to project her inner conflicts surrounding dependency and defence.

The referral

Christine was referred for art therapy by a child development worker who informed me that her 'loud attention seeking' was creating difficulties for her mother. She also provoked negative attention from other residents and staff. It was hoped that art therapy would help her to understand or discuss her feelings and associated behaviour.

Christine's mother, Mrs Lee, was eager for her to start art therapy. She met with me to discuss the referral and, significantly, used the time to focus on *her* 'need to talk to someone'. Mrs Lee discussed the concerns and difficulties she experienced with Christine, offering insightful suggestions which connected these to events in her past. These anxieties included: hearing impairment, contributing to Christine's loudness and behavioural problems at school; sibling rivalry and an over-possessive attitude towards her friends (she had recently suffered a traumatic loss of her close friend due to this); a lack of self-esteem; bereavement – her maternal grandmother had died a few months previously.

Mrs Lee made no direct reference to how her relationship with Christine had been affected by her own heroin and crack dependency. I felt that, in requesting 'treatment' for Christine's 'problems', she was both avoiding this issue yet simultaneously acknowledging her need for support, perhaps in the hope that art therapy would compensate in some way for what she had been unable to provide.

Family background

Mrs Lee had seven children from three relationships: four boys, aged twelve, fourteen, eighteen and twenty, Christine who was eleven, and two younger girls (twins) who were four. The children had been taken into care some months before and visited the Centre occasionally at weekends. Mrs Lee hoped the care order would be revoked once she had completed the programme. The fourteen-year-old boy had behavioural problems and was at a residential unit. Christine and her brother Mark stayed at the Centre. There was a great deal of aggressive rivalry between them. I was informed that Mrs Lee had a history of violent relationships.

Christine felt that the boys received more respect and attention than her, and that her younger sisters were favoured because they were 'little and cute'. Christine's and Mark's father had left when Christine was six. Her contact with him was sporadic.

Christine was tall, with a lean build and upright posture. She had quick beady brown eyes and dark hair which just covered her ears. She was always on the move and used energetic haphazard gestures. Although I recall moments of extreme frustration, my memories of her are warm; she had a friendly inquisitive nature – chatting away with contagious enthusiasm and humour, in a slightly babyish voice.

It was easy to see how her open exuberance could be distracting as her lively presence demanded full attention. Christine's desire for approval could also leave her vulnerable in certain situations as she often seemed to lack awareness of appropriate self-protective boundaries with 'new' people.

The initial meeting

After finishing my conversation with Mrs Lee, we heard Christine loudly ask, 'is *my* art lady here?' We then saw a smiling face peering in through the outside window.

In the assessment, which took place the following week, Christine wriggled around excitedly on a bean-bag. 'I'm the only person doing art therapy!' she exclaimed. 'Are you an artist, will you be teaching me every week?' I explained about therapy and the boundaries. There was a feeling of urgency in her responses as if she wanted whatever I offered regardless of content. When I emphasised using the space to express what she felt, Christine jumped in quickly: 'Does that mean I can swear and you won't mind if I spill the paint accidentally?' I felt uncomfortable and put on the spot.

'It seems swearing holds some importance for you,' I commented.

'Well, mum swears, when she's angry. Me and Mark aren't allowed but he doesn't always get told off.'

I asked what materials she liked. 'Felt pens, I'm good at drawing…but Mark's better than me.' Beneath the jovial exterior, a vulnerability became apparent in her face and she looked relieved when I said, 'I wonder why you think that when people have such different ideas about how a picture looks.' 'Yeah,' she said, and then hesitated before saying, 'Mark wants art therapy, Will you do it with him too?' 'It's important for you to have a space that's just for you,' I said. She then talked about missing her house in London and feeling 'strange and cramped' at the Centre.

Discussion

Boundaries had immediately become an issue. Christine's dependant craving for nurture was evident in the positive and unguarded nature of her transference. This was manifest in her initial eagerness to begin art therapy and lack of concern about issues of confidentiality.

She quickly assumed I was to be trusted, despite only having seen me briefly the week before. Without any caution her initial means of relating to me was to immediately present me with her vulnerability and insecurities about Mark and other children.

However, I was also struck by the way in which she simultaneously 'exploited' her vulnerability as a potential defence. In presenting me with her 'weakness' and insecurity she was unconsciously testing out how much she could use me as a protective 'ally' against others.

I had felt put on the spot by her and was cautious regarding the counter-transference, aware that she was beginning to pick up on differences in and outside the therapeutic space which were potentially useful as splitting devices. She would then, unconsciously, be able to protect her 'vulnerable' self by setting up divisions in external relationships. She had already stated the need to be allowed privileges Mark did not have, and had wanted me to authorise swearing despite knowing this would upset her mother.

Session 1

Issues concerning boundaries, persecutory feelings and defence emerged in this session. Christine accidentally kept calling me 'Liz', but denied doing so when I drew her attention to it. She drew a 'nice' stick woman with careful cautious movements and asked questions, reassuring herself about the confidentiality of sessions: 'So you don't tell my mum or the staff what I say?' Satisfied by my reiterating the boundaries, she then explained her picture was her aunt in London. 'She used to take me out, I miss her.' (In a later session I discovered this to be an early transference to me!) I picked up on a fleeting look of sadness and acknowledged how 'it can be very painful leaving people and places'. The comment did not register, it was as if it was too much to contemplate. I felt she had pushed me aside; completely changing tack, she reached for the paints.

Christine was briefly absorbed in a hypnotic silence. Gradually her movements became more vigorous. Squeezing red and black paint directly onto the paper and then aggressively beating brushes on to it, Christine painted a 'black sky' and 'red devils'.

'I don't like having to go to bed at nine o'clock here, I have horrid nightmares about my mum hitting me. She treats me like a baby.... Hitting me in front of people here.'

There followed a succession of messy images as anger and resentment spilt out. Later, I heard that Christine had been shouted at by her mother for having paint on her clothes.

When I said it was time to stop, she seemed reluctant to leave the room. 'What time are you coming next week?' she asked. Once again I reassured her that I would be coming and about the consistency of time and place each week. She then darted upstairs without saying goodbye.

Discussion

The issues that arose in this first session persisted in various forms throughout other sessions, but the way in which Christine communicated about them changed over time. In the early stages, defensive splitting was an obvious trait. I was the 'good' therapist who had come to save Christine from her 'wicked mother'. Negative transference or anger towards me was expressed inexplicably through her themes and the process of image-making. These also contained the 'bad', messy parts of herself.

Images of devils, 'attacking witches', 'scary skeletons', and the angry use of red and black paint, all contained unconscious elements of the 'victim and 'aggressor' within herself. The subject matter was also used to explore feelings surrounding illness and death. They held the promise of escape from her inner fears and conflicts.

Christine continually expected indifferent or angry responses to her mistakes and the images she had made. Her low self-esteem triggered a protective response from me and she projected strong feelings of dependency. Each week I found myself literally defending 'her' therapeutic space from Mark who peered through the outside windows. This 'protection' bonded her growing dependency but also fuelled a flicker of self-confidence. As this confidence progressively ignited into a flame, I recognised the possibilities of questioning her defences more openly and acknowledging my own contradictory responses to her behaviour. I experienced maternal satisfaction as I watched her gain 'nourishment' in the materials, yet I was often simultaneously anxious and resentful at her attitude.

In this early unconscious phase Christine got paint everywhere; I would spend a long time cleaning up after her. I was also concerned about my limited budget as, oblivious to price, materials would be 'wasted accidentally'. I was also indirectly experiencing pressure from Mrs Lee and the staff about 'Christine's mess-making'. Examining my negative and positive responses became essential in deciphering Christine's relationship with her mother and the staff. I was acutely aware of the splitting and scapegoating processes that were emerging. These were a re-enactment, covering-up mutual dependency and insecurities. In time, I was forced to battle with *my own* feelings of professional exclusion and victimisation to avoid harmful collusion in these dynamics.

Session 7

Appearing self-conscious and disturbed, Christine kept disappearing into the kitchen. When she brought back a can with sharp edges I expressed concern that she may cut herself. I noticed an element of enjoyment in her dismissive response: 'I want you to look away now, I'm drawing.' I insisted on taking the jagged lid off the can before I turned around (aware, however, that this might also imply a lack of trust). She haphazardly held on to the can and began to laugh in a haunting manner, 'like a wicked witch'.

For a split second the atmosphere in the room felt like a horror film, and reality blurred with her fantasy. I sensed Christine's fears of falling into a state of chaos, her lack of boundaries, and was aware of her dependency on me to redefine the reality, to put her fears safely back into a world of fantasy.

As the can was handed over, we both experienced a sense of relief, and she burst into warm laughter. Christine then talked about having been kept awake by 'horrid nightmares'. 'I don't want to talk about them, though,' she said. Here Christine was beginning to test out her potential power, erecting a protective boundary between herself and my possible 'maternal' intrusion.

'You can turn round now,' she said. The image she had drawn on the paper was of a house covered with glitter, with the tin stuck on top. 'The house where people are brought back from the dead,' she told me. I commented that death seemed to be on her mind a lot.

'I had a twin sister when I was born but she died, I'm lucky it wasn't me'. I acknowledged the sadness about losing her sister, adding that it would have been very sad if she had died.

'My nan died in our house and I saw her dead body, my mum was upset and let me see! Nan used to stare at me, "funny", I didn't like it'.

I wondered aloud if she had asked me to look away earlier because it made her feel 'funny' – uncomfortable inside when people focussed on her. She told me she felt as if people stared at her in school: 'Makes me feel funny'. I thought about secrecy, which is often an issue for drug-using parents who naturally want to avoid stigmatisation of themselves and their children. What did Christine tell children at school about where she lived and why? This difficulty obviously would have an efffect on her self-confidence.

After this, the session became very messy with Christine creating mixtures of paint and glue, and at one point splashing my clothes. Although apologetic, she said in a 'mummy' voice: 'I bet you get mucky even in your best clothes don't you?' She once again laughed 'wickedly' when I wondered aloud if her mother said this to her. In the last three minutes of the session she begged for more time while desperately creating a 'pretty' image with trees and birds.

I felt Christine wanted to cover up the fear and feelings that she had let out in this session. She could not, however, cover up the mess she had made earlier in the kitchen.

Mrs Lee appeared as we were cleaning up and proceeded to criticise Christine aggressively. The atmosphere became heavy with anger and tension. I was left feeling emotional and tormented with guilt, filled with sadness for Christine. I recognised the need to give Mrs Lee feedback about the therapy and discuss the issue of 'mess' for it had become an issue which resonated in and outside the therapeutic relationship.

Discussion

The strong feelings evoked after this session prompted me to arrange a meeting with Mrs Lee. I hoped that the outcome would mean that she would feel more allied with the therapy. During our meeting I picked up on an unconscious envy towards Christine receiving support. Mrs Lee spoke of her guilt in not having told Christine why they were at the Centre (Christine had been told Mrs Lee had 'a smoking problem'). While she portrayed it as a realistic move to 'protect' Christine, it was also a defence for herself, adding to the difficulties of indirect or contradictory communication between them and also to Mrs Lee's unconscious fears about 'mess' (and thus, 'secrets') spilling out.

We considered these unconscious reasons why she might find it difficult to tolerate Christine's mess, 'clumsiness' and 'not hearing'.

After exploring why Christine needed a 'space' to externalise her inner mess, I also acknowledged the genuine difficulties in this situation. We agreed on some practical solutions to resolve these issues, and to give Christine an active role in this by taking responsibility for herself. This included Christine wearing old clothes and reserving more time to clean up before ending the session.

In addition, I arranged regular reviews for Mrs Lee and Christine so that they could directly communicate with each other and with me about the sessions. I accepted this would have consequences for the therapeutic relationship but felt it appropriate given the tendency for splitting and confused communications that were prevalent at this time.

The same week I attended a case review where many strong and contradictory feelings arose. The staff team were split on several issues including the 'mess' and how to resolve other residents' resentment/jealousy about Christine receiving art therapy. Also we discussed Mrs Lee's inability to communicate her concerns to me directly.

Fortunately the staff eventually acknowledged my observations, accepting that Mrs Lee's indirect communication with others contributed to Christine's inner conflict and disruptive acting out, and how this led to her becoming scapegoated by her mother, residents and staff. Thus some of the tension that had arisen became resolved, with staff members suggesting how we could best work to prevent this happening again.

After the discussion with her mother Christine used the materials in a significantly different way which more openly expressed her anger towards me.

Session 8

Christine was late. I went upstairs as I felt that she needed reassurance that I was still 'exclusively' for her, and not for Mrs Lee. She explained smugly, 'I'm getting old clothes'. Mrs Lee kissed her before we went down. It seemed as if they both needed to 'show' the strength of their alliance to me.

Christine began by playing hide-and-seek games with the materials, and then asked me to look away, she continued talking while she drew. 'I really miss my auntie,' she said. I wondered aloud whether she thought her auntie, or myself could 'hold her in mind' even if we weren't directly present, or 'looking'. She pretended not to hear, and thoughtfully mixed paints inside a container in concentrated silence (maybe showing her need to have these painful feelings held inside – 'contained'). I watched her in an atmosphere of subdued silence and considered the possibility that she had been told not to be messy. As if reading my thoughts, she asked, 'What did you talk about with my mum?' I explained to her what had been agreed. Although she did not directly show discomfort about the meeting and the agreements which had been made, I sensed a questioning and ambiguity about her mother being involved.

Christine responded symbolically, her subdued manner changed as she poured the mixed contents from the container all over the plastic sheet protecting the carpet. 'Oops,' she laughed, adding paper and squeezing it in, then digging her fingers aggressively into the plastic sheet to make a hole. 'If the sheet is leaking we'll have to stop the session and clean the carpet,' I warned, trying to keep calm. She stopped, and I covered the hole.

She spent the duration of the session making mixtures of red and black paint with glue. With five minutes left, she carried on working, desperately searching for materials which were scattered around her.

'Just let me finish this one,' she pleaded, her hands covered in sticky red paint.

'It just doesn't feel like there's enough of anything Christine,' I reflected thoughtfully, but felt my anxiety rising and my patience running out.

As she hurriedly put the images in front of me for 'approval', a confused mixture of warm concern and angry resentment washed over me. 'They are very powerful and quite beautiful,' was all I had time to say before we stopped.

Discussion

Christine's desperate need for my approval of her images at the end of the session had made her appear vulnerable, which then increased the difficulty I had faced in addressing the powerful 'attacks' she had made, by using the materials and challenging the boundaries at the end of the session. Instead, I was the one who was left feeling strangely guilty for ending the session before we had viewed her images together.

In her discussion of projective processes, Case (1994: p.5) observes how a client is able to move from a concrete 'claustrophobic experience, an experience of being inside the mother's body...where language has little use' to a more abstracted one where the therapist is experienced as a container. She notices how in the first stage a struggle between creation and destruction occurs, usually resulting in the concrete destruction of real objects or attacks on those in external relationships (the therapist).

I felt that both Christine and her mother were initially still at this stage. The potentially nurturing dependence between mother and child therefore was conflicted and chaotic resulting in chaos and hostility between them. Case draws attention to the role of the therapist in accepting, containing and processing the hostile 'aggressive missile', inherent in the language of projective identification (ibid.: p. 7).

As Christine's therapy progressed she and Mrs Lee were both able to use me in this way, as an object who contained some of the hostility between them, so that they then could stand back and reflect on their relationship in a more objective manner.

In the following weeks, I became concerned about the forthcoming meeting with Mrs Lee, feeling that Christine's vulnerable side, her defensive 'false self' would be exposed, and that her spontaneity in sessions would be affected. As the time for the meeting approached, I became aware of how potentially powerful Mrs Lee's response to Christine's artwork could be.

Session 13

As Christine entered the room, she stuck a 'NO ENTRY' sign on the door. She had brought boxes with her and, making 'wings', she flapped around excitedly and said without stopping for breath: 'I'm a bird. Guess what? Good news to tell you, I've been chosen in a dance competition at school. ... Now I'll have to perform in front of people at a concert. Everyone can come ...you can come too'.

'Would you like me to come?' I handed her the control, and she threw it back at me.

'You can if you like...you don't have to though.'

I acknowledged her anxious ambiguity about having been 'chosen'. 'Yeah, I'm really nervous about performing in front of them all, they'll think I'm stupid.' I sensed that her nervousness extended to the meeting we were to have with her mother after this session.

While making 'a homely house' out of boxes (a symbol of security perhaps?), she asked, 'Are you bored?' I asked her why she might think this. 'Well, you just sit there quietly,' she replied. This led to a consideration of the many possible meanings behind silences in the presence of others.

'I normally think people are bored with me...or annoyed,' she said. I wondered to myself if that was her common experience of silences with Mrs Lee.

'Perhaps that makes "not talking", quite hard then?' I answered.

'Yeah, they call me Christine chatterbox at school,' she said, looking hurt. 'My mum will be seeing my pictures today!'

After reminding her she had a choice about whether to show her images or not, I realised her dilemma. Her 'choices' seemed to be conflicted and mixed up with Mrs Lee's expectations of 'seeing what Christine was up to'. 'I'll only show Mum the "good stuff",' she said thoughtfully. 'It's important for you that Mum likes what you've done,' I said.

She nodded. Hurrying to finish before the session ended, she became agitated as her image became, in her words, 'wrong'. 'You stupid thing, I'm so stupid', she said. 'It's very frustrating when it doesn't work as you want it to Christine but that doesn't mean you are stupid,' I replied.

She managed to 'put it right' before rushing upstairs to get Mrs Lee.

The review meeting

Christine laid all her chosen images out and held her mother's hand while she showed her each one. By talking constantly about them, Christine left little opportunity for comment. Acknowledging Christine's emotional needs here appeared difficult for Mrs Lee, who kept repeating 'that's good' in a disinterested, removed tone (thus giving Christine confused double messages). The times she appeared most present and interested were when she reprimanded Christine or spoke negatively of her. This threw some light on Christine's 'need' to evoke anger, as her experience suggested that this was the only way to sustain other people's interest in herself.

At one point, an irritable Mrs Lee abruptly interrupted Christine, telling that she should not have changed back into her clean clothes so soon. Christine looked helplessly at me for support and I felt her confidence slipping away. Mrs Lee also talked about

Christine as if she was not present, informing me what she thought was 'wrong' with her. This made me feel panicky and uncomfortable. Christine's defence was to 'pretend not to hear' or to ignore it by constantly chattering loudly.

By talking over Christine in this way, Mrs Lee may have precipitated her feelings of 'not being present' which Christine expressed in many ways: not hearing, wishing she was somewhere else, feeling 'dead' or detached from her emotions. When this happened she found it more difficult to accept responsibility for what she felt or did.

Mrs Lee did not appear to acknowledge the significance of Christine's 'distorting reality' because she was unable to facilitate her play and fantasy. At one point in the meeting they angrily disagreed about whether or not Christine's best friend had 'dumped her' for someone else. I reflected on the possibility that it may have felt like this to Christine.

Topics which arose included her grandmother's death, Mrs Lee's miscarriage of a twin when Christine was born, Christine having had 'two daddies' and remembering 'Bob' (who I later discovered spent some time living with Mrs Lee but had committed suicide a year before). At this point Christine sat on her mother's lap and they rocked together singing songs that 'Bob had played on the keyboard'. Mrs Lee became embarrassed at this, and by some of the things Christine remembered. 'She remembers what she wants to,' she told me.

Before the meeting had finished, Mrs Lee said the artwork should be exhibited to staff and residents at the end of her therapy. Once again I was left with confused feelings that Christine had been insensitively exposed and placed 'on show'.

Discussion

I had a number of thoughts after this meeting. First, that the strong sense of 'being on show', was an element of Mrs Lee's transference both to me and the situation. In society, women are subtly judged often on the performance or achievements of their children – by themselves, relatives, friends and outside institutions. For women who are drug dependant there is the additional pressure (and common experience) of having been assessed by probation or social services on their ability to be 'good parents', often with dramatic consequences, as in Mrs Lee's case. This might then contribute to the difficulty such parents experience in establishing a separate identity and recognising appropriate boundaries, between their needs and those of their children.

In these circumstances normal protective and introjective patterns of communication between parent and child can become distorted. The child may feel 'pressured' to become how he or she is represented 'in the parents' projection' (see Ogden 1979, 1982). A 'false self' as described by Winnicott (1947) could develop as a defence against these projective identifications from the parent.

To some extent this meeting served to deepen the therapeutic alliance. It was me to whom Christine had been 'exposed'. My acceptance and acknowledgement of her pain and conflicted dependency on Mrs Lee enabled Christine to drop some of her defensive 'false self' image. Her own vulnerability became less 'scary' to her when held within the therapeutic space and 'seen' mirrored in her pictures with me there.

Over the next few sessions the 'wicked mother' image crumbled slightly as Christine moved towards integrating the negative and positive aspects of herself and her relationships with others.

Session 17

I reminded Christine that the next session would be the last before a two-week break. She responded by aggressively cutting into the plastic which protected the carpet. Then, engaging me in games of hide-and-seek, she explored symbolically her feelings about the separation, vigorously screwing paper around art materials and hiding them under the plastic. 'This is a guessing game ... you're not to look, then guess which ones have disappeared,' she said.

This manic activity was perhaps a defence against 'being abandoned', having me 'disappear'. She then found a puppet in the toy box and violently cut its hair off. 'I hate this granny puppet!' she said. I wondered if she had felt abandoned by the death of her granny and similarly at me for 'going away'. She denied this:'I haven't thought about her much,' she responded. As if relieved by her manic activity Christine then became calm and silent, absorbed in her painting.

'I'll do a picture for you then one for my mum', she said. 'I love my mum,' she added in a defensive tone and as if she was seeking reparation. The images were an offering, I thought, to compensate for earlier attacks on me, also perhaps a reaffirmation of her loyalty to her mother.

Together we looked at the mixture of colours in the symmetrical butterfly images that she had made and reflected on the mixture of 'good' and 'bad' feelings aroused in relationships with parents. The symmetry was also significant in terms of 'mirror images' and issues of 'identity' between mother and daughter. Across the top of a piece of paper, Christine wrote, 'Carly is my best cousin'. 'We used to go swimming together when I lived in London,' she explained. She painted a picture to illustrate this. I pointed out that the two figures in the picture looked the same. 'We were like twins, we even used to wear the same clothes.' She looked sad and lost, and I remembered the loss of her 'other half', her identity as a twin. 'I wish she'd have stayed alive. I'd love to have someone to play with all the time like my little sisters do,' she said.

At the end of the session Christine also wished, in a questioning tone, 'that we hadn't had to leave London for mum to give up smoking.' I felt this was an acknowledgement about how her needs conflicted with her mother's, and also a questioning of what she had been told by Mrs Lee and why they were at the Centre. It appeared that Christine had been more able to contain and acknowledge painful feelings of anger, separation and loss in this session.

In terms of paint, there was not a lot of 'mess' to clean up afterwards. However, I left the Centre that day feeling 'messy' and 'uncomfortable' inside, thinking about how I had been drawn into upholding pretences about why Christine was at the Centre. Was I carrying her anxiety away for her? And how much of the anxiety came from Mrs Lee?

Session 18

Arriving late, Christine had run on ahead of her mother to be on time. The plastic sheet had been mislaid by other residents. 'Don't worry,' she said, 'I'm not going to get messy today'. Feeling uneasy, I reminded Christine of my absence in the coming two weeks. She suddenly looked on the verge of tears. 'Who will do art with me then?'

The pang of guilt I felt steadily grew throughout the session. As Christine carelessly squirted paints onto the paper, I said, 'Perhaps you're feeling upset about the break?' 'Not if you're going somewhere you'll have fun,' she said. Her mature manner made me feel like a child. As she painted I found myself asking her meaningless questions and sensed her valid irritability at being interrupted. The role reversal became striking. As she completed a 'I love my mum' picture I suddenly felt rejected and inadequate. There followed a picture *for me*, which strangely reassured me.

Realising the strength of the protective identification, I was relieved when Christine began to own some of the insecurity. 'Do you do art with other children?' she asked, then went on to ask if I had any children. I wondered aloud about the connection between having to share me and having to share mum with her siblings. 'Mark gets to do things I don't, just 'cos he's older,' she complained.

At this point her artwork became messier and she flicked paint directly at me, as if to provoke a response. While acknowledging her frustration and anger I also warned that we would have to stop if she continued to express herself in this way. Christine was then able to reflect on how anger could be expressed indirectly: 'Like when people draw things at school to annoy you, they don't say it out loud.' She got covered in paint and we stopped early so that Christine could go and wash.

I expected her to return to help me clean up but she did not reappear – perhaps sensing the need to be the one to 'leave' first so as to avoid the feeling of being the one who is left – abandoned by me.

I went upstairs to say goodbye and promised to send Christine a postcard while I was away. At the time I was thinking she needed a reassuring concrete symbol that I 'held her in mind' (however my response may equally have been triggered by guilt in the countertransference). Her jovial, casual response, added to the sense of guilt, inadequacy and insecurity I felt as I left.

Discussion

In this session projective identification was clearly being used as a defence against Christine's feelings of dependency and insecurity. These were brought about by my forthcoming absence and disruption to her therapy but obviously went deeper, triggering memories of painful separations and losses in her past.

Counter-transference effects on the therapist and within the institution

On my return, my own insecurities took on a more 'real', concrete form when I was informed that Christine's sessions might be discontinued due to lack of funding. With the manager away on leave I was given no clear explanation as to why funding had become a problem.

Over the next few weeks there were breaks in the regularity of Christine's sessions, some of which were unexpectedly cancelled by staff, from whom I received very mixed messages. Like Christine, I was left in the dark, helplessly guessing and fantasising about 'the real reasons' for this disruption. Was it a dissatisfaction with my work, professional rivalry or Mrs Lee's disapproval?

Some weeks later, my supervisor pointed out how my passive position in this situation might be connected to strong emotions and projected identification within the counter-transference. This spurred me into taking action.

On her return, I met with the Centre manager to discuss the importance of continuing Christine's therapy until she left and how it was essential to maintain the consistency of her sessions. She explained to me that the staff had been on tenterhooks while the Centre's annual finances were being justified to Phoenix House. Continuation of the sessions was then agreed.

It had been with considerable difficulty that I had informed Christine about the possible threat to her sessions. So we were both relieved by this development. Before this time, however, there was a very trying period in her therapy.

Somehow we both held on to the therapeutic alliance as many issues arose around dependency and rejection. These interacted with external events. The uncertainty about funding in particular, which related to my own feelings of insecurity, fed into Christine's renewed vulnerabilities: at the same time as coping with disruption in her art therapy sessions, she also faced dramatic changes in her family situation. There was renewed contact with her father and the prospect of her brother Mark leaving to live with him. Also, she was being reunited with her siblings at weekends.

Mrs Lee was now near to completing the rehabilitation programme and so Christine was also forced to contemplate leaving the Links Centre, returning to her old home and school in London;

at the same time this would coincide with ending art therapy. Obviously all of this created very powerful dynamics.

In hindsight, I reflected on how, through talking directly to the manager, I had unconsciously functioned as a role model for Christine, who appeared more assertive, better able to maintain boundaries and to take 'space' for herself. This contributed to Christine's confidence in coping with her fears of separation and loss when the therapeutic relationship was coming to an end.

Session 20: Following the break

'It's good you're back.' I was surprised by Christine's openness in front of Mark and Mrs Lee (who followed her into the room). I felt the session was being invaded as Mark asked if he could stay. 'No!' Christine reacted quickly, now more able to protect 'her space'. She made a sign, 'Christine only for Art Therapy', which caused some tension when she put it on the door as Mrs Lee left.

During most of the session she made big sticky glitter circles, using up nearly all the materials I had just brought. This indicated her need to 'fill up' again, and comfort herself after my absence.

'Can we get some more glitter?' she asked. 'That depends on the budget,' I explained; my words were double-edged as at the time I was considering the difficulty in explaining to her that the sessions were possibly under threat. (I felt guilty about this later on, as I realised that my response here may have been different if I had not been preoccupied by issues of funding.)

Towards the end of the session some of the paper shapes Christine was cutting out 'went wrong', and in an agitated state she threw down the pair of scissors. 'Perhaps you're anxious and angry at being left again at the end of the session?' I said. She turned a tin over and began to bang on it loudly so I could not be heard. She then stomped out of the room. First feeling numb, then emotionally torn and quite traumatised, I sat down and let the feelings run through me. Christine returned five minutes before the session was due to end. She accused me of not liking coming to see her, 'Because you always finish exactly at six o'clock! You never give me extra time'. I asked if she often felt people who 'went' away did not like her or would not return again. While we cleaned up, Christine said that she'd been pleased about the postcard I had sent while I was away, and she then talked about her father and how he never wrote to her, 'only to Mark'.

Discussion

After this session I realised how Christine was productively making 'use' of me within the therapeutic relationship. It was evident that I was 'holding' on to her projected but unsatisfied emotional needs in a number of ways. However, throughout this time I also had to consider if I 'was acting out' and whether my own defences were being triggered in a way that made me blind and lose my objectivity. If so, was I failing to prevent a re-enactment of old dynamics and unhelpful emotional responses with Christine?

The parental concern and anxiety about separating which Christine wished her parents to show was now being felt by me in the counter-transference. My initial anxiety about addressing the possible threat to her therapy had mirrored Mrs Lee's secrecy, avoidance and indirect communication with Christine over many issues. The 'intrusive' and perhaps mistaken nature of my verbal interventions also reflected Mrs Lee's behaviour towards Christine. These 'here and now' responses were perhaps partly triggered by a real anxiety over the prospect of the therapy ending prematurely.

Once again I underestimated Christine's ability to be independent and able to cope with separation, for she had, in fact, made considerable progress in working through her insecurity and difficulties, despite my concerns. This was verified later in positive feedback from Mrs Lee and staff, regarding her behaviour and ability to 'talk about feelings' more directly.

At this point I considered the possibility that there were perhaps errors in my handling of the projective identifications. That my own defences had been triggered causing me to over-identify with Christine and the dynamics between herself and Mrs Lee. The loud banging on the tin was, perhaps, to shut out my intrusive interpretations and pressure for Christine to conform; not only to my own projections about her loss, and the causes of her behaviour, but also to my wish for Christine to 'get better' and equate that with a verbalisation of her feelings.

Winnicott (1947) reminds us that this pressure to succeed can perpetuate a 'false self' identity in the client, and that premature interpretations may provoke unhelpful rigid defences. Sometimes, however, it is only in retrospect that the therapist is able to identify the significance of her/his interactions during the session and begin to process or readapt initial responses so that they become more 'useful' to the client. In art psychotherapy the art medium has a unique role to play in acting as a buffer when the therapist makes such initial errors, holding the therapeutic alliance and containing client feelings until the therapist can recognise his/her own acting out and adapt his/her responses accordingly.

Christine's messiness and images continued to be accepted by me and held within the therapeutic space (despite some of my premature and indigestible 'therapeutic' interventions) therefore, her projective identifications were still being contained and processed at an unconscious level. Simultaneously my verbal reflections and feedback did continue to offer Christine some conscious understanding of her 'split off' emotions, even when my interpretations were occasionally difficult for her to accept. Fortunately, in Christine's case, the words and images eventually came together. In the following sessions Christine's ability to reflect more objectively and verbalise her feelings rapidly increased.

Session 23

This session took place after I had been absent for one week (due to a member of staff unexpectedly cancelling the session because Christine might not return in time from a Centre outing that she had gone on. Unfortunately, she had returned before I would have been due to arrive). Christine was waiting for me by the front door.

'Can I help you get things out?' she eagerly asked. On entering the playroom, I noticed that she had been there beforehand and that she had written several questions on the blackboard. These all began: 'How do you feel about…?

I wondered aloud, 'perhaps you have some questions to ask me?' She shook her head but looked upset as I wondered about how she had felt regarding my absence. When I explained why I had not come the week before, she said, 'you should have come because I was here at five o'clock!' She left no room for further discussion and began to use the art materials while conducting a running commentary about what she was making.

'I'm the presenter on *Art Attack* [a TV programme],' she explained. I was painfully aware that many of the materials were running out. She became very frustrated, wincing and groaning as she attempted to violently squeeze the last dregs from a tube of paint. Eventually she threw it across the room. 'Perhaps *you* felt "attacked" Christine, when I didn't turn up last week?' I asked. She ignored me or 'didn't hear', and I resigned myself to the symbolic 'spilling out' of emotion, quickly slipping paper under her now dripping images in an attempt to protect the carpet.

I picked up on a strange sense of her enjoyment at seeing me running around after her. Was she 'getting her revenge?': regaining her control by making me feel as anxious as she had felt last week?

As the situation escalated, she flicked paint towards the wall. I picked up on her feelings – both fear and excitement – that she may have angered me. Our eyes suddenly met in unspoken acknowledgement of her provocations and I could not help but smile as I felt a mixture of sadness and warmth towards her. To my surprise she became upset. Tears welled up in her eyes. 'I bet you're fed up and annoyed with me?' she said. I said 'No,' but I did wonder (aloud) why she was intent on trying to make me angry with her. 'Is this a way of showing me you are both angry and upset about me being away?' I asked. She nodded in agreement, and bit her lip to stop herself from crying. When we went into the kitchen to clean up she said: 'Sometimes I do that to my mum you know, annoy her because I don't think she likes me. People don't like me much you know?' This made me feel sad, and I asked why she thought this was the case:

'Mum doesn't care about me any more. I know because she always takes Mark's side, so I annoy her to get my own back. It's the only way.'

I questioned this and asked if she could think of other ways of expressing herself.

'You could perhaps talk to your mum like you are talking to me now about how you feel inside.'

'People might think I'm silly if I *said it* though.'

A rare moment followed in which we discussed her fears of talking about her feelings and also the possibility that how others perceived her might differ from how she perceived herself. We went on to consider how different people may also respond to her differently depending on who they were and what the situation happened to be. We agreed that she would try and use the sessions to test out her fears and say what she was feeling. Though I realised this would be difficult for her, the session ended with a sense of elated companionship between the two of us.

Session 26

When I entered the room Christine announced, 'I will be leaving soon'. I felt a pang of sadness and panic. 'We will have to say goodbye too, Christine, I wonder how you feel about this?' I said. 'Can we do something special?' she asked with a hint of despera- tion. 'You could take me out one day.' I said we could do something to say goodbye in the session.

'My sisters will be coming back home. I've really missed them but we'll all be happy together now.' There was a note of uncer- tainty in her voice. She talked about how she had not much liked her sisters before, but last weekend she felt surprised as she had been excited and happy to see them.

'Mark's leaving before me. He's going to live with my dad now.' I was surprised and sensed her envy at Mark receiving special atten- tion from their father. 'I wonder if you'll miss Mark? I asked. She acknowledged that she would when he went to live with their father.'You rarely talk about dad,' I commented. 'He used to get really mad and that was scary,' she said.

I felt I was being told not to pursue this matter as she began filling the space with words, pretending to be the presenter on *Art Attack*.'I'm going to leave this picture so that the first coat can dry,' she informed me, putting a thick sticky image to one side. 'We'll come back to it later,' she said. This first image was of a woman and a boy. I wondered to myself if it was her mother and Mark.

She then drew one large and one small figure and asked me how to spell 'daddy', which she wrote in a bubble coming from the small figure's mouth. Feeling invited by this, I referred again to the fact that she did not mention her father very often. She tossed the picture aside and reached for the red paint.'I'll be shocked to see him again. We are going to see him when we take Mark there,' she said, squirting paint on the paper. At this point her movements became more haphazard. 'He was scary,' she laughed.

She now had red paint all over her hands and pretended to have hurt herself. I asked if she had sometimes felt hurt by her father and that maybe it would also hurt when she left the Centre and art therapy. I felt that she needed me to acknowledge these emotions for her before she could fully identify and digest them herself. Now, however, Christine seemed to be able to introject and 'digest' her emotions once a mirror was held up to show her the feelings she had originally projected onto me. She said she had lots of feelings.

'All mixed up like the colours,' I said. By now she was squirting different colours on the paper making a thick mixture. Her urgency and the intensity of feeling in the room seemed to make her oblivious to the fact that she was getting paint everywhere, including on herself and her clothes. She held up her hands in a menacing way, 'Dracula hands!' she laughed. 'Things seem very frightening at the moment?' I said. I thought about the attacking vampire, how her messy clothes perhaps were going to be a source of her attacking and simultaneously being attacked by Mrs Lee after the session. Christine went back to her drying image. With only two minutes left she pleaded for more time in her usual way. 'It is difficult to finish sessions and it will be hard for us to say goodbye Christine.' She laughed in agreement.

In the sessions leading up to the end of Christine's therapy and her stay at the Centre, she appeared to have developed a more positive identity which enabled her to integrate both the 'good' and 'bad' aspects of leaving. She was, therefore, able to contemplate the ending without suffering from feelings of devastating dependency and exhibiting rigid defences which such separations had previously evoked for her.

Session 30

When I arrived Christine was playing in the lounge with Mark. 'Oh no!' she laughed, 'I forgot about you.'

I went to get the art materials out. When I returned to the art room Christine had hidden. I pretended to search for her and eventually she bounced out from behind the curtain, laughing loudly. 'I won't be here next weekend,' she said in a boastful voice. 'I'm going to see my family in London and I forgot you were coming today!' 'Perhaps you have mixed feelings about art therapy sometimes?' I said, acknowledging her ambiguity and growing independence. 'Maybe you would have preferred to carry on playing with Mark today instead?' She looked at me and sheepishly smiled and nodded in agreement, then asked if she could go to the toilet. Perhaps this was an outlet for uncomfortable guilty feelings she experienced through recognising her own needs in separating from me.

When she came back, these feelings seemed to spill out uncontrollably as she knocked over all the water and some of the paint. 'Do you think this could be a way of telling me something which is hard to talk about?' I asked. 'Maybe you're worrying about how I will react, that you might upset or displease me. What happens to all these feelings Christine?' 'Yeah…sometimes it's hard to tell mum stuff like that. I feel bad, I've had accidents and not told anyone, staff or my mum. I've hidden them instead in case I get told off.' She looked at me cautiously. Then her sense of relief filled the room as she told me about how in the past she had hidden spilt drinks and wet knickers so as to avoid confrontation.

She had begun to tear the paper into bits, and to put the pieces into a lunch box. 'It's a lucky dip!' she explained. We reflected on how being more direct with people could be risky, like a 'lucky dip', in that you could not control their reactions. Christine started to talk about the 'sad little girl' on a kidney donor advert she had noticed, who unwraps her parcel to find nothing there.

Later, I thought about her forthcoming expectations of having a reunited, happy family on leaving the Centre and wondered if these would materialise.

The subject of unfulfilled expectations and concern about the responses of others continued into the final sessions. In one session Christine brought in some silver stars. ' I always use everything up,' she said. 'Maybe you wish you could "make" some more sessions happen with them [the magic stars],' I asked, reminding her of the few sessions we had left. 'You always say things like that!' She sounded irritated. She began to paint a big black wall with pretty flowers on top. Looking at her image I commented: 'That wall looks very hard to climb.' She began to say that it was difficult to leave but she was also glad to go. In silence, she picked up a sheet of paper and at the top wrote 'dark night'. She began to cover it in black paint, and she looked as if she was about to cry.

'We've been meeting a long time Christine, it's very sad to say goodbye.' I suddenly felt overwhelmed by emotion. She began to stick silver stars onto the black background.'There are goods bit about leaving, too,' I continued. 'It's sad,' she mumbled, handing me her image. 'You can keep this one, from me, as a goodbye gift.'

She needed to mark the ending and also to be assured that I would have a concrete reminder of her. 'It's beautiful,' I said. 'I'll put it on my wall'. 'Will you keep *all* my work?' she asked. I suggested that we could both look at her work together in the last session before we said goodbye, but I explained that it was up to her what she wanted to do with it.

I sensed her uncertainty about stating what she really wanted and this made me wonder if she would be able to ask for my support in exploring her fear of separation and loss as well as those fears involving the future.

The image that she was making became so wet that the paper began to disintegrate. My instinct was to help but I resisted, waiting for her to ask 'me in'. 'Yes, you can help me, actually,' she invited. As I did she became upset: 'I woke up crying this morning, I had a pain in my tummy last night and I was sick. I didn't tell my mum as she would have said I was lying.' 'It sounds very painful, your tummy, and also the fact that you don't feel you can tell mum about it,' I replied. After this she engaged me in her activities by asking me to pass her the art materials. 'When you're in pain and are upset it makes you feel like having things done for you... being looked after and tucked up in bed,' I said. She laughed and began to talk about some rather painful issues, including her feelings of exclusion as a result of her mother having a lover and her desire to have a 'real dad' to play with.

'I've had three dads,' she told me. 'One died after falling asleep, a bit like my granny did.' We reflected on the pain of these losses and how leaving the Centre and saying goodbye might reignite feelings like these again. Christine asked if I would make her a cup of tea with two sugars at the beginning of the last session as a way of marking 'the end'.

Although she still tended to express her feelings through physical symptoms and act out a little at times of separation and stress, on leaving the Centre, Christine's ability to use symbolism more appropriately, and to communicate her feelings verbally, had greatly improved. This was evident in the last therapy session, by which time any sign of disruptive behaviour was rare, and Mrs Lee reported a great improvement in her relationship with Christine.

The final sessions

In the session leading up to her last week, Christine often developed tummy aches or headaches. After I had reflected on the need to be physically comforted when upset, she acknowledged, 'I get ill when I'm upset. It makes me feel sick when I'm worried'.

She talked a lot about her hopes and fears in having to say goodbye to everyone. Many of the images and discussions centred around feelings of rejection that she had felt in her relationship with her father.

As promised, we began her last session with 'comforting', hot sweet tea. We were both conscious of 'acting out' the need to be physically comforted. Christine divided her first image into 'good' and 'bad', drawing a witch 'sick in bed' on the bad side. We then talked about the good and bad aspects of her leaving the Centre and ending therapy.

Throughout the session her image-making became increasingly messy and my interventions to protect the carpet were met with demands to, 'speak louder, I can't hear you. The doctor says my ears are really bad.' Her deafness gradually increased as the session continued; I was 'shut out' literally by this and by her becoming totally absorbed in her painting.

With ten minutes of the session left, the atmosphere suddenly became one of sadness. Feeling pained and uncertain, I asked myself whether I should 'intrude' with words or leave Christine with these painful feelings verbally unacknowledged? I watched in silence as she continued to paint. She glanced up only occasionally to check the clock. With three minutes left, she leaned back and said, 'finished'. I went and sat next to her as she described the image.

There was a child crying 'lots of tears' at the top of a big bean stalk. A woman with an umbrella stood underneath saying, 'I'm coming'. 'The woman's going to rescue the child,' Christine explained. 'Maybe this is a wish for someone to "be there" to "rescue" you when you're sad?' I said, 'To take the pain away', but my words felt superfluous.

She presented me with a farewell present, an attractive glittery-glue patterned image, and we put the rest of the pictures in a big bag. She had kept all the 'good ones' and significantly threw the remainder away.

She asked: 'Will you come upstairs to say goodbye before you go?' I did this with a heavy heart. In a sad and emotional state, I experienced a panicky feeling of wanting urgently to 'get away'. She was surprised by a little 'good luck' card I gave her and she hung out of the bedroom window, waving energetically, and calling out 'goodbye', until I was out of sight.

For some hours afterwards I felt unsettled and became preoccupied with doing housework. I felt out of touch with myself, both physically and emotionally.

Discussion

The attempt to idealise what is lost can be part of the grief process, which perhaps was reflected by Christine discarding her 'bad images', that is, only taking the good ones with her. It was encouraging that before ending therapy, she had been able to acknowledge successfully the sadness she felt when separating, and link this quite insightfully to painful endings in her past.

Her use of projective identification to communicate how she felt had become more appropriate and I left feeling that she had achieved a lot through therapeutic work and that we had both learnt something from it.

Reflection on Christine's process

On referral to art therapy, Christine presented with psychological and behavioural features commonly observed in children who have experienced emotional trauma, deprivation and rejection. Such features are discussed by Case (1990). What aspects of art therapy make it such an effective approach to use in working with adults and children who exhibit such features? In the following points, I will outline how I see art therapy as an intervention helping Christine to resolve some of these behavioural traits, and some of the related difficulties she experienced around issues of dependency and defence in relationships:

1   The consistency provided by the therapeutic relationship and boundaries of the sessions enabled Christine to work through the trauma of separation and loss, both in her past and current relationships. As a result, she became less insecure and found it easier to establish and maintain close, trusting relationships. This coincided with an increased ability to learn and think things through; in her therapy she had become able to sustain longer periods of silent concentration, through absorbing herself in the image-making process.

2   Her re-enactment of old and self-destructive behavioural patterns in new situations lessened, as did the difficulty Christine had experienced in being objective and using symbols appropriately.

3   Initially she had shown a tendancy to 'act out' and become a scapegoat by evoking anger and negative responses from others.

Christine had demonstrated this in therapy through her 'challenging messiness' and insatiable use of the art materials. She communicated her inner chaos and her need for emotional nurture through symbolic means. Once engaged in the sessions Christine became more aware of this through reflecting on her relationship with me. She questioned both how and why she tested the boundaries of the session by using the art materials as she did.

Christine's 'split-off' emotions fluctuated ambiguously and rapidly between extremes of good and bad, tightly controlled order and chaos without boundaries. Within the therapeutic space, the art medium itself provided her with a unique and highly appropriate form of containment because conflicting feelings could be physically expressed, held and, literally 'seen' as we reviewed her images together. As they were accepted without retaliation or judgement, Christine became able to accept her own internal contradictions and different aspects of herself. Later, she occasionally relapsed into 'messy' use of the materials when there were breaks in the consistency of the sessions or if she was upset about separation and loss.

4   Conscious and unconscious attempts to manipulate and control others improved as Christine acknowledged and more directly expressed or contained her own feelings. Through hide-and-seek games in sessions Christine worked on an unmet infantile desire for someone 'to know' how she felt without having to be told directly. The 'non-verbal' expression of feelings fulfilled Christine's need to be 'present' and seen by me, yet not 'exposed' through the danger of having her defences explicitly and uncontrollably challenged. The art material played a central role in helping Christine to work through conflicts around dependency and defence. In her use of them, she was able to open up at her own pace. Feeling that she remained in control of the therapeutic and artistic process enabled her to explore internal conflicts. This simultaneously promoted a sense of independence and greater self-esteem.

5   As her self-confidence gradually grew, Christine became less dependent on denial or defence mechanisms. She became less fearful of rejection and making mistakes.

Defensive denial of her feelings had been expressed concretely, and took two main forms:

- The development of a thick 'second skin' (Bick 1968). This was acted out often via somatization, 'not hearing' or manic chattering so as to avoid her feelings during periods of silence. For this reason cathartic aspects inherent in art psychotherapy were particularly beneficial for Christine. Sensations of touch and movement involved in making the images put her 'back in touch' with her feelings. It provided both physical and emotional release, simultaneously offering concrete containment in the images produced and the process of making them.

- By splitting-off and projecting unbearable feelings on to others. In therapy this was demonstrated in her transference to the therapist and image-making process. Initially, themes included horror, death and nightmares. Images of witches, skeletons and devils were common. At different times Christine had perceived herself or others as 'wicked'. Joy Schaverien (1992) discusses how the art process and image can be 'projected into', used by the client, used to 'contain' split-off feelings (both good and bad). In this way they might become a talisman or scapegoat. Similarly, Schaverien suggests that transferences to the therapist may be held within the imagery.

Although witches continued to be prevalent in her drawings, later on in Christine's therapy the way they were portrayed and perceived changed. There was more of a reference to 'good' and 'bad' witches which corresponded to Christine's increased ability to recognise good and bad aspects in herself and others. Within the therapeutic relationship she had begun to trust that these 'frightening' projections from herself could be accepted, contained and processed.

Making images had provided Christine with a 'safe' medium through which to re-enact the compulsive patterns of defence which she had become dependent on within relationships. Finding a new and more constructive channel through which to express these old defences can bring about a deep shift in consciousness when set within a reflective, therapeutic setting. Fundamental changes in perceptions and behaviour can then follow. Previously, Christine may have been negatively exhilarated by seeking 'bad' or 'angry' responses from others.

As the medium was fun to use Christine experienced a sense of achievement from engaging in the artistic process. She gained a substitute 'high' which rapidly contributed to increasing her ego, strength and self-respect. This then perpetuated new more objective patterns of learning and experiencing herself to others. Interpretations and reflection in the sessions were aimed at helping Christine to access her emotions and gain some insight into how she expressed feelings. She then experimented with more direct ways of communicating and later extended this outside the therapeutic setting.

Mrs Lee and staff at the Centre also reported changes in Christine's outlook and behaviour as a result of her attending art therapy. Towards the end of her therapy Christine became progressively self-contained. Eventually she began to verbalise how she felt rather than resorting to destructive 'acting out'.

At certain stages in Christine's therapy it became essential that the therapist was able to alert the staff team to the powerful effect of projective identification in the counter-transference, which extended to relationships outside the therapeutic space. This is very important in order to prevent harmful re-enactment within the institutional dynamics. This would ultimately have interfered with Christine's therapeutic progress.

Art therapy for Christine ended prematurely when she left the Centre when her mother's programme finished. However, the way she coped with the final separation indicated that her prognosis was quite good; she had gained considerable insight through art therapy.

For her future progress, a lot depended on the quality of support she and Mrs Lee would receive on their return to London. It was recommended that Christine continue with art therapy as soon as possible if further somatizing and behavioural problems were to be avoided. The tendency for her to revert to physical forms of expressing emotion when anxious suggested that difficulties in adolescence and adulthood could centre around abusive relationships or more direct forms of self-harm, involving the misuse of substances, for example, alcohol and drugs, or manifest itself as an eating disorder.

Exploring the issues of dependency and defence which developed throughout Christine's therapy, this study has emphasised processes of splitting and projective identification which emerged in the transference. These mechanisms of psychological defence are characteristic in the paranoid schizoid mode and in this mode, internal experience is generated through very literal or concrete forms. Drugs are one such example of a concrete form through which clients may express issues of dependency and defence. When parents are drug dependent they can also unconsciously project their internal conflicts around dependency and defence on to their relationship with their child.

An important initial feature of the work with Christine was Mrs Lee's unconscious over-identification with her daughter which became a major obstacle to changing the vicious cycle of hostile dependency between them. Vulnerable aspects of herself which she found too painful to acknowledge consciously, triggered intolerant angry attacks from Mrs Lee when seen mirrored in Christine.

These attacks were part of her own desperate defence against the painful separations, rejections and dependency she had experienced in her past and present relationships. In Christine, they reproduced a need for similar psychological and emotional defences which took the form of splitting and projection. They fuelled an internalised aggressor with an associated tendency to feel comfortable re-enacting the victim role by provoking angry responses from others.

For Christine, a therapeutic relationship, combined with the physical aspects of the image-making process, provided a unique form of containment. This made it possible to facilitate intensive therapeutic progress with complex issues and defences which would otherwise have been extremely difficult to access with more verbal therapies.

In art therapy Christine externalised and experimented with these dynamics. In doing so, she found a means of drawing some boundaries between herself and her mother, finally separating enough to develop a more integrated sense of her own self in relation to others. This in turn enabled Mrs Lee to become more reflective about her own identity in relation to Christine. She appeared to become less defensive about her own emotional vulnerabilities and therefore was more able to facilitate Christine's emotional needs without acting in a hostile or dependent manner.

Becoming more objective about the relationship enabled Mrs Lee to make practical changes to prevent the addictive and self-harmful patterns of hostile dependency which had developed between them. Indeed these were also the patterns she had expressed in her use of drugs. Simultaneously she had adopted practical solutions in order to prevent her own self-harm through drug use.

Conclusion

Within this area of clinical practice, where clients' emotional conflicts are expressed through compulsive physical rituals with concrete substances, art psychotherapy can clearly offer specific benefits, as can be seen by the following summary.

Art therapy offers an alternative to verbal communication

Direct expression of raw emotions can 'be seen' literally within the images. This gives the client an important choice about whether to reflect on them silently (intra-psychically) or, alternatively, to discuss them with the therapist. This is very appropriate for drug dependant clients who may have become out of touch, disassociated from their feelings or initially find them difficult to discuss due to fear of judgemental responses about their drugs use.

The artistic process provides an element of anonymity in psychotherapy

As images are not addressed to particular individuals they can remain inexplicit, facilitating the drug dependant clients conflicting desire to *be seen* but not prematurely exposed.

It facilitates intra-psychic exploration promoting self-confidence

Drug dependency may result in social isolation and withdrawal diminishing the clients' self-confidence and sense of control. The use of art materials in therapy can provide clients with a 'private' space from which to emerge gradually at their own pace. It encourages self-reflections within the presence of the therapist therefore supporting self-acceptance and confidence.

Emotions can take on a concrete aspect which are 'contained' and held in imagery

This is particularly helpful for drug dependant clients who may feel chaotic or that they lack boundaries. Feelings are physically held up – 'mirrored' – to the client through the image.

Images are not transitory

The image can be reviewed by client and therapist chronologically and can signify changes in the client or show how they have developed over time. This can be very important to clients who wish to 'see' or acknowledge progress in their mental and emotional state, while following a rehabilitation programme.

Art psychotherapy offers cathartic release on many levels, meeting the specific needs of clients at particular times

When attempting to become drug free or during relapse, drug-dependant clients' emotional states are often erratic. They may rapidly alternate between being unable to discuss their feelings rationally and/or expressing them through cravings and other non-verbal forms. This ideally requires emotional outlets in therapy that are either verbal or physical, or both.

The image-making offers a safe yet pleasurable alternative to releasing pent-up anxiety and emotions through drug use. In the use of creative activity, the client can gain a sense of euphoria and individual purpose/identity. The artistic process can facilitate an element of ritualistic repetitive behaviour without being self-harmful or addictive.

Images have meaning on many levels

Individuals may recognise previously unconscious/unrecognised aspects of the self in reviewing imagery with the art therapist. They can 'hold' seemingly irrational, contradictory feelings simultaneously (for example, hope, the desire to fight anger, defence and, on the other hand, dependency, acceptance and understanding).

The art therapist can 'accept'/ receive the image and what it holds non-verbally

Transference of emotions to the image and therapist therefore involves a physical act on a proverbial level which goes back to early infantile nurturing. This unique aspect of the therapeutic relationship in art psychotherapy is particularly helpful for drug dependant clients.

Throughout this chapter I have considered how drug dependency can result from early childhood trauma and/or emotional deprivation (often passed through generations in cycles of deprivation from parent to child). The forms of defence used in drug dependency are physical and pre-verbal.

In art psychotherapy the therapist/image are constantly receptive and receiving. Being able to comprehend experiences without words is essential at times when verbal intervention, interpretation or explanations by the therapist may evoke early defences and rob the client of an experience in finding him or herself.

Through art psychotherapy the client may experience acceptance and self-discovery, affirmation and control while in a regressed state.

Bibliography

Balint, M. (1952) *Primary Love and Psychoanalytic Technique*, New York: Liverwright Publishing Co., 1965, pp. 90–102.

——(1968) *The Basic Fault*, London: Tavistock, pp. 56–70.

Bick, E. (1968) 'The Experience of the Skin in Early Object Relations', *International Journal of Psychoanalysis*, 49 (2–3): 484–6.

Bion, W.R. (1957) 'Differentiation of the Psychotic from Non-psychotic Personalities', *International Journal of Psychoanalysis*, 38: 266–75.

——(1959) 'Attacks on Linking', *International Journal of Psychoanalysis* 40(5–6): 90–1, 102–5.

——(1962) *Learning from Experience*, London: Heinemann, pp. 119–30.

Case, C. (1990) 'Reflections and Shadows', in C. Case and T. Dalley (eds), *Working with Children in Art Therapy*, London and New York: Tavistock/Routledge, pp. 133–5.

——(1993) *Theoretical Advances in Art Therapy*, Warwick University, unpublished paper, October.

——(1994) 'Art Therapy in Analysis: Advance Retreat (In the Belly of the Spider)' *Inscape*, 1: 3–10.

Fairbairn, R. (1949) 'Steps in the Development of Object Relations: Theory of the Personality', *British Journal of Medical Psychology*, 22(26): 31. (Republished 1952 in *Psychoanalytic Studies of the Personality*, Routledge and Kegan Paul, pp. 152–61.)

Klein, M. (1927) 'Symposium on Child Analysis', *The Writings of M. Klein, Volume 1*, London: Hogarth Press, pp. 139–69.

——(1940) 'Mourning and its relation to Manic Depressive States' *Contribution to Psychoanalysis,* London: Hogarth Press, pp. 71–80.

——(1946) 'Notes on Some Schizoid Mechanisms', in *The Writings of Melanie Klein, Volume 3*, London: Hogarth Press, pp. 1–24.

——(1957) *Envy and Gratitude*, London: Tavistock, pp. 56–7.

——(1975) 'The Importance of Symbol Formation in the Developing Ego' in the *Collected Works – Volume 1*, London: Hogarth Press, pp. 156–9.

Langs, R. (1975) 'Therapeutic Misalliances', *International Journal of Psychoanalysis and Psychotherapy*, 4: 77–105.

Ogden, T. (1979) 'On Projective Identification', *International Journal of Psychoanalysis*, 60: 357–73.

——(1982) *Projective Identification and Psychotherapeutic Technique*, New York: Jason Aronson, pp. 89–92.

Schaverien, J. (1992) *The Revealing Image*, New York: Tavistock/Routledge, p. 22.

Winnicott, D.W. (1947) 'Hate in the Countertransference', in [Collected Papers of D.W. Winnicott] *Through Paediatrics to Psychoanalysis*, New York: Basic Books, pp.162–9.

——(1965) 'The Theory of the Parent–Infant Relationship' in *The Maturation Process and the Facilitating Environment*, London: Hogarth Press and the Institute of Psychoanalysis, pp. 72–90.

——(1971) *Playing and Reality*, Harmondsworth: Penguin, pp. 50–62.

The future

Diane Waller and Jacky Mahony

Although it will be old news by the time this book is published, we felt it worth noting that, as we were putting the finishing touches to *Treatment of Addiction*, a significant Government-level appointment had been made of a drugs specialist – drug czar, Keith Helliwell – with one of his tasks being to produce a British policy on drugs. At the same time, it was reported that a Government minister's son had been implicated in dealing cannabis. Although the name of the minister had appeared on the Internet and in Scottish newspapers, an embargo was placed on naming him in the English press. However, it was revealed to be the son of the Home Secretary, Jack Straw, who had recently opposed the legalisation of cannabis. The minister's picture and that of his son, accompanied by such captions as, 'My Agony', 'Humiliation for a man of principle' and 'Oxford-bound, the idealist with luminous yellow hair' (*Daily Mail*, 3 January 1998), appeared in all the daily papers and the item took place of priority in the national news.

In the same month, there were reports in both the *Guardian* and the *Daily Telegraph* (2 January 1998) of several deaths resulting from drunkenness, including drunken driving, and a report of a young person who had fallen under a train after allegedly taking Ecstasy. The *Guardian* also reported an attempt to limit the growth of opium poppies in Pakistan. There were two articles about tobacco; including a defiant piece by Emily Mortimer (p. 22) who declared that she was going to continue smoking.

In the *Daily Mail* (3 January 1998: 12–13) there was an article by the journalist, Ann Leslie, titled, 'Why I think cannabis should be made legal', next to an editorial comment, 'Why we must go on holding the line', which warns: 'With a greater availability of drugs there would certainly be many more addicts. The human and financial costs would be enormous. Britain would become a magnet for countless foreign potheads'.

The same would, we assume, apply for British potheads.

These kinds of sentiments are currently to be found in all the British tabloids and in the 'quality' press', the theme being that something has to be done about all these addicts – and potential addicts. *The Mail*'s answer – in tune with New Labour – is,

> that parents must be made more responsible for the activities of their children. Such new responsibility will, though, entail a social revolution. It will require fewer households in which both parents work full-time; it will require fewer single-parent house-holds too. It does not necessarily have to be the mother who makes the career sacrifice; in some cases it would make economic sense for the father to be at home.
>
> (*The Mail*, ibid.: 15)

However, if New Labour's 'back to work' for single mothers policy is successful, then neither parent will be at home.

Around the same time as *The Mail* article, CNN news showed an item about the new president of the combined Ciba-Geigy-Sandoz pharmaceutical company, based in Switzerland and renamed Novartis, and the amount of money committed to research, including genetic engineering and organ transplants. We saw Dolly, a cloned sheep. Novartis supply many of the drugs which are used to treat major illnesses. The president, a young, lively looking man, enjoyed art, especially Oriental art which he collected. Another news item which caught our eye recommended that HIV-testing should be carried out more frequently, due to a new cocktail of drugs which could potentially control the virus at an early stage.

So it is that we find drugs (good and bad), tobacco and alcohol everywhere in the news. For the Home Secretary, his son's involve-ment in illegal drugs must be an embarrassment, especially since he is so implacably opposed to them. It at least shows that alleged drug dealers can come from the highest-placed families, which might be some comfort for those families whose children engage in glue-sniffing or who take Ecstasy at raves. Is the Minister part of the new social revolution – or should he sacrifice his career to be with his 17-year-old son?

What has become clear during the writing of this book, is that the area of addiction is clouded by moral judgements and hypocrisy which can lead to the most puzzling and indeed intrusive interventions in the name of treatment. Therapists are not exempt from making moral judgements but yet often behave as if they are. It would be better if they were open about their prejudices, if they have them.

This is not to underestimate or belittle the devastation caused by addictions. Families of drug users – including alcoholics – suffer a great deal as their relative's behaviour often becomes intolerable. Glue-sniffing, injecting, lack of personal hygiene, the use of dirty needles, stealing, hiding equipment, being sick and brain damage, are impossible for most people to tolerate. Alcoholism leads to secrecy, violent behaviour, liver damage and, sometimes, an early death. It is not surprising then, that parents fear that their children will get involved in the 'drug scene' and end up in prostitution, in prison, or dead.

As Angelika Groterath notes in Chapter 1 of this book, economics play a central role in the drug problem. The economic plight of some countries means that production and export of substances, such as opium poppies and coca beans, which can be sold for illegal purposes is essential to that country's maintenance. The organised distribution and sale of these substances does not take place only among a few members of the Mafia. In any case, these substances often have a medical value: for example, morphine as a painkiller. Many people are making a great deal of money out of the drugs industry: sport has benefitted from tobacco sponsorship which is now coming to an end with a European ban on all advertising – except for Formula One racing. But tobacco companies can easily sell their products in Africa, the Far East and in 'developing countries' and so are unlikely to fade away. Alcohol is available cheaply, and 'Alcopops' (low alcohol beverages) can be purchased easily. Every day, people cross the English Channel to Calais, Boulogne and Dieppe in France to buy cheap wine and spirits 'for their personal consumption'. This means a good trade for the ferries and the hypermarkets and for the governments who levy a hefty tax.

While there continues to be such massive social support for drugs for pleasure, escapism and the relief of pain, we should hardly be surprised if people turn to them in times of stress, either to medically prescribed drugs or to illegal ones. Nor should we be surprised if they take them because their friends do, or to help them stay up all night; it is a way of rebelling or getting a 'buzz'. This is not a new phenomenon.

As therapists, although we need to be aware of the context of drugs and addiction, we should also think about the way in which we can support people who are in misery because of their addiction or because their life situation has led them to become addicted. In this book we have attempted to show some examples of how different interventions might be helpful. We would certainly recommend that arts therapies get a higher profile in places where drug addicts are treated, not because we see them as a panacea, but because there are specific ways in which they can assist in the expression and containment of painful feelings, as well as enhancing creative potential. Centres where drug-addicted clients have access to a range of therapeutic interventions, including homeopathy and 'alternative' medicines, as well as arts and group psychotherapy – and individual therapy or counselling, too – would seem a good idea. These could be adapted for all age ranges and should be open to families as well.

We would like to see the problem of addiction to drugs taken out of the isolated position it still holds within our health and social care system so that people with such problems do not suffer from guilt as well as the misery caused by their habit and the reasons for acquiring the habit. There are many signs that 'harm reduction' as a policy is being accepted, with some clients receiving methadone or maintenance amounts of a drug at the same time as receiving support. If we recognise that ambivalence and manipulative behaviour are normal when we do not want to stop doing something but know we need to, and that the more guilty we feel the more manipulative we then become, then psychotherapy can be made available. The loss and emptiness which causes some people to turn to drugs and then to become addicted to them, has to be acknowledged and the person supported through this loss.

We have suggested how the arts therapies can help by enabling very raw feelings to be contained through the making of images or by symbolically enacting them in dance or psychodrama, and that the non-judgemental and perhaps even 'outsider' role of the artist can facilitate the person being safe. We also caution that these therapies are not magic and that professionals should support each other in the interests of their clients – whoever their clients are, not just addicted ones.

Projects which respect and value their clients, such as the ones mentioned here in this book, which technically come under the 'voluntary sector' or the National Health Service, and others which are beginning to emerge, could play an important role in helping those whose addictions are ruining their lives: whether these are the more 'sensational' addictions (heroine, cocaine, etc.) or the ones which quietly make people miserable, such as compulsive shopping and eating.

People who visit Weight Watchers are, after all, suffering from guilt and low self-esteem, and are caught in a cycle of bingeing, dieting and berating themselves for their lack of willpower. However, the damage to their health is not as dramatically obvious as, say, a heroin addict's habit, and they are not criminalised. It seems to us very important then, to understand the economics of drug abuse, and the strong conflicted and often irrational feelings that are generated by the drugs problem. We hope that the papers found in *Treatment of Addiction* – which in themselves represent differing views on the role of therapy in treatment – will help in stimulating debate among therapists, counsellers and specialist drug workers, so that we can continue to learn from each other.

Index